W9-BRK-198

TEACHER IN AMERICA

Teacher in America

Jacques Barzun

Dulce est desipere
in loco ... parentis.

UNIVERSITY
PRESS OF
AMERICA

LANHAM • NEW YORK • LONDON

University Press of America,® Inc.

4720 Boston Way
Lanham, MD 20706

3 Henrietta Street
London WC2E 8LU England

Library of Congress Cataloging in Publication Data

Barzun, Jacques, 1907-
  Teacher in America.

  Bibliography: p.
  Reprint. Originally published: Boston : Little,
Brown, 1944. With new introd.
    1. College teaching—United States.   2. Education,
Higher—United States.   3. United States—Intellectual
life.   I. Title.
LB2331.B374   1986   378'.12'0973   86-15853
ISBN 0-8191-5447-4 (pbk. : alk. paper)

Reprinted in 1986 by arrangement with Little, Brown and Company, New York, New York

All University Press of America books are produced on acid-free
paper which exceeds the minimum standards set by the National
Historical Publications and Records Commission.

CONTENTS

Contents

TEACHER IN AMERICA

1. *Profession: Teacher*

> The bore of all bores was the third. His subject had no beginning, middle, nor end. It was education. Never was such a journey through the desert of the mind, the Great Sahara of intellect. The very recollection makes me thirsty.
>
> — T. L. PEACOCK

EDUCATION is indeed the dullest of subjects and I intend to say as little about it as I can. For three years past, now, the people of this country have knitted their brows over the shortcomings of the schools; at least that is the impression one gets from newspapers and periodicals. And by a strange necessity, talk about education never varies. It always seems to resolve itself into undeniable truths about "the well-rounded man" and "our precious heritage." Once in a while, in a fit of daring, the man who lectures you about education points out that the phrase "liberal arts" means "liberating." Then he is off on a fine canter about freedom of the mind and democracy. Or again, hypnotized by your glazed eyeballs, he slips into the old trap of proclaiming that "education" comes from the Latin word meaning to "lead out." Alas! the Latin root has nothing to do with "leading out"; it means simply — to educate. But no matter, it is all in a good cause: "Education should be broadening." Of course! "It should train a man for practical life." Of course again! "Education should be democratic — but nothing radical, naturally. Education must be thorough, but rapid too. No waste of precious time conning over our precious heritage." Those for whom these fundamental principles are rehearsed never argue: they are too drowsy.

This narcotic state is not due merely to the fact that we have latterly had too much educational discussion. After all, we have also been chewing the cud of peace plans, labor problems, and expert strategy. No. I am convinced that at any time brooding and wrangling about education is bad. It is as bad as it would be to perpetually dig around the roots of government by talking political theory. Both political and educational theory are for the rare genius to grapple with, once in a century. The business of the citizen and the statesman is not political theory but politics. The business of the parent and the teacher is not education but Teaching. Teaching is something that can be provided for, changed, or stopped. It is good or bad, brilliant or stupid, plentiful or scarce. Beset as it is with difficulties and armed with devices, teaching has a theory too, but it is one that can be talked about simply and directly, for it concerns the many matters of human knowledge which affect our lives, from the three R's to electronics. To deal with it in that fashion is in fact what I am going to do in this book: very simply and literally I am going to tell tales out of school.

Education is obviously something else, something intangible, unpredictable. Education comes from within; it is a man's own doing, or rather it happens to him — sometimes because of the teaching he has had, sometimes in spite of it. When Henry Adams wrote *The Education of Henry Adams*, he gave thirty pages out of five hundred to his schooling. Common usage records the same distinction. No man says of another: "I educated him." It would be offensive and would suggest that the victim was only a puppy when first taken in hand. But it is a proud thing to say "I taught him" — and a wise one not to specify what.

To be sure, there is an age-old prejudice against teaching. Teachers must share with doctors the world's most celebrated sneers, and with them also the world's unbounded hero-worship. Always and everywhere, "He is a schoolteacher" has meant "He is an underpaid pitiable drudge." Even a politician stands higher, because power in the street seems less of a mockery than power in the classroom. But when we speak of Socrates, Jesus, Buddha, and "other great teachers of humanity," the atmosphere somehow changes and the politician's power begins to look shrunken and mean. August examples show that no limit can be set to the power of a teacher, but this is equally true in the other direction: no career can so nearly approach zero in its effects.

The odd thing is that almost everybody is a teacher at some time or other during his life. Besides Socrates and Jesus, the great teachers of mankind are mankind itself — your parents and mine. First and last, parents do a good deal more teaching than doctoring, yet so natural and necessary is this duty that they never seem aware of performing it. It is only when they are beyond it, when they have thoroughly ground irremediable habits of speech, thought, and behavior into their offspring that they discover the teacher as an institution and hire him to carry on the work.

Then begins the fierce, secret struggle out of which education may come — the struggle between home and school, parent and child, child and teacher; the struggle also that lies deep within the parent and within society concerning the teacher's worth: Is this man of knowledge to be looked up to as wise and helpful, or to be looked down on as at once servile and dangerous, capable and inglorious, higher than the parent yet lower than the brat?

Most people meet this difficulty by alternately looking up and looking down. At best the title of teacher is suspect. I notice that on their passports and elsewhere, many of my academic colleagues put down their occupation as Professor. Anything to raise the tone: a professor is to a teacher what a cesspool technician is to a plumber. Anything to enlarge the scope: not long ago, I joined a club which described its membership as made up of Authors, Artists, and Amateurs — an excellent reason for joining. Conceive my disappointment when I found that the classifications had broken down and I was now entered as an Educator. Doubtless we shall have to keep the old pugilistic title of Professor, though I cannot think of Dante in Hell coming upon Brunetto Latini, and exclaiming "Why, Professor!" But we can and must get rid of "Educator." Imagine the daily predicament: someone asks, "What do you do?" — "I profess and I educate." It is unspeakable and absurd.

Don't think this frivolous, but regard it as a symbol. Consider the American state of mind about Education at the present time. An unknown correspondent writes to me: "Everybody seems to be dissatisfied with education except those in charge of it." This is a little less than fair, for a great deal of criticism has come from within the profession. But let it stand. Dissatisfaction is the keynote. Why dissatisfaction? Because Americans believe in Education, because they pay large sums for Education, and because Education does not seem to yield results. At this point one is bound to ask: "What results do you expect?"

The replies are staggering. Apparently Education is to do everything that the rest of the world leaves undone. Recall the furore over American History. Under new and better management that subject was to produce patriots — nothing less. An influential critic, head of a large university, wants education to generate a classless society; another asks that education root out racial intolerance (in the third or the ninth grade, I wonder?); still another requires that college courses be designed to improve labor relations. One man, otherwise sane, thinks the solution of the housing problem has bogged down — in the schools; and another proposes to make the future householders happy married couples — through the schools. Off to one side, a well-known company of scholars have got hold of the method of truth and wish to dispense it as a crisis reducer. "Adopt our nationally advertised brand and avert chaos."

Then there are the hundreds of specialists in endless "vocations" who want Education to turn out practised engineers, affable hotelkeepers, and finished literary artists. There are educational shops for repairing every deficiency in man or nature: battalions of instructors are impressed to teach Civilian Defense; the FBI holds public ceremonies for its graduates; dogs receive short courses in good manners, and are emulated at once by girls from the age of seven who learn Poise and Personality. Above and beyond all these stand the unabashed peacemakers who want Kitty Smith from Indiana to be sent to Germany, armed with Muzzey's *American History*, to undo Hitler's work.

These are not nightmarish caricatures I have dreamed but things I have recently seen done or heard proposed by representative and even distinguished minds: they are so many acts of faith in the prevailing dogma that Education is the hope of the world.

Well, this is precisely where the use of the right word comes in. You may teach spot-welding in wartime and indeed you must. But Education is the hope of the world only in the sense that there is something better than bribery, lies, and violence for righting the world's wrongs. If this better thing is education, then education is not merely schooling. It is a lifelong discipline of the individual by himself, encouraged by a reasonable opportunity to lead a good life. Education here is synonymous with civilization. A civilized community is better than the jungle, but civilization is a long slow process which cannot be "given" in a short course.

No one in his senses would affirm that Schooling is the hope of the world. But to say this is to show up the folly of perpetually confusing Education with the work of the schools; the folly of believing against all evidence that by taking boys and girls for a few hours each day between the ages of seven and twenty-one, our teachers can "turn out" all the human products that we like to fancy when we are disgusted with ourselves and our neighbors. It is like believing that brushing the teeth is the key to health. No ritual by itself will guarantee anything. Brushing won't even keep your teeth clean, by itself. There is no key to health and there is none to education. Do you think because you have an expensive school system there shall be no more spelling mistakes? Then why suppose that you can eradicate intolerance more easily? Free compulsory "education" is a great thing, an indispensable thing, but it will not make the City of God out of Public School No. 26.

The whole mass of recrimination, disappointment, and dissatisfaction which this country is now suffering about its schools comes from using the ritual word "Education" so loosely and so frequently. It covers abysses of emptiness. Everybody cheats by using it, cheats others and cheats himself. The idea abets false ambitions. The educator wants to do a big job in the world, so he takes on the task of reorienting Germany and improving human relations. The public at large, bedeviled as it is with these "problems," is only too glad to farm them out, reserving the right of indignant complaint when the educator breaks down or the Institute for Human Relations fails to reduce appreciably the amount of wife beating.

Dissatisfaction remains, and not unmixed with ill will. For in this vast sideshow of illusions and misplaced effort, educators find an opportunity to belabor one another in clans: College teachers cry out, "Why can't high school boys write decent English?" The Deans exclaim, "Why can't our college graduates speak foreign languages and be ready to serve in wartime? Look at what the Army is doing!" Up and down the line others say, "Discipline is the thing — the Navy knows more about training boys than we do." And the rhetorical questions continue, answered by the askers themselves: "Why is there so much juvenile delinquency?" — "It's the schools." "Why did army doctors find so many neurotics?" — "It's the colleges." "Educators are Confused," read one front-page headline a couple of years ago, and down below the explanation was: "It's the fault of out Higher Education."

This is certainly looping the loop. Like the jurymen in *Alice in Wonderland*, the parents, the children in high schools, the men and women in colleges, are bewildered by claims and counter-claims. They are stunned by solicitations to follow this or that course, for this or that imperative reason. And like the jurymen, they repeat "Important," "Unimportant," while making futile motions with their forefingers. Inside the academic precincts, plans, curriculums, and methods whirl by with newsreel speed. Labels change; the Progressives become Conservative, the Conservatives Progressive, while the Classicals form a Third Party with adherents and attackers in every camp. From a distance the academic grove looks remarkably like Chaos and Old Night.

II

Happily there is something stable and clear and useful behind this phantasmagoria of Education — the nature of subject matter and the practice of teaching.

The word helps us again to the idea. The advantage of "teaching" is that in using it you must recognize — if you are in your sober senses — that practical limits exist. You know by instinct that it is impossible to "teach" democracy, or citizenship or a happy married life. I do not say that these virtues and benefits are not somehow connected with good teaching. They are, but they occur as by-products. They come, not from a course, but from a teacher; not from a curriculum, but from a human soul.

It is indeed possible so to arrange school and college work that more play is given to good human influences than in other conceivable arrangements. But it is not possible by fiddling with vague topics to insure or even to increase the dissemination of virtue. I should think it very likely that a course in Democracy would make most healthy students loathe the word and all its associations. And meanwhile the setup (no other word will better express my contempt) takes the room and time and energy which should legitimately be used to teach somebody something teachable — English or History, Greek or Chemistry. I shall show later what subjects are teachable and what priceless by-products, leading *possibly* to democratic or marital bliss, come from their study.

Meanwhile I dwell on the necessity of teaching, that is to say on the need for teachers. There are never enough. Statistics tell us that at this moment we are one hundred thousand short — one in ten. This does not include men fighting or putting their special skill at the war plant's disposal. One hundred thousand have simply jumped at the chance for higher pay. That is their right and in a competitive system they must be free from blame. Nevertheless we have here an estimate of the number who are normally in teaching for want of better jobs. The "call" cannot be strong if a teacher will leave the classroom to floor-walk in a department store. Doctors are poor too, but they stick to their rounds and their patients.

But in truth, American schoolteachers as such may well be forgiven their recent desertion — or what looks like it — when we remember how so many college and university administrators acted under the emergency of war. In a twinkling, all that they had professed to believe in for thirty years was discarded as useless. Subjects, schedules, principles, were renounced, with tossing of caps in the air and whoops of joy. Naturally and fortunately, there were notable exceptions to this stampede and much indignation within the ranks. But the bandwagon pressure was great and solid institutions found it hard to resist. One wonders what would have happened if we had been blitzed like England — where no such academic jamboree ensued — or economically hampered like Canada — where academic calm has continued to reign.

I am inclined to think, and again I shall give my reasons later, that this excitement signalized a release from long pretense. With us many people who pass as professional teachers are merely "connected with education." They live on the fringes of the academic army — campus followers, as it were — though too often it is they who have the honors and emoluments while the main body lives on short rations. Dislocation by war naturally mixes up the doers with the drones and produces the academic riot that our newspapers depict. To judge fairly, it would be well to draw a veil over the scene since Pearl Harbor and say that on that day the United States suspended all serious educational projects — excepting of course the people's wise award of a traveling fellowship to Mr. Wendell Willkie. Looking at the situation in this way would give us perspective, and something like a fresh start — again from the base of Teaching as against Education. For if anything is more alarming than the demand for education as a cure-all, it is the chuckle-headed notion that many educators have of teaching.

To think of a fresh start raises a host of problems — about administration, advancement, public and private rewards; about methods, subjects, teachers' colleges, and Ph.D.'s; about young men and women; about national culture and individual research — which I shall touch upon in the light of my experience and observation.

But before any of it can have any meaning for the layman, the basic facts of teaching must be set forth, as free as possible from the cant that surrounds them. Naturally, in trying to strip them, I cannot help criticizing and condemning other modes of dealing with the same facts. But at no point do I mean to imply that I have made an original discovery, or that there are not thousands of American teachers who would not say the same thing in much the same way. I have met many of them. corresponded with them, imbibed their wisdom and even stolen their anecdotes. I do not pretend that teaching is a lost art. On the contrary, almost all the younger men in higher or secondary education today are committed to teaching as a freely chosen vocation. And each year more and more college undergraduates show an interest in the ways of the profession with a view to following it if they can. It is for them as much as anybody else that I write this book, though it is addressed to parents and students as well.

Teaching is not a lost art but the regard for it is a lost tradition. Hence tomorrow's problem will not be to get teachers, but to recognize the good ones and not discourage them before they have done their stint. In an age of big words and little work, any liberal profession takes some sticking to, not only in order to succeed, but in order to keep faith with oneself. Teaching is such a profession. Why does it exist and what is it like? The public thinks it knows from its own experience of school. Ideally, teaching is ever the same, but teachers have changed since the days when aged Headmasters reminisced in mellow volumes, and the question I must really answer is, What is teaching like now?

2. Pupils into Students

Madam, we guarantee results —
or we return the boy!
— PRESIDENT PATTON,
late of Princeton

To PASS from the overheated Utopia of Education to the realm of teaching is to leave behind false heroics and take a seat in the front row of the human comedy. What is teaching and why is it comic? The answer includes many things depending on whether you think of the teacher, the pupil, the means used, or the thing taught. But the type situation is simple and familiar. Think of a human pair teaching their child how to walk. There is, on the child's side, strong desire and latent powers: he has legs and means to use them. He walks and smiles; he totters and looks alarmed; he falls and cries. The parents smile throughout, showering advice, warning, encouragement, and praise. The whole story, not only of teaching, but of man and civilization, is wrapped up in this first academic performance. It is funny because clumsiness makes us laugh, and touching because undaunted effort strikes a chord of gallantry, and finally comic because it has all been done before and is forever to do again.

All the knowledge, skill, art, and science that we use and revere, up to Einstein's formulas about the stars, is a mere repetition and extension of the initial feat of learning to walk. But this extension does not take place by itself. Most of it has to be taught, slowly and painfully. There was a time when Mr. Einstein was not quite sure what eight times nine came to. He had to learn, and to learn he had to be taught. The reason teaching has to go on is that children are not born human; they are made so. The wretched foundlings that were occasionally discovered in rural parts of Europe a hundred years ago walked on all fours and grunted like beasts.

And we not only want human offspring but more particularly Western, American-speaking, literate, twentieth-century men and women, endowed furthermore with all sorts of special religious, moral, and intellectual characteristics. In short we want a very definite product, and it is our ability to make the plastic young animal develop certain desirable traits which makes men fall into the educational fallacy I denounced earlier. We speak of "molding the mind of a child" and G. B. Shaw denounces us as abortionists. But both he and we are wrong. Though the young mind is plastic and skillful handling can accomplish miracles, instruction *and* distortion are alike limited by forces of which we know nothing, except that they exist. We bottle up our ignorance and label it Heredity and Environment and there we stop. We should add something about will and temperament and then forget about the limitations, in order to concentrate on what *can* be done. Then we may ask, How is it done? And finally, What should we teach, and to whom? When we have answered these questions as reasonably and practically as possible, we shall, I think, find that the sulphur-and-brimstone nebula of Education has disappeared like a pricked bubble.

II

Since I am going to tackle these concrete questions in a somewhat autobiographical manner, I had better indicate here and now the sources of my experience. One never knows what accidents turn out to be advantages, and I am not yet sure my early apprenticeship was not a disadvantage, but the facts must be stated, for they contributed to the result and may be freely used against me.

I taught my first class at the age of nine. All I remember about it is that it had to do with arithmetic and that the room seemed filled with thousands of very small children in black aprons. The explanation is that with the shortage of teachers in France towards the middle of the last war, there were sporadic attempts at establishing the so-called Lancaster system of using older pupils to teach the younger. Lancaster himself, who lived a hundred years before, was only trying to meet the teacher shortage of the Napoleonic Wars, but he became an educational fanatic who believed that "any boy who can read can teach, although he knows nothing about it." I don't know what the "it" refers to, whether the art of teaching or the subject matter, but in any case this maxim, like so many others in education, is only half true.

It served, however, to apprentice me to my trade. Not that I stayed very long in it that first time. Indeed, my maiden effort possibly drove me into the retirement of a protracted illness. I recovered, only to relapse, not once but many times — into the habit of teaching. Having learned English and come to this country to rejoin my father, previously sent on a good-will mission, I found myself exchanging French lessons for further work in reading and speaking American. I had the good fortune to come in contact with a fine group of high school teachers, and since advanced mathematics and beginning philosophy are taught earlier abroad, I was able to tutor boys of my own age in those subjects also.

All this while I vaguely felt the force of Milton's angry words: "I hate a pupil teacher." But whenever I made mental casts in the direction of more easygoing professions, like diplomacy or finance, I was brought back to my destiny. In my second year in college, I had my first academic offer. I happened to be coaching two graduate students in the French educational theorists on whom they were to be examined — Rabelais, Montaigne, and Rousseau. My students, middle-aged men, apparently spoke of me to their sponsor and I received a note asking me to call on him. He was head of a department in a large university and I thought at the time that he scarcely lived up to the dignity of his position. For when I was announced by his secretary and he saw me, he laughed in my face. He had not been told that I was about seventeen and he was on the point of offering me an instructorship.

This experience should have soured me against all academic entanglements but circumstances prevailed. The period just before 1929 in this country, and particularly in the metropolis, offered the active-minded college man innumerable opportunities to achieve financial independence even before the bachelor's degree. So I found myself writing and tutoring in very profitable fashion before I thoroughly knew that I had chosen the two most back-breaking jobs in the whole world. Combined with study, this was an adventure of distinctly sociable character. A group of us — all classmates — maintained a perfectly legal and honest tutoring mill, whose grist renewed itself as we managed to put the backward rich through the entrance examinations of famous colleges not our own. School authorities smiled on our work and we ended by taking on all kinds of academic cases. No subjects were barred. If a retired minister came who wanted to read *Hamlet* in Esperanto (one did) we supplied an instructor who spoke the language like a native. At times our facilities were strained and some of us found ourselves tackling subjects with a bare head start over the pupil. But it was excellent practice and most broadening to the tutors. As a natural subsidiary enterprise we undertook high-class literary hackwork. We compiled statistics, contributed to the lesser encyclopedias, and worked up the raw material for public addresses by public men. We referred to ourselves as Ghosts, Incorporated.

When the time of my graduation came, in 1927, the die was cast. I knew I wanted to keep right on with both occupations, though no longer as piece work. Meanwhile I had formed an attachment to the Muse of History and was encouraged in it, chiefly by two men — Harry James Carman, now Dean of Columbia College, and Rexford Guy Tugwell, then Professor of Economics in that institution and now Chancellor of the University of Puerto Rico. Commencement emotions were hardly past when the director of the Summer Session asked me whether I was willing to teach an introductory course. I said I should like nothing better. He wanted to know with whom I had taken that same course. I told him. "You can teach it anyway." That was my *Hoc age*. I have been at it ever since, with breaks for study and travel and excursions into neighboring institutions.

It is over a quarter of a century since I first obeyed the summons to teach and I can only hope the habit has not become a compulsion. "Oh to sit next a man who has spent his life in trying to educate others!" groaned Oscar Wilde. My belief is that the last thing a good teacher wants to do is to teach outside the classroom; certainly my own vision of bliss halfway through a term is solitary confinement in a sound-proof cell. But feeling this way, I often wonder what originally made the impulse to teach take root. In the lives of so many good men one reads that they "drifted into teaching." They drift out again. It is clear that teachers are born, not made, and circumstances usually permit rather than compel. It is impossible to think of William James *not* teaching or of his brother Henry consenting to give a simple explanation. For many people, doing is far easier than talking about it.

From which I conclude that the teaching impulse goes something like this: a fellow human being is puzzled or stymied. He wants to open a door or spell "accommodate." The would-be helper has two choices. He can open the door, spell the word; or he can show his pupil how to do it for himself. The second way is harder and takes more time, but a strong instinct in the born teacher makes him prefer it. It seems somehow to turn an accident into an opportunity for permanent creation. The raw material is what the learner can do, and upon this the teacher-artist builds by the familiar process of taking apart and putting together. He must break down the new and puzzling situation into simpler bits and lead the beginner in the right order from one bit to the next. What the simpler bits and the right order are no one can know ahead of time. They vary for each individual and the teacher must grope around until he finds a "first step" that the particular pupil can manage. In any school subject, of course, this technique does not stop with the opening of a door. The need for it goes on and on — as it seems, forever — and it takes the stubbornness of a saint coupled with the imagination of a demon for a teacher to pursue his art of improvisation gracefully, unwearyingly, endlessly.

Nor is this a purely mental task. All the while, the teacher must keep his charge's feelings in good order. A rattled student can do nothing and a muddled teacher will rattle or dishearten almost any student. The teacher must not talk too much or too fast, must not trip over his own tongue, must not think out loud, must not forget, in short, that he is handling a pair of runaway horses — the pupil and a dramatic situation.

Patience is a quality proverbially required for good teaching, but it is not surprising that many good teachers turn out to be impatient people — though not with their students. Their stock of forbearance gives out before they get home. What sustains them in class is that the situation is always changing. Three successive failures to do one thing may all seem identical to the bystander, but the good teacher will notice a change, a progression, or else the clear sign that the attempt must be postponed until some other preliminary progress has been made.

It is obvious that the relation of teacher to pupil is an emotional one and most complex and unstable besides. To begin with, the motives, the forces that make teaching "go," are different on both sides of the desk. The pupil has some curiosity and he wants to know what grownups know. The master has curiosity also, but it is chiefly about the way the pupil's mind — or hand — works. Remembering his own efforts and the pleasure of discovery, the master finds a satisfaction which I have called artistic in seeing how a new human being will meet and make his own some part of our culture — our ways, our thoughts, even our errors and superstitions. This interest, however, does not last forever. As the master grows away from his own learning period, he also finds that mankind repeats itself. Fewer and fewer students appear new and original. They make the same mistakes at the same places and never seem to go very far into a subject which, for him, is still an expanding universe. Hence young teachers are best; they are the most energetic, most intuitive, and the least resented.

For side by side with his eagerness, the pupil feels resentment arising from the fact that the grownup who teaches him appears to know it all. There is, incidentally, no worse professional disease for the teacher than the habit of putting questions with a half-smile that says "I know that one, and I will tell it you: come along, my pretty." Telling and questioning must not be put-up jobs designed to make the teacher feel good about himself. It is as bad as the Jehovah complex among doctors. Even under the best conditions of fair play and deliberate spontaneity, the pupil, while needing and wanting knowledge, will hate and resist it. This resistance often makes one feel that the human mind is made of some wonderfully tough rubber, which you can stretch a little by pulling hard, but which snaps back into shape the moment you let go.

It is exasperating, but consider how the student feels, subjected to daily and hourly stretching. "Here am I," he thinks, "with my brains nicely organized — with everything, if not in its place, at least in a place where I can find it — and you come along with a new and strange item that you want to force into my previous arrangement. Naturally I resist. You persist. I begin to dislike you. But at the same time, you show me aspects of this new fact or idea which in spite of myself mesh in with my existing desires. You seem to know the contents of my mind. You show me the proper place for your contribution to my stock of knowledge.

Finally, there is brooding over us a vague threat of disgrace for me if I do not accept your offering and keep it and show you that I still have it when you — dreadful thought! — *examine* me. So I give in, I shut my eyes and swallow. I write little notes about it to myself, and with luck the burr sticks: I have learned something. Thanks to you? Well, not exactly. Thanks to you and thanks to me. I shall always be grateful for your efforts, but do not expect me to love you, at least not for a long, long time. When I am fully formed and somewhat battered by the world and yet not too displeased with myself, I shall generously believe that I owe it all to you. It will be an exaggeration on the other side, just as my present dislike is an injustice. Strike an average between the two and that will be a fair measure of my debt."

At any stage in learning, this inner dialogue between opposite feelings goes on. It should go on. Teaching is possible only because there is a dialogue and one part of the mind can be used to rearrange the other. The whole secret of teaching — and it is no secret — consists in splitting the opposition, downing the conservatives by making an alliance with the radicals. It goes without saying that I am not using these words here in their workaday sense. My meaning applies to the multiplication table as well as to anything else. The conservative part of the pupil's mind is passive, stubborn, mute; but his radical minority, that is, his curiosity and his desire to grow up, may be aroused to action. The move forward is generally short; then the conservatives return to power; they preserve, they feel pride of ownership in the new acquisition and begin to think they had it as a birthright. This rhythmical action is one reason why teaching and learning must not go on all the time, nor at an accelerated pace: time and rest are needed for absorption. Psychologists confirm the fact when they tell us that it is really in summer that our muscles learn how to skate, and in winter how to swim.

If I have dwelt on the emotions of teaching and being taught, it is because many people believe that schooling only engages the mind — and only temporarily at that. "I've forgotten," says the average man, "all I ever learned at school." And he mentally contrasts this happy oblivion with the fact that he still knows how to open oysters and ride a bicycle. But my description of teaching applies equally to physical things and to metaphysical. We may forget the substance of American History but we are probably scarred for life by the form and feeling of it as imparted by book and teacher. Why is it that the businessman's economics and the well-bred woman's taste in art are normally twenty-five years behind the times? It is that one's lifelong opinions are those picked up before maturity — at school and college.

This is why a "teacher's influence," if he does exert one, is not so big a joke as it seems. Notice in the lives of distinguished men how invariably there is a Mr. Bowles or a Dr. Tompkins or a Professor Clunk — whom no one ever heard of, but who is "remembered" for inspiring, guiding, and teaching decisively at the critical time. We can all see the mark left by a teacher in physical arts like tennis or music. The pupils of Leopold Auer or Tobias Matthay can be recognized at forty paces by their posture and even in a dark room by the sound they make. For in these disciplines the teacher usually falls back on direct imitation: "Hold your hand like this," or more simply, "Watch me." Well, much good teaching is of the "watch me" order, but the more abstract the knowledge, the less easy it is to imitate the teacher, and the genuine student wants to do the real thing in a real way *by himself*.

Consequently, the whole aim of good teaching is to turn the young learner, by nature a little copycat, into an independent, self-propelling creature, who cannot merely learn but study — that is, work as his own boss to the limit of his powers. This is to turn pupils into students, and it can be done on any rung of the ladder of learning. When I was a child, the multiplication table was taught from a printed sheet which had to be memorized one "square" at a time — the one's and the two's and so on up to nine. It never occurred to the teacher to show us how the answers could be arrived at also by addition, which we already knew. No one said, "Look: if four times four is sixteen, you ought to be able to figure out, without aid from memory, what five times four is, because that amounts to four more one's added to the sixteen." This would at first have been puzzling, *more* complicated and difficult than memory work, but once explained and grasped, it would have been an instrument for learning and checking the whole business of multiplication. We could temporarily have dispensed with the teacher and cut loose from the printed table.[1]

This is another way of saying that the only thing worth teaching anybody is a principle. Naturally principles involve facts and some facts must be learned "bare" because they do not rest on any principle. The capital of Alaska is Juneau and, so far as I know, that is all there is to it; but a European child ought not to learn that Washington is the capital of the United States without fixing firmly in his mind the relation between the city and the man who led his countrymen to freedom. That would be missing an association, which is the germ of a principle. And just as a complex athletic feat is made possible by rapid and accurate co-ordination, so all valuable learning hangs together and *works* by associations which make sense.

Since associations are rooted in habit and habits in feelings, we can see that anything which makes school seem a nightmare or a joke, which brands the teacher as a fool or a fraud, is the archenemy of all learning. It so happens that there is one professional disease, or rather vice, which generates precisely this feeling and whose consequences are therefore fatal. I refer to Hokum and I hasten to explain what I mean. Hokum is the

---

[1] I find that General Grant complained of the same thing: "Both winters were spent in going over the same old arithmetic which I knew every word of before and repeating 'A noun is the name of a thing,' which I had also heard my Georgetown teachers repeat until I had come to believe it." (*Memoirs*, New York, 1894, p. 20.)

counterfeit of true intellectual currency. It is words without meaning, verbal filler, artificial apples of knowledge. From the necessities of the case, nine tenths of all teaching is done with words, whence the ever-present temptation of hokum.

Words should point to things, seen or unseen. But they can also be used to wrap up emptiness of heart and lack of thought. The student accepts some pompous, false, meaningless formula, and passes it back on demand, to be rewarded with — appropriately enough — a passing grade. All the dull second-rate opinions, all the definitions that don't define, all the moral platitudes that "sound good," all the conventional adjectives ("gentle Shakespeare"), all the pretenses that a teacher makes about the feelings of his students towards him and vice versa, all the intimations that something must be learned because it has somehow got lodged among learnable things (like the Binomial Theorem or the date of Magna Carta) — all this in all its forms gives off the atmosphere of hokum, which healthy people everywhere find absolutely unbreathable.

In a modern play, I think by A. A. Milne, this schoolmarm vice has been caught and set down in a brief dialogue which goes something like this: —

GOVERNESS. Recite.
PUPIL. "The Battle of Blenheim." (*Long pause*)
GOVERNESS. By?
PUPIL (*silence*).
GOVERNESS. By Robert Southey.
PUPIL. By Robert Southey.
GOVERNESS. Who was Robert Southey?
PUPIL (*pause*). I don't know.
GOVERNESS. One of our greatest poets. Begin again.
PUPIL. The Battle of Blenheim by Robert Southey one of our greatest poets.

As this example shows, hokum is subtle and I will forbear to analyze it. It hides in the porous part of solid learning and vitiates it by making it stupid and ridiculous. I remember once giving a short quiz to a class of young women who had been reading about the Renaissance. I asked for some "identification" of names and put Petrarch in the list. One girl, who had evidently read a textbook, wrote down: "Petrarch — the vanguard of the new emphasis." I spent a good hour trying to explain why this parroting of opinion was not only not "correct" but blind hokum, hokum absolute. It was not an easy job because so many teachers and books deal exclusively in that cheap commodity. The child's instinct is first to believe the Word, spoken or printed; then with growing good sense to disbelieve it, but to trust to its hokum value for getting through by "satisfying" the teacher. Great heavens, what satisfactions!

To carry my anecdote one step further, I believe I made a life-long friend and a convert to decent learning by persuading my student that almost any honest mistake would have been truer than the absurdity she was palming off. She might better have been trivial: "Petrarch was an Italian"; or flippant: "Wrote poems to a girl named Laura"; or downright mistaken: "Also spelled Plutarch," rather than do what she did. My difficulty — and this is the important point — was in convincing her that I meant what I said, in breaking down the strongest superstition of the young, which is that everybody but themselves prefer make-believe and live by it.

III

So far as it concerns teachers, this superstition is not limited to the young. The reason why the "big world" scorns the "academic world" is precisely this, that remembering its school days, the big world is sure that all learning is hokum, and all teachers Old Pretenders. No doubt a good many teachers are. For some minds in any profession it is the path of least resistance to deal in shoddy phrases and use what brief authority is available to cram them down others' throats. But in teaching, this tradition — if it may be called one — has been rapidly dying out. It has been scotched like the custom of formal lecturing from cold-storage notes. Progressive education in this country, if it has done nothing else, should forever be honored and given thanks for insisting on genuine, hand-to-hand teaching, as against the giving out of predigested hokum. The older way was a hangover from the one-time union of the teaching and the preaching professions. Not that preaching is synonymous with hokum, but that when the ministry was the gateway to teaching, the Tartuffian attitude was compulsory. The teacher had to be more moral — which usually meant more conventional; he had to talk pious; to be gravely noncommittal and to support the established order in detail; he had to look and act — though the word is blasphemy — like a divine.

Since the advent of lay education — roughly the last seventy-five years — much has changed. No longer does the academic man resemble the description that Sherlock Holmes gives of his great antagonist, Professor Moriarty: ". . . clean shaven, pale and ascetic looking, retaining something of the professor in his features. His shoulders are rounded from much study, and his face protrudes forward and is forever slowly oscillating from side to side in a curiously reptilian fashion." Try as I may, I cannot think of any of my colleagues who has "retained something of the professor in his features," reptiles though they may be. They look like any other Americans; they are no more round-shouldered than bank presidents, they play golf and tennis and watch football, they marry and beget children, laugh and swear and have appendicitis in a thoroughly normal way. They are far less absent-minded than waiters in restaurants and they do not look a bit more like one another than a comparable number of doctors or mechanics.

Moreover their lives are as full of routine and excitement as that of any other group, and the excitement is not purely mental either. My own introduction to collegiate teaching, for instance, was marked by a seriocomic sequence reminiscent of Hollywood.

A big bruiser of a student whom I had failed came to my office threatening bodily harm, then hounded me by phone, wire, and letter, pleading that I should pass him "in the name of Christian brotherhood," for he had "powerful friends in Brooklyn." Nothing happened, but two years later, the tide as it were turned in my favor. I mean that another student, an impressive-looking, middle-aged man in an Extension course, made a point of showing his gratitude, first by inviting me to his Turkish restaurant and then by intimating that if I had any enemies he would only be too glad to get rid of them for me gratis. Unfortunately by then I had mislaid the address of my disgruntled Brooklynite.

Even if the academic man is popularly thought of as a Hamlet sicklied o'er with the pale cast of thought, do not underrate thought. Remember how many corpses Hamlet managed to pile up by the end of the play and what relief it was. Given the chance, men of thought readily turn men of action because their minds do not shrink from the unfamiliar; think of all the professors now in government service, dealing on the whole as well as any regular bureaucrats with thoroughly live situations. Or returning to the hurly-burly of human passion, think of the academic tradition of private murder, begun (fittingly at Harvard) in 1849 with Professor Webster's despatching of his colleague Parkman. Oliver Wendell Holmes – the elder and the greater one, that is, the doctor – has some wonderful testimony on that case and he is himself a witness to the variety, power, and unpredictability of the teaching faculty. They have furnished every kind of talent, crankiness, and devotion, and they have also, I trust, contributed their share to the nation's suicides, lunatics, and embezzlers. I even read last week in the news that a professor in the Army had been a hero. It is true that the young man was called an *ex*-professor, but we may put that down to the understandable jealousy of journalists.

A student of mine, to whom I once pointed out some of these facts to rebut the customary charge of being out of the world, answered with what seems at first a plausible distinction between the teacher and the man of action. "Anyone," he wrote me, "who does not spend most of his life working at something to which he is either indifferent or antagonistic cannot claim to share the common experience of mankind. Do I sound bitter? I am." The final comment gives the game away, and the argument is moreover based on a misconception. First, there are millions of people who work at things they like. Most professional men are in that class, and they pay for the privilege by working harder and cheaper than other people. Second, it is utterly untrue that teachers lead a life of elegant leisure, doing only what they like.

In recounting my apprenticeship I called teaching backbreaking work and later I hinted that steady teaching is a task that would fray the nerves of an ox. These are both sober statements. An hour of teaching is certainly the equivalent of a whole morning of office work. The pace, the concentration, the output of energy in office work are child's play compared with handling a class, and the smaller the class, the harder the work. Tutoring a single person — as someone has said — makes you understand what a dynamo feels like when it is discharging into a nonconductor.

Most teachers in colleges teach three hours daily five days a week, and their friends gape and stare: "You're through for the day at twelve!" The fact is that at twelve o'clock a teacher who has done his stint is as limp as a rag. In the next chapter I shall show in more detail what he has done to get into this state. In speaking now of the bare effect, I am not thinking of feeble constitutions or neurotic personalities, but of the average man or woman who might readily find other employment. Nor shall I go on to harrow the reader with accounts of primary and high school teaching, characterized by huge, unruly classes, longer hours, and usually — for the women at least — housework on getting home; and private schools impose other chores to fill the teacher's day. I stick to college teaching, which is supposed to be a sinecure. At noon, the best effort of the day has been put in. Then comes lunch, usually spoiled for relaxation by being combined with a committee meeting. The afternoon goes to conferences with students, a mass of clerical work, professional correspondence, and snags of all sorts involving plant and personnel — all this very akin to hospital work because in both places time and considerateness for persons are the dominant concerns.

By five or five-thirty, this do-nothing king of a professor goes home — to his family if he has one, to his books and papers, which he cannot help having. If he is a young instructor, he has many new preparations — perhaps four hours' work to every three class hours. If he is an old hand, he not only reprepares for surety but he is exploring some field of his own; he is reading and reviewing books, keeping up with periodical literature, carrying on debate with his colleagues all over the world, and supervising the written work of his advanced students. He has worked seven hours abroad and probably will work four more at home, while his businessman neighbor is quietly enjoying bridge with friends or worry by himself. No teacher gets through his day's work that day and hence no teacher has ever lived who did not regularly sigh, "Thank God it's Friday!"

"Yes, yes, of course, but he has four months in the summer with nothing to do." On any campus around the first of June, this is a dangerous remark to make. Most teachers are then gasping for their three weeks' rest before the Summer Session opens. And those who are taking what is ironically called "the summer off" are planning only a modest vacation. Getting acquainted with one's family, swimming and loafing or fishing, are an absolute necessity, if the teacher's battery is going to be recharged for the next bout. But the four months cannot be devoted wholly to this body culture. The wretched slave has dragged with him to his summer camp: one Ph.D. candidate's manuscript stuck in mid-passage and so bad he will himself rewrite it; six current nonprofessional books which he must read if he is not to become an illiterate; three folders full of notes to be organized for his own next work; and two new volumes in his field, one in German and one in French, which he gullibly accepted for review last December. Teaching in America is a twenty-four-hour job, twelve months in the year: sabbatical leaves are provided so you can have your coronary thrombosis off the campus.

In England, they arrange things somewhat better. Terms are shorter and vacations longer. More people loaf, and teaching is on the whole as active and probably a good deal more effectual. For in our American university, with a few exceptions justified by age or eminence or incurable laziness, the faculty reaches the end of term frazzled and the students dizzy with work. Not that all students work, but that those who do, overwork. As for the instructor, he hurtles from term to term, wishing he could echo in his own behalf the tremulous cry that William James uttered near the end of his career: "For thirty-five years I have been suffering the exigencies of being . . . [a teacher], the pretension and the duty namely, of meeting the mental needs and difficulties of other persons, needs that I couldn't possibly imagine and difficulties that I couldn't possibly understand; and now that I have shuffled off the professional coil, the sense of freedom that comes to me is as surprising as it is exquisite. . . . What! not to have to accommode myself to this mass of alien and recalcitrant humanity, not to think under resistance, not to have to square myself with others at every step I make — hurrah! it is too good to be true."

3. Two Minds, One Thought

Gentlemen: I shall not ask you
to believe but defy you to deny.
— PROFESSOR SEELEY
to a new class

IT IS A PITY that our novelists have been so chary of showing
human nature in the classroom. Had they done so, I should not
have to write this chapter. I could point to well-known tales in
which the intellectual drama of teaching was depicted in full,
emotion and intellect fused into one. But I can think of only
two stories that even touch on the subject. One is Kipling's
"Regulus" in the "Stalky" series; the other is Lionel Trilling's
"Of This Time, of That Place" in *Three Readers*. Perhaps there
is something revealing in the lack I deplore, for there is no dearth
of school stories and even movies. But they are always about setting dormitories on fire and narrow escapes from learning. In
Dickens's *Our Mutual Friend*, certain outside personal relations
of master and pupil are brilliantly recorded, but we have no
account of what goes on in the minds of the two participants
when the teacher actually performs.

No doubt what goes on is something of a mystery. What I
described in the last chapter had to do with the parts of the
machine and the motive power that moves the parts. Their
grinding should of course never become conscious, any more
than digesting breakfast should. But the most notable part of
teaching is very conscious indeed. It is the imparting of knowledge. The mystery there, is that no one can tell when or
how this happens. It is simply true of human beings that they
can communicate. Hence those educators who have recently pro-

posed to "teach communication" in the colleges are forgetting that communication is just what teaching is.[1] Its ideal aim is to have two minds share one thought. This of course can never be perfectly realized in practice. The teacher's age and mental associations differ too much from those of his students; his students differ among themselves, and no two people anywhere ever reach perfect mutual understanding.

How then do you pour a little bit of what you feel and think and know into another's mind? In the act of teaching it is done by raising the ghost of an object, idea, or fact, and holding it in full view of the class, turning it this way and that, describing it — demonstrating it like a new car or a vacuum cleaner. The public has an excellent name for this: "making the subject come to life." The student must see the point, must re-create Lincoln, must feel like Wordsworth at Tintern Abbey, must visualize the pressure of the atmosphere on a column of mercury. The "subject" should become an "object" present before the class, halfway between them and the teacher, concrete, convincing, unforgettable. This is why teachers tend so naturally to use physical devices — maps, charts, diagrams. They write words on the board, they gesture, admonish, and orate. Hence the fatigue and hence the rule which I heard a Dean enunciate, that good teaching is a matter of basal metabolism. The man who yawned during his own lecture was correctly reproved by him who said: "The professor confirms our judgment but usurps our prerogative." And another of the same caliber was neatly told off as "having the facts but not the phosphorescence of learning."

Still, this power to throw light is not the whole story. There must be something to throw light on. There must be a subject matter and the word *matter* is there most significant. Not everything can be made into an "object" for purposes of teaching. I

---

[1] Roget's *Thesaurus* sums up the matter in a casual note: "Teaching, for example, although a voluntary act, relates primarily to the communication of Ideas." (Ed. Boston, 1879. *Introd.*, xvii–xviii, *n.*)

dogmatically asserted earlier that it is impossible to teach tolerance or democracy. The reason is that these are not subject matters at all but virtues or attitudes. I shall have more to say about what makes a proper subject and I think it will help resolve many doubts about what the "right curriculum" is. But surely no human quality is a matter for curriculum in the sense I mean. Would any faculty offer a course called "Wit, Elementary and Advanced"? Or "Firm Principles – Old and New"? Then why speak of teaching toleration? All these things are aspects of subject matter. You can study wit from the Greeks to Will Rogers, or compare the firm principles of Stoics, Christians, and Atheists. Similarly, you can explain what Voltaire did for toleration in his campaign to rehabilitate the Protestant Calas. You can even raise a warm glow of approval for the deed. But what you are teaching is history or literature or philosophy. You could not hope to make a genuine course of study by stringing together two dozen instances of struggle for toleration. At the third instance you would lose your class. Why? Because in a real subject there must be order, progression, increasing complexity, new principles at every step. This in turn is true because the human mind is built on dramatic lines. It wants plot, climax, and denouement. Without them attention wanders and teaching dies. Can you imagine a play composed of nine opening scenes? Each might be most alluring but no audience could stand the strain of bafflement or have zest for ever-new beginnings.

Not long ago I sat in on a long discussion of this very topic: should we teach subjects or attitudes? One man with a warm heart even preferred to ask, "Should we teach subjects or boys and girls?" This play on words confuses the whole issue. The only way to teach somebody is obviously to teach him something. Shall it be an attitude? I answer No because the only way to build up attitudes – once simply known as good habits – is by repetitious moralizing, and repetition, as I have said, is undramatic. Even Aesop had to write fables to his maxims. Besides, the only attitudes worth teaching are flexible ones, adaptable to different circumstances. A tolerant person may not be perfectly tolerant but he will surely tolerate more things than those his parent or teacher happened to mention. This means that the only way to instill any human virtue is to have parents and teachers and friends who are themselves tolerant and just, and who in all reasonable opportunities evince that character.

Yet the teaching of subject matter cannot go on without the building up of certain habits. Whether they are moral habits or intellectual is a question of definition; they constitute the element of "training" that we hear so much about. Accordingly, the habits stressed by the teacher must be so general in scope and so clearly necessary for pursuing and possessing knowledge that his insistence on them looks like a genuine part of the business in hand. There are only two such habits. One is thinking; the other is attention. Some might say the two are aspects of a single condition, which is that of being wide-awake. But I believe it is useful to distinguish them because in practice the one power occasionally gets in the way of the other — as when in a discussion group a very active-minded student thinks so violently that he pays no attention to another's objection. It is true that like all gifts of nature the ability to think cannot be imparted; it can only be developed, and one of the oldest complaints against schools is that they stop the natural thinker and try to make him a learned dunce. But this is no monopoly of the schools; the family, the church, the community, do it too. By the law of probability, some teachers are bound to be more stupid than their best students, and since a pint pot cannot hold a quart, the more limited mind will try to compress and head off the richer.

It is only fair to add that determined thinkers are few. For most people, thinking is dreary uphill work; their mind is set in motion by only a rare stimulus. I remember an easygoing classmate of mine, nicknamed "Q," who was thickness personified, but who apparently could think like lightning on the football field. There he was brilliant, but coming out in a group from an examination, once, someone asked him, "Say, Q, how much did you know?"

"Know! I didn't even suspect anything."

Overhear a group of average students talking about their teachers and you will find the near majority agreed on warning the rest: "Don't take *his* course: he tries to make you think." Again, in the communistic pooling of knowledge that goes on before final examinations, the demand is "Give me the dope" — that is, tell me the minimum of ready-made catchwords with which I can fool the old boy into supposing I know something. No college student need feel offended at this revelation: how many of his teachers are great thinkers? How many books in the library enshrine genuine hard thought? Thinking is rare; that is one reason it is precious. Besides, there are moments in all our lives when the line of least resistance is clearly indicated. As one Ph.D. candidate said when grilled in a picayune manner about his footnotes: "I did not discover America, I took it second hand from Christopher Columbus."

Nevertheless, without some power of thought, study is effort wasted, and drearisome besides. I tell students that I can certainly "give them the dope" but that they will feel the narcotic effects. In the long run, the harder way is more fun; and I am struck by the fact that the great public senses this, rushing out to buy almost any book that offers to teach "the art of thinking" or "mathematics for the million" or "how to read a book." Thinking means shuffling, relating, selecting the contents of one's mind so as to assimilate novelty, digest it, and create order. It is doing to a fact or an idea what we do to a beefsteak when we distribute its parts throughout our body. We are presumably stronger and better for it, readier for attack and defense, as well as more competent to assimilate more of the same protein without strain.

You will tell me that thinking is on the contrary something anemic and finicky and disabling. To which I reply that that is not thinking but brooding. Brooding is thinking in a circle instead of toward the point of effortless mastery. The philosopher Whitehead very justly says: "It is a profoundly erroneous truism, repeated by all copy books and by eminent people when they are making speeches, that we should cultivate the habit of thinking of what we are doing. The precise opposite is the case. Civilization advances by extending the number of important operations which we can perform without thinking. . . ." This is particularly true in mathematics, where the ability to pass rapidly from our starting point to our goal is the result of previous thinking, just as muscular power is the result of previous practice.

Now to learn to think while being taught presupposes the other difficult art of paying attention. Nothing is more rare: listening seems to be the hardest thing in the world and misunderstanding the easiest, for we tend to hear what we think we are going to hear, and too often we make it so. In a lifetime one is lucky to meet six or seven people who know how to attend; the rest, some of whom believe themselves well-bred and highly educated, have for the most part fidgety ears; their span of attention is as short as the mating of a fly. They seem afraid to lend their mind to another's thought, as if it would come back to them bruised and bent. This fear is of course fatal to sociability, and Lord Chesterfield was right when he wrote to his son that the power of attention was the mark of a civilized man. The baby cannot attend; the savage and the boor will not. It is the boorishness of inattention that makes pleasant discussion turn into stupid repetitive argument, and that doubles the errors and mishaps of daily life.

Those who urge that schools should once again give "discipline" really mean attention. In that form, their proposal is worth considering. I am bound to say that with all its grave faults, the French secondary school system does successfully emphasize the importance of attention. Perhaps it limits it too much to verbal matters, but in the *lycée*, as soon as children are old enough to know what they are about, a *faute d'inattention* is accounted worse than an error in substance. In this country, good training in science achieves the same result, but again limits it too narrowly to technical matters. *All* subjects have their fine points, and letting the careless ride roughshod over them is doing a poor favor to subject and student. It is not enough to say that when the matter is interesting the pupil will be interested and will attend: every branch of learning involves drudgery and it is there that attention is most required. A blunder is harmless; it almost corrects itself, but repeated falling away from precision through scatterbrains is like the adulteration of food — less nourishment, possible danger, and invariable bad taste. It is needless to add that the teacher must not rest content with demanding attention: he must command it. Easier said than done, even for those with "commanding personality." Stonewall Jackson could lead an army but not a class.

II

Yet "any damn fool," said the Admiral with a friendly pat on my shoulder, "can teach Naval History." I knew what he meant by this subtle encouragement, but I disagreed. I had visited a midshipmen's school and heard a petty officer, who was not a damn fool but not a teacher either, instruct in the subject. He had his nose in a book and was reading aloud: " 'On the eleventh of February, Commodore Perry made for an anchorage twelve miles farther up Yedo Bay — ' This is important; take it down: 'On the eleventh — of February — Commodore Perry — made for an anchorage — ' "

This may have been the Admiral's idea of a lecture; certainly many people now alive have been taught in this fashion. But it proves nothing except that anything may be done badly. What is bad here is of course the absence of meaningful stress, or, as I said before, of drama. Given the three basic ways of conducting a class, success will depend on the degree to which the chosen way has dramatic form. This does not mean histrionics, though neither does it exclude them wholly.

Let me explain. The three basic ways are the lecture, the discussion group, and the tutorial hour. In a lecture, a silent class is addressed, more or less like a public meeting. In a discussion group, comprising from five or six to not more than thirty students, the members of the class speak freely, putting or answering questions on points which the teacher organizes so as to form a coherent account of some topic. It may be that for this purpose discussion by the class is broken at intervals by lecturettes from him. In a tutorial hour, the instructor is really holding a conversation, usually with one student, certainly with not more than three or four. This is in the best sense a free-for-all and it presupposes a good stock of knowledge on the part of the students. I may seem to have left out the recitation class, common to the lower schools, in which every pupil in turn answers a part of the day's lesson. But this is really a form of examination. Its teaching value is that of any good examination and I shall speak of it later under that head.

If some few years ago I had listed lectures as a legitimate mode of teaching, I should have been set down by my progressive friends as an old mossback corrupted by university practice. But now several of the progressive colleges have officially restored lecturing — Bennington notably — and I suspect that unofficially they were unable at any time to do altogether without it. Lecturing comes so natural to mankind that it is hard to stop it by edict. It simply turns into bootleg form. Many teachers think that because they sit around a table with only a dozen students they are running a discussion group, but they are lecturing just the same if the stream of discourse flows in only one direction.

Now what makes a lecture legitimate and good? The answer is — a combination of eloquence and personality. The petty officer reading aloud from a book was out of his element. But if Charles Dickens, famous for his public readings, had held that textbook of Naval History, the class would have *seen* Commodore Perry steaming up the bay in defiance of Japanese orders; they would have known without being told that it was important; they would not have had to take it down. And this is the justification of large-scale lecturing.

The lecture room is the place where drama may properly become theater. This usually means a fluent speaker, no notes, and no shyness about "effects." In some teachers a large class filling a sloped-up amphitheater brings out a wonderful power of emphasis, timing, and organization. The speaker projects himself and the subject. The "effects" are not laid on, they are the meaningful stress which constitutes, most literally, the truth of the matter. This meaning — as against fact — is the one thing to be indelibly stamped on the mind, and it is this that the printed book cannot give. That is why their hearers never forgot Huxley lecturing, nor Michelet, nor William James. Plenty of facts can be conveyed, too — the more highly organized the better; but in the hands of a great lecturer it is feelings and principles that illuminate the soul as does a perfect play or concert.

Again, the tone of a whole philosophy may be given by a manner, and many manners are good. In Carlton J. H. Hayes's course on Nationalism, for example, I shall never forget the introductory lecture on the peoples of antiquity and the nature of their tribal bond. The lecturer enumerated them — the Chaldees, the Persians, the Phoenicians, the Greeks, the Hittites, and others — peoples, city-states, and empires but not nations; human groups with a language, a past, and a destiny. Then, stopping dramatically, and leaning forward over the desk, he asked: "Where are the Hittites?" Contrast this with John Dewey's manner, effective in a precisely opposite way — through a steady bagpipe drone, full of small variations, a kind of rustic Debussy with wonderful insinuations that linger in the ear. From the late F. J. E. Woodbridge one had defiant, almost angry impersonations of the world's philosophers. Or yet again, from John Erskine princely introductions to the poets, with an accompaniment of great passages that we had not managed to find for ourselves.

To this day, throughout the country's colleges one hears of courses famed chiefly for their delivery: "You *must* take so-and-so before you leave." This love of spectacle is perfectly sound and there is no truth in the belief that artistic brilliance invariably conceals emptiness of mind. Students know better, and when a man commits the sin of nonteaching that Milton denounces in *Lycidas*, they detect the false rhetoric and are quick to scorn it as it deserves. To try to abolish the varied forms of lecturing virtuosity in the name of a theory cut to fit more common gifts is surely a mistake. What led to the attempt was that formerly *all* college teaching was through lectures. Many were bad and nothing is worse than a bad lecture. Everyone can conjure up from his own past the memory of incoherent mumblings that make time stand still and inspire suicidal thoughts.

At the same time, it is also true that lectures alone will not suffice to teach, for the lecture method assumes that every member of the class comes in the same state of preparation and leaves with the same increment of knowledge. The fact is otherwise. Only individual attention to each student can keep the whole class abreast and truly teach. A lecture is a sizing of the canvas in broad strokes. The fine brush and palette knife must be used close up to finish the work of art. This is why a normal three-hour-a-week class is usually broken up into small groups for the "third hour" after the two lectures.

Unfortunately, the third hour is too often entrusted to a "section man," usually a graduate student earning his keep by doing nothing else than this quiz and rehearsing work. This is the cheapest way of dealing with large numbers but it is bad practice. The lecturer should himself be available for questioning by his students; he should himself discover their failures and misconceptions; he should run his whole show as one enterprise and be responsible for conveying his subject to as many men, personally known to him, as possible. If we remember the axiom, Two Minds Sharing One Thought, we can see that teaching by proxy is as impossible as learning by proxy. Besides, the "section man" device is a piece of academic wickedness towards the man for reasons I shall give later on.

The idea of breaking a large class into small groups gives us the second mode of teaching, by means of informal discussion. As a general rule, I believe that all introductory courses should be taught thus. It is expensive but worth it. Only in a small group can the student learn to marshal his thoughts, expose his weaknesses, argue out his beliefs, and gain that familiarity with the "ropes" of a given subject which, if not learned early, will never be learned at all. The expense of staffing many small groups in the first two college years is partly compensated by the lesser amount of academic floundering and failure and by the central fact of teaching success.

Handling a discussion group requires a special talent, too. Here the drama is more subtle but equally imperative. The hour's discussion must not go off in all directions like a leaky hose. It must have a pattern, beginning at a given point and logically reaching another, from which to start again the next day. Now it is relatively easy to impose a pattern on a lecture; the scheme of it can be written out beforehand and even memorized, because no one will interfere with it. But in a discussion, every one of twenty-five or thirty men has a right to shove the tiller in any direction he pleases. Since there must be an atmosphere of freedom, the instructor must not act like a priggish moderator with a gavel. He must be willing to go up sidetracks and come back. His imagination must swarm with connecting links, factual illustrations, answers to unexpected questions. He must moreover know how to correct without wounding, contradict without discouraging, coax along without coddling. Every once in a while, a group of men will contain a crank or a fanatic: he must be turned to good teaching use without being made to feel a goat. Every once in a while, the class will want to take the bit in its teeth and hold a political or ethical debate, none too close to the issue. This must be tolerated. Every once in a while, the instructor will feel so strongly on a given matter that he will want to lecture. This must be nipped in the bud.

An advanced discussion group — say twelve men in a senior colloquium in economics meeting for two consecutive hours — is a test of any discussion leader. His role is that of an orchestra conductor, except that neither he nor his men have a score before them. Yet the result of the evening's noise must be as intelligible as a symphony. This takes mutual accustoming on the part of leader and led. Calling on the right man for the right thing, balancing opinions, drawing out the shy and backward, keeping silent so that the group itself will unwind its own errors — and doing all this in the casual "colloquial" manner which the title of the course prescribes — is an art that only comes with long practice. It calls for the best teachers in their prime and I am convinced furthermore that it accomplishes more than any other form of teaching.

Compared with this the "tutorial" is far simpler though physically more exhausting. Two or three or four men can talk so much more fully to one another that errors are more quickly corrected and ground is covered faster. Indeed, there is less temptation to error because there is no audience, no attitudes to strike before one's fellow students. The foursome have probably studied the topic together anyway and they are reporting progress. The instructor usually finds little to amend and therefore feels bound to add, to fill out, to interpret the body of facts. This leads to more questions and he finds himself being pumped absolutely dry. No matter how much he knows or how fully he has thought, he is relentlessly pushed until his back touches the wall of the great absolutes. For students are ever seeking final answers and they know how to ask questions which no wise man would dare answer.

Not all tutors are wise, however, and the principal danger is that unprepared or malicious students will use a common trick to defeat the purpose of the meeting. If a man is known to have some pet view or favorite topic, he will be brought to the brink of it by artful dodges and then pushed over. While he climbs his way out the students can respectfully daydream. I am told that one man at a Midwestern university can be wound up by his students like a grandfather clock. He runs down daily and hourly on the same topic like a weight on its chain, and no one is the worse, or the better, for the ticking.

I do not know whether this is a saving of energy for him as well as the students, but I do know that the other and truer discharge of duty is a wearing process. At most progressive colleges, at least until recently, teachers were committed to whole days of half-hour tutorials, each with a single student. Every student was at work on a different phase of a given subject and, by virtue of the time and freedom allowed, was ravenous for knowledge. I can guarantee from experience that at the end of such a day the instructor is a gibbering idiot. The output of words alone, the quick modulations, the sense of multitudinous insistent claims on one's best thought, and what James meant by "having to square oneself with others at every step," would in time surely kill the poor goose. One perceptive student, commenting on certain events at the time, said to me: "At F—— [a progressive school] the teachers die young; at J—— [a nonprogressive one] the students hang themselves: that seems to be the basic difference between old-fashioned and Progressive Education."

In all three modes of teaching — by lecture, by discussion, and by tutoring — it is evident that the effective agent is the living person. It is idle to talk about what *could* be done by gadgets — gramophone disks or sound films. We know just what they can do: they aid teaching by bringing to the classroom irreplaceable subject matter or illustrations of it. The disk brings the music class a whole symphony; the film can bring Chinese agriculture to students in Texas; it could even be used more widely than it is to demonstrate delicate scientific techniques. But this will not replace the teacher — even though through false economy it might here and there *dis*place him. In theory, the printed book should have technologically annihilated the teacher, for the original "lecture" was a reading from a costly manuscript to students who could not afford it. Well, why is it so hard to learn by oneself from a book? Cardinal Newman, himself a great teacher, gives part of the answer: "No book can convey the special spirit and delicate peculiarities of its subject with that rapidity and certainty which attend on the sympathy of mind with mind, through the eyes, the look, the accent, and the manner, in casual expressions thrown off at the moment, and the unstudied turns of familiar conversation."

Clearly no Hollywood technique will yield casual expression. But there is more to live teaching than a manner: the manner must fit. Teaching is not a process, it is a developing emotional situation. It takes two to teach, and from all we know of great teachers the spur from the class to the teacher is as needful an element as the knowledge it elicits. In its most advanced phase, even the forbidden fault of thinking aloud becomes the most desirable product of the occasion. William James used to be so stimulated to original thought in class that his mind would race ahead of the subject, he would have to interrupt himself and ask the group, "What was I speaking about?" Here the very disconnection and break of form becomes the highest virtue, leaving mere correctness and continuity far behind.

But always, if the "sympathy of mind with mind" is to play its role, the teacher's utterance must fit and therefore cannot be premeditated. For this reason, a quick wit can achieve results beyond foretelling. I recall a class in comparative literature in which the lecturer began by dwelling on the magic importance of words in the history of the race. "Primitive man," he said by way of illustration, "will never tell you his name, for fear you will use it to cast a spell on him. He will not repel but evade your question." At this point, the speaker paused and looked at Q sitting with his head hidden behind an open newspaper. "What is the name of the gentleman in the back row reading the paper?"

Down came the sheet. "Who, me?"

"Gentlemen, what did I tell you!"

For the same reason of fitness, no lecturing or dialectic device should become a trick. It is easy perhaps not to overdo wit; harder to avoid those phrases and mannerisms of vocal and physical emphasis which students remember long after they have forgotten the thing emphasized. Ideally a teacher should speak with the tongue of an angel and look like one. In saying this, I deny a common half-truth which seems to me to rest on false democratic feeling. I refer to the elder-brother notion that the teacher is simply a student who has been at it somewhat longer than his charges. I have heard a teacher tell a class that all he could do, really, was by a timely word here and there to help his juniors avoid this or that pitfall. And I seemed to hear the echo answer, "Piffle!"

It is of course a fact that the teacher is *not* an angel and actually *is* an older student. But he is even more truly a leader, a superior officer, a responsible head meant to inspire confidence. He is, or ought to be, the captain of the ship. Students no more than passengers want the "captain" to go about his duties with an apologetic cough. This does not mean that the teacher must be overbearing or that he must pretend omniscience. A good teacher is free to admit his ignorance openly and frequently. But what he knows, he knows better than his students, knows it in a far different manner, and knows that he knows it. The word "authority" is liable to abuse, but there is a sense in which the teacher must have authority as well as be one. The giving of full authority to beginning teachers is of the utmost importance, for them and for the class. If they are supervised, badgered, "taken down," how can they develop assurance and — what is equally important — a sense of professional responsibility for their words and acts?

The worst instance of maladministration in this respect was reported to me by a former student of mine, who was taken into the Army to teach celestial navigation (the very post for an angel) to trained bombardiers. He was a good man and, though not an astronomer, had mastered his subject. Unfortunately he was only a technical sergeant while all his students were lieutenants. Some accepted his authority well enough, others were insolent and resentful. But all thought it an imposition: they could not imagine themselves needing the knowledge. So that whereas a superior officer could have reconciled them to the drudgery, the presence as teacher of a mere sergeant, who could rely only on tactfulness, was simply an incitement to grumbling and academic sabotage.

In civilian teaching, of course, nothing gives authority like knowledge; and each instructor, if let alone, develops the manner suited to his talents. This implies that all "methods" in the "educator's" sense of the word are wholly beside the point. Some teachers can and must do what others would reject as unpractical. Some classes induce an ease and a familiarity which would be fatal with another group. In any case, the teacher must to a large extent accept himself, with all his shortcomings, before he can expect others to accept him. If he has himself on his mind, the class will automatically follow his thought and think about his hair or his necktie instead of his subject. I once opened by mistake a textbook on teaching methods, and my eye fell on Rule 24, which was that you must keep your hands hanging naturally at the side of your body. A footnote further suggested that if this proved difficult, touching the seam in one's clothing with the little finger would serve as a reminder. How many young teachers, men and women, have been made miserable by such "advice"? I wonder. Yet how difficult to make clear the paradoxical truth about an angelic presence, namely, that while it is good not to be a bundle of mannerisms, it is better to be one-self and forget Rule 24.[2] Given a mastered subject and a person committed heart and soul to teaching it, a class accustomed to think, attend, and be led; the result will be, under God, as near to the discourse of men and angels as it is fit to go.

Mastery of subject matter brings up the next large tract I must cross, hoping it will not prove to be another stretch of Peacock's Great Sahara of the mind. What must teachers teach, why, and how? Since I shall deal with a quantity of subjects ranging from spelling to music and science, it may well seem contradictory to stress mastery as a prerequisite to authority. My excuse must be that although I have taught or coached in a good many of these subjects, I am not speaking exclusively from my direct experience. I have listened to others, particularly students, and observed my fellows. Besides, there are varying degrees of mastery, and the right standard to ask of a graduate instructor would be misapplied to a teacher in an elementary school. Finally, even though I shall not mind making mistakes and being corrected, I shall say more about certain subjects and far less about others, in proportion to my sense of having experience at my back. In any event, I am setting down a personal record, not codifying the law and the prophets.

[2] It may interest college graduates who remember their teachers' oddities to know that the habit of rattling keys in a pocket or pacing up and down is not the sign of "nervousness" that it seems. Rattling keys may be annoying, but some means of letting the body steadily discharge motor energy is a psychologically sound aid to concentration. It helps to carry off through one path the responses to all the minor stimuli that might otherwise interrupt the train of thought. I suggest that lecturers be held to noiseless immobility only when classrooms are soundproofed and students stop shuffling feet, banging doors, and dropping books.

4. How to Write and Be Read

Here and there a touch of good
grammar for picturesqueness.
— MARK TWAIN

Writing comes before reading, in logic and also in the public mind. No one cares whether you read fast or slow, well or ill, but as soon as you put pen to paper, somebody may be puzzled, angry, bored, or ecstatic; and if the occasion permits, your reader is almost sure to exclaim about the schools not doing their duty. This is the oldest literary tradition, of which here is a modern instance: —

WHAT KIND OF TEACHING IN THE PRIMARY SCHOOLS?

BY "DISGUSTED"

Recently a letter came into my office from a boy who described himself as a first-year high school student. He wanted *infirmation* about *Africia*, because for his project in the social studies class he had *chozen Africia*. If we could not help him, *were* could he write? In closing, he was ours *sinceerly*. His handwriting was comparable to that of my 6-year-old nephew.

Too bad, but I am not alarmed. This student of "Africia" may or may not learn to spell: it is not nearly so important as his diction and his sentence structure, which the plaintiff withheld, though they would have better enabled us to judge what the schools were really doing. What I fear about this boy is that when grown-up and provided with a secretary who can spell, he will write something like this: —

Dear Sir: —

As you know, security prices have been advancing rapidly in the recent past *in belated recognition of the favorable fundamentals that exist.* [Italics mine]

What is decadent about this I shall shortly explain. Meantime, the fact should be faced squarely that good writing is and has always been extremely rare. I do not mean fine writing, but the simple, clear kind that everyone always demands — from others. The truth is that Simple English is no one's mother tongue. It has to be worked for. As an historian, I have plowed through state papers, memoirs, diaries, and letters, and I know that the ability to write has only a remote connection with either intelligence, or greatness, or schooling. Lincoln had no schooling yet became one of the great prose writers of the world. Cromwell went to Cambridge and was hardly ever able to frame an intelligible sentence. Another man of thought and action, Admiral Lord Howe, generally refrained from writing out his plan of battle, so as to save his captains from inevitable misunderstanding. Yet Howe managed to win the famous First of June by tactics that revolutionized the art, and led directly to Nelson's Trafalgar plan — itself a rather muddled piece of prose. Let us then start with no illusion of an imaginary golden age of writing.

Which leaves the problem of doing the best with what nature gives us. And here I have some convictions born of long struggle, with myself and with others. First, I pass by all considerations of penmanship and elementary spelling to remark only that I think it a mistake to start children writing on typewriters, and worse yet to let them grow up unable to do anything but print capitals.

Above the beginner's level, the important fact is that writing cannot be taught exclusively in a course called English Composition. Writing can only be taught by the united efforts of the entire teaching staff. This holds good of any school, college, or university. Joint effort is needed, not merely to "enforce the rules"; it is needed to insure accuracy in every subject. How can an answer in physics or a translation from the French or an historical statement be called correct if the phrasing is loose or the key word wrong? Students argue that the reader of the paper knows perfectly well what is meant. Probably so, but a written exercise is designed to be read; it is not supposed to be a challenge to clairvoyance. My Italian-born tailor periodically sends me a postcard which runs: "Your clothes is ready and should come down for a fitting." I understand him, but the art I honor him for is cutting cloth, not precision of utterance. Now a student in college must be inspired to achieve in all subjects the utmost accuracy of perception combined with the utmost artistry of expression. The two merge and develop the sense of good workmanship, of preference for quality and truth, which is the chief mark of the genuinely educated man.

This is obviously a collective task, in which every department and every faculty has a common stake. But it is not enough to give notice that these are the faculty's sentiments. Even supposing that all teachers were willing and able to exert vigilance over written work, there would still be many practical problems of detail. And first, what motive for writing well can the student be made to feel? There is only one valid motive: the desire to be read. You will say that most students have no urge either to write or to be read. True, but (*a*) they know that they have to write and (*b*) most of them want to be well thought of. They should accordingly be made to see that reading the ordinary student paper can be a nuisance and a bore to the teacher, and that the proper aim of writing should be to make it a pleasure. This is another way of saying that most school writing is bad because student and teacher play at writing and reading instead of taking it seriously. The teacher expects second-rate hokum and the student supplies it. Let the teacher assert his rights just as the students do: in many college classes the men protest — quite rightly — when they are asked to read a dull or ill-organized book. Similarly, the instructor may warn the students that when they turn in filler and padding, jargon and lingo, stuff and nonsense, he will mark them down, not only in his grade book, but in his violated soul.

Naturally, this conscious brutality must go with a helping

hand; in fact a revision of all usual practices is in order. The embargo on hokum will already work a healthy elimination of bad prose. Then the long Term Paper must be discarded and replaced with the short essay, not more than five typewritten pages in length. Students always ask how long a final paper should be and they are absolutely right in believing that most instructors are impressed by mere bulk. But when one knows how difficult it is to articulate even three measly thoughts around a single point, it is folly to ask eighteen-year-olds to produce thirty- or forty-page monographs that shall be readable. What they produce is an uncarded mattress of quotations, paraphrase, "however's," and "Thus we see's." Size being aimed at, there is no time for rewriting or reordering the material culled from half a dozen books, and the main effort goes into the irrelevant virtues of neat typing, plentiful footnotes, and the mannerisms of scholarship.

The short paper — and I speak from a large pile accumulated over twelve years — aims and arrives at different ends. It answers the reader's eternal question: Just what are you trying to tell me? It is in that spirit that student writing must be read, corrected, and if need be rewritten. When first presented, it must already be a second or third draft. The only reason I can think of for the somewhat higher average of good writing in France is that the *brouillon* is a national institution. The *brouillon* (literally: scrambled mess) is the first draft, and even the concierge writing to the police about anarchists on the third floor begins with a *brouillon*, later found by his heirs.

Of course it is no use telling an American boy or girl that the essay must be written, laid aside, and rewritten at least once before handing in: the innocents do not know what to do after their first painful delivery. So the simplest thing is to ask early in the term for a good five-page essay, which turns out to be pretty bad. This is fully annotated by the reader and turned back before the next one is called for. But the corrections on it are not merely the conventional *sp.*, *ref.*, *punc.*, and *awk.* which the writers have seen in their margins from the seventh grade on. The comments are intensely and painfully personal, being the responses that an alert reader would feel if he were encountering the essay in print. The result is that even the best students feel abashed, if not actually resentful. To which one can only say that they should resent the neglect in which all their previous teachers have left them.

This neglect has not damaged their grammar so much as their vocabulary. Since the last thing any writer learns is the uses of words, it is no wonder if untutored youths of ability write like the stockbroker whom I quoted about "favorable fundamentals that exist" — spineless, vague, and incoherent prose. Indeed, the exact parallel comes this moment under my hand, taken from a very able student's report on Newman's *University Sketches:* "A University that rests on a firm financial foundation has the greater ability to unleash the minds of its students." Despite the difference in names, the stockbroker is that boy's putative father. Their failure comes from a like inattention to meaning — their own and that of the words they use.

This means that words and tone are the main things to be taught. Spelling, grammar, and punctuation do not precede but follow in the order of importance. They follow also quite naturally in the order of facility. Accordingly, the teacher-critic must slowly and carefully explain to the student what each word conveys in its particular context. I find that in the essay just cited I have written such comments as: "I can't follow — This repeats in disguise — 'avocational fruit' suggests alligator pears: why? — We now have about eight 'problems' on hand: Begin! — What! more issues and problems? — Commercial lingo — Who is 'we'? — Why 'cradle': the metaphor is lost — Who says this? — 'Patina' is not 'clothing' — Don't scold and then trail off in this way — This is your point at last." In addition, images are changed, synonyms proposed, and bad sentences recast, sometimes in alternative ways, in order to show precisely how the original misleads and how clarity is to be reached.

Tone grows naturally out of diction, but the choice of words betrays feelings of which the young writer is usually unaware. "Are you pleading, denouncing, coaxing, or laughing? Do you back up this exaggeration? Why suddenly talk down, or turn pedant? If you want to change the mood inside the piece, you must modulate, otherwise your reader will stumble and you will lose him." The student who learns to quiz himself in this fashion over his first draft is learning not only something about English, about writing, and about thinking, but about the human heart as well.

At the risk of tediousness I repeat that what has to be done is to dramatize the relation between writer and reader. The blunt comments are just a device to break the spell of routine, and though they administer an unpleasant shock at first, they are also flattering. "Somebody cares about what I want to say." The teacher is no longer a paid detective hunting stray commas.

To point these lessons up in minute detail to a student of average powers is of course time-consuming — but what else is the teacher there for? Time spent on reading and writing, in any subject, is never a waste, and the reward almost always comes, often astonishingly great. The excitement aroused by the discovery that words live is like finding that you can balance on skates. A new world of motion and of feeling is opened out to the student, a source of some anguish balanced by lifelong delight. George Gissing writes somewhere that he saw an excursion steamer advertised as being "Replete with Ladies' Lavatories" and he comments on how many people could pass by the sign without a smile. My own favorite recollection is of a guarantee pasted on a modest shop window: "Hats fitted to the head exclusively" — fun in every ad and at the company's expense.

The pleasure to be taken in words is as innocent and satisfying as the moral effect is clear: unless words are used deftly to set the imagination on its travels, language, literature, conversation, and friendship are full of snares. Much of our modern anxiety about the tyranny of words and of our desire for foolproof Basic comes from the uneasy suspicion that we have lost the art of diction and with it the control over our own minds. This is more serious than it seems, for there is no doubt that the world outside the school largely checks what present instruction attempts, as we shall see. But having spoken of the imagination, let me first meet a likely objection to the advice here proposed. I can fancy some reader for whom school compositions were torture shaking a skeptical head and saying: "Most young children have very little to say and school assignments blot out even that little." I agree and the second great practical problem is, What to ask boys and girls to write about?

The don'ts are easy. Don't ask them for "A vacation experience," or "My most embarrassing moment," or "I am the Mississippi River." Such topics will only elicit the driest kind of hokum, though to be fair I must say that they are an improvement on the older practice of expecting infant moralizing and "What the flag means to me." Although as a child I enjoyed writing — history chiefly — I can remember the blankness of mind that overtook me when we had to do a *dissertation morale*. I still have a school text with some of those themes checked as having been done — for example: "*The Faithful Dog.* — A poor man has resolved to drown his dog. Thrown into the river, the dog tries to scramble up the bank, but his master lunges out to kill him with a stick. In so doing, he slips and falls. The dog saves him. Remorse of the owner."

I regret to say that French school life is stuffed with such thorns as these, but I am not sure that the opposite "progressive" extreme of turning children into researchers on their own is desirable either. The eleven-year-old son of a friend of mine once told me that he was writing a "project" on Papyrus. Why papyrus? Well, the class had been "doing" Egypt and each child was assigned one aspect of Egyptian civilization. Where was the information to come from? From encyclopedias, museums, friends, and paper manufacturers — hence such letters to strangers as the one about "Africia" quoted earlier. As I see it, two things are wrong with this scheme. One is that it gives a false freedom; the other is that it hardly trains in the art of composing. Did this boy care at all about Egypt, let alone about the technicalities of papyrology? A child should select a topic that truly engages his interest. To eliminate pretense he must be helped to do this by means of questions and suggestions. At any age, it is very reassuring to be told that you don't really want to write about the Tariff. After two or three casts a real subject emerges, satisfactory to both parties.

Next should come into play the single good feature of the French dissertation, namely its furnishing a plan or program. Depending on the child's age a briefer or longer table of contents should be set out for each theme, either in logically organized form, or pell-mell for the student himself to disentangle. After all, what is wanted is prose, not a riot of fancy. In my experience, even examination questions are answered better when they consist of five or six sentences outlining a topic for discussion. This means further that brevity should never be accounted a fault in itself. After thirty, we can all spin tall tales, mostly secondhand,[1] but students, even of college age, have had very little conscious experience of life or books and it is no wonder their minds are bone dry. One should moreover keep in view the possibility that in some of them brevity may come from genius. American schoolmarms who relate the anecdote of Lincoln's "failure" with the Gettysburg Address are just as likely to say at one glance, "Jane, this is too short." How do they know? Perhaps they unwittingly agree with the Gettysburg crowd that Everett's speech, being longer, was better.

[1] No course, therefore, should ever be called Creative Writing. Let us have at least a collective modesty and leave to charlatans the advertising of "How to Write Powerful Plays."

Some secondary schools, particularly the private ones, require the writing of verse as well as of prose. If the students are really shown how to go about versifying and are not expected to be "poetic," there is no harm in it. Verse writing is excellent practice for the prose writer and the striving for correct rhythm and rhyme gives the student of literature a feeling for words that may not otherwise be obtained. What can be done in this way before college by a gifted teacher has been shown by the experience of my friend, the poet Dudley Fitts, formerly at Choate and now at Andover. In collegiate circles, it is now well known that a freshman prepared under him is a literate, sometimes a polished writer, who can be safely allowed to skip into advanced work. No doubt Fitts has had his failures like all of us, but it is the successes we are looking for and that count in leavening the mass.

II

I am not so foolish as to think that carrying out my few suggestions would get rid of illiterate A.B.'s. I am too conscious of my initial point about "Education," which is that the school does not work in a vacuum but rather in a vortex of destructive forces. As regards writing, we in the twentieth century must offset not only the constant influence of careless speech and the indifference of parents, but the tremendous output of jargon issuing from the new mechanical means at man's disposal. Worst of all, circumstances have conspired to put the most corrupting force at the very heart of the school system. It is not newspapers, radio scripts, and movies that spoil our tongue so much as textbooks, official documents, commencement speeches, and learned works.[2]

The rise, at the turn of the century, of what James called "the

[2] See Mr. Maury Maverick's excellent denunciation of what he calls Gobbledygook in the *New York Times* for May 21, 1944. The rebuttals attempting to show that roundabout expressions spare shocks to the sick are hardly to the point. The healthy ought to be able to stand directness and even mention of "death and taxes." "Loss of life" and "fiscal levies" cost just as much in the end.

softer pedagogy" is responsible for a debasement of language beyond all bounds of forgiveness. The desire to be kind, to sound
new, to foster useful attitudes, to appear "scientific," and chiefly
also the need to produce rapidly, account for this hitherto un-
heard-of deliquescence. In the victims, the softness goes to the
very roots of the mind and turns it into mush. And among the
"new" educators thus afflicted, the Progressive vanguard has
naturally outstripped the rest. I shall not multiply examples from
catalogues, reports, and speeches, though over the years I have
gathered a blush-making collection. I want only to identify the
evil because it spreads like the plague.

It consists mainly of what our forefathers called "cant phrases,"
strung together without continuity, like wash on a line. At a
faculty meeting, a teacher asks the Director of Admissions why
there seem to be more music students applying than before. The
Director replies, "Well, I should say that the forces undergirding
the process are societal." Or a committee chairman wants to
know what we do next. "I think," says the secretary, "that we
should go on to institute actual implementation."

Teachers steeped in this medium are bound to ooze it out
themselves, particularly if weekly and daily they receive official
instructions like these: "Specify the kinds of change or perma-
nence the student seems to crave, reject, or fear; the reasons given
for liking-disliking, giving up-persistence; complaining-boasting.
. . . It cannot be too strongly emphasized that the observations
of characteristics associated with age and background are not
being made in the general area of adolescent behavior but under
specific and limited conditions — those set by the aims, emphases,
and assumptions of one particular faculty.[3] Moreover, the observations of what appear to be the interests of freshmen conceal a
possible ambiguity. The term 'interests' may refer to fairly superficial interests in the sense of surprise, pleasure, enjoyment,

---

[3] I regret to say that "faculty" here means "faculty member" — a usage
so far confined to the progressive schools.

which are comparatively temporary; or 'interests' may involve an awakening curiosity which leads to consistent inquiry along the lines of some project." The reader must imagine not merely a paragraph taken at random, but pages and pages of similar woolly abstractions, mimeographed at the rate of nine and one-half pounds per person per semester. If the words "specific" and "objective" were blotted out of the English language, Progressive Education would have to shut up . . . shop.

As for students in teachers' colleges, the long climb up the ladder of learning comes to mean the mastering of this ghoulish *Desperanto*, so that with the attainment of the M.A. degree, we get the following utterance: —

In the proposed study I wish to describe and evaluate representative programs in these fields as a means of documenting what seems to me a trend of increasing concern with the role of higher education in the improvement of interpersonal and intergroup relations and of calling attention in this way to outstanding contributions in practice.

Some readers might think this quotation very learned and highbrow indeed. But in fact it says nothing definite. It only embodies the disinclination to think. This is a general truth, and nothing is more symptomatic of the whole jargon than the fantastic use and abuse it makes of the phrase "in terms of." The fact is worth a moment's attention. "In terms of" used to refer to things that had terms, like algebra. "Put the problem in terms of *a* and *b*." This makes sense. But in educational circles today "in terms of" means any connection between any two things. "We should grade students in terms of their effort" — that is, *for* or *according to* their effort. The *New York Public Library Bulletin* prints: "The first few months of employment would be easier . . . and more efficient in terms of service . . ." — that is, would yield more efficient service. But no one seems to care how or when or why his own two ideas are related. The gap in thought is plugged with "in terms of." I have been asked, "Will you have dinner with me, not tonight or tomorrow, but *in terms of* next week?" A modern Caesar would write: "All Gaul is to be considered in terms of three parts." [4]

From this Educator's patois, easily the worst English now spoken, we ought to pass to the idiom of textbooks, since they are written either by educators or by teachers. Happily, there is a standard set by other books — trade books — and it is not true that all textbooks are as badly written as those on education. On the contrary, it is very encouraging that the leading ones in every field are usually well planned *and* well written. The success of Morison and Commager's *Growth of the American Republic* is only the most recent case in point. Students, nevertheless, are asked to read many ill-written books. There is no excuse for this, though it is by no means the only source of error. We must remember that students do not read only books; they read what every man reads, and this would do no harm — it does no harm — when the mind is trained to resilience by the kind of writing practice I have advocated.

Unfortunately, with the vast increase in public schooling since 1870, an entirely new notion of what is good English has come to prevail. Awakened by free schooling, the people have shown worthy intentions. They want to be right and even elegant, and so become at once suspicious of plainness and pedantic. They purchase all sorts of handbooks that make a fetish of spelling, of avoiding split infinitives, of saying "it is I" (with the common result of "between you and I") — in short, dwell on trivialities or vulgarisms which do not affect style or thought in the slightest. But with this intolerance towards crude and plain error goes a remarkable insensitivity to inflated nonsense. Most bad journalism is only highbrow verbosity, yet the popular mind continues to believe that the pedantry which it likes is simple

---

[4] The objectionable phrase is now to be found in newspapers, business reports, and private correspondence. It is a menace *in terms of* the whole nation.

and the simplicity which it finds hard is complex. Here is the opening of a serial thriller in a Boston paper: —

Strange things happen in Chinatown. But even that exotic and perverse district seldom presented drama as fantastic as the secret that hid among the silk and jade and porcelain splendors of the famous House of the Mandarin on Mulberry Lane.

There is a certain art in this, and I take note of "porcelain splendors" as the *mot juste* for bathtubs on exhibit. But the passage as a whole contains nothing but arty and highfalutin words, joined by the good will of the reader rather than the mind of the writer. Still, every newspaper reader feels he understands it. Take now a well-known sentence composed of common words, all but two of them single syllables: "If there are more trees in the world than there are leaves on any one tree, then there must be at least two trees with the same number of leaves." Read this aloud and almost any listener will respond with "Huh? Say that again." For this sentence records a thought, and the Chinatown "drama" did not.

The close logic in the truly "simple" sentence makes the contrast sharper, but it would be just as sharp between a feeling clearly put and a feeble attempt to thrill. Thus there is a superstition that the novels of Henry James are written in a "difficult style." Yet if you examine them, you will find that the words and sentences — in *The Ambassadors*, for example — are in themselves quite usual. But the feelings they convey are unusual and subtle, and require attention. At the same time they also compel it, which is all that an artist takes pains for in writing.

Conversely, the only thing that can be asked of a writer is that he should know his own meaning and present it as forcibly as he can. The rule has not changed since Byron affirmed that "easy writing makes damned hard reading." Hence there is great value, as I think, in having college graduates recognize good prose when they see it, know that a tolerable paragraph must have gone through six or seven versions, and be ready to follow athletically on the trail of articulate thoughts, rather than look for the soapy incline to muddled meaning.

One does not have to go very far for the enjoyment of precise, sinewy writing. The same newspaper that furnishes tripe for the morning meal also brings such rarer tidbits as these: "They [the robot bombs] are of much the same shape and size as a small fighter plane, with stubby wings. They come over with tails aglow from the propelling rocket force, like little meteors moving at a nightmare pace by dark, and by day like little black planes with tails afire." This is perfection; and here is poetry: "Mr. McCaffrey, himself the father of two children, *and therefore schooled in apprehension,* ran across the street . . . shouting a warning."

When the daily reporter, harried by falling bombs or hustled by a city editor, can write like this, it is depressing to return to agencies closer to the school and find verbal laziness encouraged and imbecility taken for granted. One publisher of reference works sends out a circular stressing the fact that his books give the pronunciation of "all difficult — 'hard-to-say' — words." Is this where we are after fifty years of quasi-universal literacy? Is the word "difficult" so difficult that it has to be translated in its own sentence? The question is one for readers, and it is to the subject of reading that I now turn.

5. *How to Read and Be Right*

> For better or worse the beginner
> now reads until he can read, and
> dances until he can dance — or
> until it is perfectly clear that he
> cannot.
>
> — DR. WENDELL H. TAYLOR
> of Lawrenceville School

"THE SUBSTANCES of what we think, though born in thought, must live in ink." A publisher said that, but it is true. What we are most pleased with in our Western civilization is found largely on shelves and is held together by buckram binding. So at this late date any lowbrow snorts about books and bookishness are quite futile except as a relief from bad temper. Besides, "books" is a variable term which might better be replaced with "print." Print surrounds us, and the three-year-old crawling around on the floor with a copy of *Life* wants to know — pointing to the airplane — what *that* says. Grown up, he will have to know what the sign says which reads: "Danger: Live Wire"; and even halfway between, as Hilaire Belloc pointed out in the fable of the little girl, it is a practical advantage not to run away from "Lemonade: 5 cents" in the belief that it is a warning about a wild bull.

But reading, like all human activities, refers to a wide range of performance, from the workaday to the masterly. Although the Army turned down only two hundred and forty thousand for deficient schooling, the level of reading in the camps for the ten million is reported as pretty low. The comics were the best sellers and *Life* magazine enjoyed only a *succès d'estime*. Doubtless there are many and complex psychological reasons for this state of affairs, but some things about the physical and mental art of reading surely contributed their share.

The schools nowadays teach reading by one or the other of two methods — the old one of memorizing letters and combining them: c-a-t, cat; and the new one of learning whole words as signs, like Chinese characters. If you send your child to a "modern" school, you will be spanked for showing him the alphabet. The new way has its good point. In later life, all efficient reading is done the "Chinese" way of visualizing whole words and phrases at a glance. If you see an adult moving his lips as he reads, you may be sure that his mind is laboriously grinding out the syllables, missing the ease and some of the fun. In this regard, reading is like athletics: the less you know what you are doing, the better you do it.

The older way, however, did not prevent the acquiring of the one-glance reading habits, and it did help to learn spelling and pronunciation. So that my choice, if I had any, would be for starting the old way and making sure that the child does not bog down at the letter or the syllable stage. This should be possible because what has greatly improved since my youth is our knowledge of eye and brain co-ordination. In every good college now, there is a coach in "remedial reading" to catch up students who read too slowly, or backwards (mirror-image), or who transpose letters, or who move their lips, or who are color-blind without knowing it. Let us hope that twenty-five years from now there will be no need of this assistance, the difficulties having been taken care of in the lower schools. Already the use of glasses has become more rational, after the first flush of enthusiasm for sticking them on every baby nose. And in the same direction, Aldous Huxley's important account of the Bates method in *The Art of Seeing* is having an excellent influence.

Let us assume then a normally equipped young reader. When, what, where, and how much should he read? Rousseau said that a child ought not to read until the age of ten or eleven, *after* he has had an experience of things. What Rousseau says is always worthy of the most attentive consideration, and here again, though formally wrong, he is intrinsically right. The art of reading consists in getting from the printed word as nearly as possible a sensation equivalent to the real thing. If a child reads, "The giraffe loped along easily, holding her head a little to one side," it is desirable that he should have seen a giraffe. That is in fact the only excuse for a zoo. Without the image, the words remain only so much mumbo jumbo. In Rousseau's day, verbal education was at its worst and "object lessons" were nonexistent. He revolutionized teaching theory and practice by pointing out in detail the error and its remedy.

But nowadays, with pictures on every page, machinery in every house, and toys designed by child-infatuated corporations, the infant grows up among "real" objects like a nabob among jewels. Almost every word he reads refers to something which he has seen, heard, touched, and tried to swallow. Rousseau's problem does not occur. But his principle remains sound, and it is still to be applied to the reading which goes on after the first period of infant exploring. Ideally, at every stage, the reader should use printed matter to reinforce his experience of life, to organize it, and to extend it. Books point to things known or imagined, to feelings felt or conceivable, to answers hoped for or certified. A man or woman deprived of these common goods because the ways of print are, as we say, a closed book, is in the position of the thirsty girl and the lemonade.

What misleads us about bookishness and justifies Whitman's warning about "the spectres that stalk in books" is the bad habit of taking the contents of books as things in themselves, trusting to words as magic, failing to test them by life or light them up with imagination — in short, preferring hokum to truth. But the power to imagine vividly and correctly comes in part from the habit of reading. It is a circular process and one to which children must be inured.

Let me say at once that all books are good and that consequently a child should be allowed to read everything he lays his hands on. Trash is excellent; great works containing passages of tragic or passionate import are admirable. Unless a child is clearly morbid, he will take in what he can and dismiss the rest with a lordly indifference that should make the celebrated author writhe in his grave. Do I draw no line anywhere? Only at vocabulary. There are some few modern works that use words which if unknown might puzzle in a disturbing way, or if known might act too powerfully on the imagination of a child. But this is hardly a real question for any sane parent.[1]

It is more difficult to know what to do about the large number of books, written for children, which base their appeal on slang and bad grammar. A certain quantity of this type of trash does no harm, but it is a good idea to thin down double negatives with a little conventional idiom from the pages of Dumas or Conan Doyle. Above all, don't worry about style. Sham medieval is as good as snappy Wild West badinage. Tom Swift and the Rover Boys — if they still exist — are as readable as the Henty books and far better than "approved" namby-pamby like *Freckles* or *Black Beauty*. Doubtless my examples date me, but in the matter of youthful reading a man cannot transcend his century or his habitat, even if he wished to. I learned about my native land from the *Bibliothèque rose* of the Comtesse de Ségur and about the more manly American continent from *The Pony Express* and *Frank Merriwell, Pitcher*.

The child who is a born reader will of course go through phases of continuous reading, which has a way of getting on the nerves of family and friends. Why it is in itself better to have a child hanging from the limb of a tree than sitting in a window seat

---

[1] I might add for what the testimony is worth that at the age of eleven there fell by mistake into my hands a fiercely naturalistic novel by Mirbeau. The behavior of the characters struck me at the time as decidedly odd, but I calmly attributed it to the inexperience of the novelist, not to mine. Most children would respond in exactly the same way.

with a book is hard to say. Reading children manage to get in plenty of baseball and swimming: only when they happen to be reading they are in everybody's eye and thereby inspire envy or reproach to the grownups buzzing or idling about. As a French philosopher remarked: "It is imperative to send children to bed at eight, so that adults may devote themselves in quiet to serious occupations, such as: bridge, cocktails, dancing and flirting." But don't ever badger a reader. The chief good that results from letting children have their fill of reading — apart from pleasure — is that they will find later reading effortless and rapid. The well-read boy has an easier time in college and the well-read undergraduate finds that as a man he can keep up with current literature on economics or medicine, without all the groans and self-reproaches of the rusty reader.

All this implies good habits. The suave churchman in *Shadow and Substance* gravely says to the villagers who have read the infamous book: "You skipped?" for they were reporting at once its danger and their freedom from contamination. But the poor souls had the right idea: the first reading of any book should be swift, even of "great books." The practised reader skips more than he reads, just so that he can concentrate on what is food for him and give his fullest attention to master works. This practice takes care of what my friend Mark Van Doren calls "the inferior books." In a certain sense there are no "inferior books" in the abstract. To calm down a toothache, the *World Almanac* is an inferior book, but it has its uses and even its worth as entertainment. What determines these merits is the reader's intent at the time, even if that intent is to let the eye wander nonchalantly over the page. As desire becomes more definite, the mind becomes more choosy, and the trained eye skips. But all this adds up to the generality that we can no more do without inferior books than we can get along without inferior people or without inferior air. With all of these, survival and, if possible, squeezing profit out of suffocation, should be our policy.

In school, of course, reading the best would seem to be required alike by professional ethics and by shortness of time. But even there it is impossible to read only the best. The child must read textbooks and very few are masterpieces. The average, as I have said, is pretty good. But there are some traditional features of academic writing which make very bad reading. The worst is the Impersonal Voice in which knowledge is uttered. Tone, once more, or absence of tone, passes for scholarliness, for impartiality and "objectivity," but it is usually a shirking of responsibility, a refuge in hokum. How can such writing be really read, that is, taken in with an active, judging mind? Professor X's manual tells me that Disraeli was a "shrewd but erratic" Prime Minister. I as a student am willing to believe him, but what do the words mean in that context? What is their force? Isn't it the writer who is erratic, like that one who in another textbook told me that Blake was a madman? Nowhere in these hundreds of pages can I gauge the Voice as a person or a mind. The Truth drones on, with the muffled sound of one who is indeed speaking from a well.

The effect is that every part of knowledge resembles every other part. History, which is the most chaotic, colorful, inspiring, and hateful panorama imaginable, comes out like a strip of celluloid film, gray and white, gray and white, with thousands of separate images all alike. No wonder it is so slow-moving and so dull to the child. How can he be expected to remember any "salient facts" when nothing sticks out? This is particularly true of modern "improved" history, for the old battle-and-kings sort could not wholly extinguish drama and suspense. As a high school teacher once said to me, "Thank God for Henry the Eighth" — one man at least who by sheer force of character has defied the burial rites of the textbook maker.

In other subjects, the same holds true with variations. Manuals of literature, philosophy, fine arts, and music teach ready-made judgments — abstract and uniform. The same patter of nouns and invertebrate phrases fills textbooks in mathematics, composition, hygiene, and the physical sciences. You can read millions of textbook pages and never find a personal touch or concession: "Admittedly," "to be sure," "I submit — " One is led to suppose — and children do suppose it — that the truth about things is "in" and reckoned up. No textbook says: "The student may feel that this is unlikely, but — " What harm in showing that the author knows what is passing in the reader's mind and means to fasten his new knowledge to the old? The answer doubtless is that textbooks have no authors, just as it might be said that they have no readers.

What do their purchasers do? They do not read, they study. And since "study" with mumbling lips, head averted, finger in the place being memorized, is a most unnatural and uncongenial act, they come round and ask the teacher how it should be done. Too often the teacher cocks an eye at the book-laden boy (the smaller the boy, the heavier the books) and asks severely, "Do you take notes?" "N-no, sir. I underline." "What! You mark up the school's books?" "Why, yes sir." And once again, the boy is penalized for knowing better than his mentor. There should of course be no distinction whatsoever between reading and studying, and all serious reading should be done pencil in hand, with a book whose ownership allows of its being marked up. Notes on reading may in some cases be useful, but they should be very few and synoptic, that is, cover much ground in brief space.

This is so true that side by side with the inflated and wickedly competitive textbook industry there has grown up a thriving subsidiary trade in outlines, graded for use in high school or college. They are bought by the students on their own initiative, to serve them in reviewing a course, in boiling down a textbook, and sometimes in putting order into the chaos projected by the lecturer. Having myself written one such outline and part of another, I know how much more difficult it is to present a vast field accurately in this form than it is to run along on a spider thread of thought either in lecturing or in writing. In an outline, the great principle of "they don't want to hear about that" works to reduce matter, not so much to the minimum as to the essentials.

Now in a well-made textbook — not necessarily a classic — the essentials form a clearly proportioned skeleton upon which the more decorative parts are hung. The book is decidedly not a "storehouse of facts." Imagine the mental starvation of the student locked up in one! For the virtues of knowledge thus organized, read D. C. Somervell's *English Thought in the Nineteenth Century* or Charles Singer's *Short History of Science*. They can be read. The student of those works does not have to wonder whether this or that plum is worth preserving. He follows and perceives what is important, for the authors have observed the canons of dramatic construction.

This is not to say that all the blame for waste motion in studying can be laid exclusively on the writers of schoolbooks. Too few boys and girls seem to know the simplest facts about reading. When a student comes around with a baffled look, saying that he has spent several hours each evening doing the assigned work but "don't seem to get anything out of it," the case is usually easy to diagnose: "Do you study in a room by yourself?" "No." "Then, do." Sometimes the answer is "Yes, I have a room of my own," in which case the next question is, "Do you keep the radio on?" "Yes." "Then, don't." Jane Austen could write novels in the family parlor and some people can think in a boiler factory, but it is foolish to take the hardest hurdles first when the power of attention is so rare.

It is a pity, too, that school reading should be done by jerks of so many pages a day, usually in defiance of all natural divisions of the subject. I notice that college texts written in England, being more like ordinary books, are better suited to reading than ours: their chapters are shorter, the type and binding are less heavily pedagogic, and an assignment can be made to embrace a whole topic. To be sure, American students sometimes find it hard to follow the lead of smoother prose. They are not used to hearing a voice and they fail to respond when their elbow is gently taken at the points of transition. They look for the glaring signposts in bold-face type that they are accustomed to: **THREE MAIN RESULTS** or **§ 52. — *Dementia Praecox.***

This expectation really means that they have never read a book attentively that was not fiction. They cannot follow a "story" unless it is animated by "people." What I have called "drama" does not exist for them apart from bodily conflict. And the idea of keeping sharply separate in the mind what the author actually says and what someone else might say under the same circumstances is entirely foreign to their minds. They seem to read without noticing the modifiers — "if," "perhaps," "occasionally," "others think." Interpretation to most students means only pigeonholing points of view with the aid of vague names like "radical" or "pessimistic" or "emotional." And they simply flounder when you ask about a text they have just read: "What precisely does it say on this point?" How indeed can they be expected to do anything but flounder when they have never been shown how to read and possibly prevented from learning for themselves?

Aware of this lack, many college teachers today take the opportunity of an elective course in philosophy or literature to teach their students how to read. The response is enthusiastic. Whether I hear students of Joseph Campbell at Sarah Lawrence College or of Donald Stauffer at Princeton, or of Philip Blair Rice at Kenyon, or of William Troy and Francis Ferguson at Bennington, talk of being "put through" a work of Hume's or Shakespeare's, the result is a sense of unforgettable discovery, of a new power to make a text yield its treasures by close scrutiny of meaning, allusion, structure, and imagery.

In *How to Read a Book*, Professor Mortimer Adler gave an elaborate formula for carrying out this procedure, though it was encumbered — as I think — with certain needless adjuncts, as well as made forbidding by too much paper work. Some wag computed that to read in the recommended manner the recommended books listed by Mr. Adler would take about one hundred and thirty years. But criticism of the technique at large can go even farther. When a student is asked to read a Shakespeare play with an instructor over a period of fifteen weeks, something is gained for the student but lost to the play. What is there to talk about during fifteen weeks? Clearly a mass of details about each verse and word. If Shakespeare uses a term of falconry, down go some notes on that lost art. If an image implies a belief in medieval medicine (for example, Hamlet's "fatness" is only perspiration after exercise), in goes the student for a sketch of the four humors. All this is excellent, for the student is getting closer and closer to Shakespeare's mind. But only in one direction. Test it by imagining a reader of the twenty-fourth century tackling John Dos Passos's *U.S.A.* and stopping to "work up" the New York transportation system. What would be left of the emotional and formal impact of a scene? A play is meant to be taken in (not necessarily seen) in two hours or so. Granted that a fine play is too complex to be fully enjoyed in that time, what is the best compromise between superficiality through speed and falsification by slow motion? Why, to read it, swiftly at first; then once again, stopping here and there; then reading it a third time, and again and again, all the way through, with intervals for assimilation. Each time the play will change and grow, and the meaning of its lesser parts will become clearer while keeping properly subordinate. It is just as bad to have a possibly unimportant line jump out at you because it was there you found out about Elizabethan nautical terms as it is to have the "soliloquies" clatter out of their place like an artificial denture.

I seem to be blowing hot and cold upon the growing academic practice of attentive reading. Surely I am not for *in*attentiveness. What then do I want? First, the practice of rereading. A college student will say: "Plato? I've had that." He must learn that you cannot step into the same river of thought twice, because neither you nor it is the same. Second, I should like to see minute analysis done only on sample passages from books, the remainder of which should be read at a normal pace. This is the French *explication de texte* and it can be used under our present scheme of courses without its becoming the far too regular drill that it is in the *lycée*. Let the instructor choose from time to time a paragraph, not especially prominent, and make the class produce *all* that they know which will throw light on the meaning of the passage.

Three things should follow. First, the student gains an idea of what *can* be done by applying one's mind and using others' ideas. He thus forms a standard for his own reading, based on what total comprehension might be. Second, he begins to discover the need for interpreting; the ways of testing a preference for one interpretation over another; and the desirability of checking doctrinaire inclinations in an uncertain world.[2] Third, he comes to see that in the realm of mind as represented by great men, there is no such thing as separate, isolated "subjects." In Shakespeare's English are tags of Latin, allusions to medicine, elements of psychology, facts from history — and so on ad infinitum. Nor is this true of fiction alone. The great philosophers and scientists are — or were until recently — universal minds, not in the sense that they knew everything, but in the sense that they sought to unite all they knew into a mental vision of the universe.

II

A practical problem of some magnitude lurks behind all this — not only behind the accurate reading of print, but the forming

[2] If anyone thinks this will produce hesitant intellects, here is the answer: "Just as our extensor muscles act most firmly when a simultaneous contraction of the flexors guides and steadies them; so the mind of him whose fields of consciousness are complex, and who, with the reasons for the action, sees the reasons against it, and yet, instead of being palsied, acts in the way that takes the whole field into consideration — so, I say, is such a mind the ideal sort of mind that we should seek to reproduce in our pupils." (William James, *Talks to Teachers*, p. 180.)

of good mental habits and the selling of textbooks. I mean the physical availability of books. In his biography of the poet François Villon, D. B. Wyndham Lewis tells us with appealing honesty that he did not read certain books on his subject because they were long out of print and "difficult to discover, except in libraries." I think I know how he felt. We in the twentieth century take public libraries for granted. We are proud of them and would be helpless without them, for there are but few large private collections left. Yet it must be admitted that having to read a book in a library is a misfortune. It is only slightly better than being read aloud to. Reading, true reading, is the solitary vice par excellence, and should be kept so as far as means permit.[3]

While remembering that I am not proposing the burning of our great collections, please consider the obstacles that libraries place in the path of true reading. The book belongs to the public and may not be marked; then it must be read on the spot, which means interruptions, although most books should be read in large chunks or at one sitting; lastly, the whole operation is done in an atmosphere of half buzz and half hush, which is distinctly worse than overhead riveting — the psychologists of hearing could tell us why. I shall speak below of further impediments caused by current library practice. I want, before that, to relate these first remarks to college work.

Clearly, if what I say is true, a small college library is better than a big one — for the students. It can have alcoves and easy chairs so that the reader sits in his own atmosphere instead of in a concourse resembling a railroad waiting room. Those long tables that divide grim scholarship into two camps, facing each other and numbered odd and even, are the death of thought. That is why the circular plan of the British Museum or the Preussische Staatsbibliothek is preferable to that of the Paris Bibliothèque Nationale or the New York Public Library. In the

---

[3] I do not exclude the sociable reading aloud of light literature or even of great works that can stand the spoken word, like *Pickwick*.

reading room of the British Museum, by some artful arrangement of bookshelves, one has the feeling of everybody having his back to everybody else. Trust the British for that!

Beyond all this a college library needs open shelves. A college dean once boasted in a newspaper interview that his instructors could always be found "surrounded by their books." Well, the students should be besieged in the same manner. They must live close to books: it is part of the definition of the word "student." They must find, on the shelves, books that they were not looking for and that they did not know existed. They must be able to go from shelf to shelf, tracking down an idea, a name, or a picture. And all this freely, in a mood of peaceful *laissez faire*. It is absurd to have in a large library one room set apart as a Browsing Room. Reading and browsing are not separate functions of a double-action intellectual stomach.

Nor is a businesslike routine conducive to mental absorption. Going up to a Loan Desk with a slip which you have had to stop and write out, handing it to an attendant who stamps the date on it with a loud bang, shoves it down a pneumatic tube, and tells you to wait, makes the student life too much like the struggle for ration cards and three-cent stamps. Ordinarily, for "standard courses," college practice is to have a reserve of identical books which are doled out to the students, sometimes with a limit of two hours' reading time. What could be more discouragingly anti-cultural? A boy's will is the wind's will and even the second volume of *Tom Jones* could not, under those adverse conditions, anchor it.

As with so many trivial hardships which are not really trivial, the answer is a matter of money. Libraries generally have not enough copies of assigned books (non-textbooks) and libraries are too apprehensive about the stealing of those they have. I say that a college ought to be proud, within reason, to have its books stolen. Why do people steal money? Because they value it. Apply this to books and you may get a measure of effective education.

Naturally, purloining should not be encouraged or even condoned; but it should be accepted as a running expense, which would find its natural limits in the average deviation from right conduct among normal American youth.

But there is another reason why not enough books are provided. The college library seeks to cater at the same time for two distinct clienteles — the students and the faculty. As soon as a college grows into a university, it wants to compete in scholarly resources with other centers. This strains the budget and current needs suffer. For the sake of a rare pamphlet or a medieval charter, which some faculty member requires, the undergraduates go bookless. It is true the pamphlet may also be of use to advanced students, but ordinarily the question does not arise because the library is buying not one item, but this or that "rare collection" at a sizable outlay, in order to own it and preserve it. In other words, the library — originally founded to *give out* books — becomes a Museum, designed to keep them *in.*

This brings me to the awesome subject of Library Science. The accumulation of books in one place has given rise to a new and honorable profession, which it would be foolish as well as unjust to condemn en masse. I, for one, owe too much to the friendly offices of librarians to attempt it. But it must be said that a love of administration, together with something like a defensive attitude, has conspired to make the librarian's relation to students rather less satisfactory than it could be. Librarians doubtless develop through their training a passionate love of books. But need it be so possessive? Why must many of the rules that they make suggest the bad governance which galls without repressing? Should a common enough attitude — the pursed lips, the tone of suspicion, the pouncing manner — become professional traits? Most important, is it so arduous a task to learn the Dewey classification system and the use of bibliographies that there is no time left for librarians to learn about the insides of the treasures they hoard? I am struck by the fact that many able librarians spend their time setting up exhibits in glass cases — and denying stack access to students worthy of the privilege. "Don't look at those books," they seem to say. "Look at these."

Or else the librarian composes a little reading list to be posted up for the edification of undecided readers. This is thoughtful, but while this is being typed and thumbtacked, the student who knows what he is about can get no hearing for his inquiry: the staff is too shorthanded and again he waits in line. It almost seems as if a clear purpose in a student disqualified him from receiving assistance. And too often, when he approaches the high priestess, it is the suppliant who has to guide the ritual. I mean that the librarian who knows only tricks and numbers is made nervous by an unexpected question and turns the tables on the inquirer by implying that he does not know what he himself wants.

Perhaps fatigue accounts for some of these symptoms. Some librarians are judged by the number of books they circulate during the fiscal year, and so they turn into library advertisers and promoters — but not in the right way.

Anyway, there should be, in college work, less reliance on library books.[4] During each of the four years, the undergraduate should become the owner of a good choice of volumes — not textbooks, but books to keep, books that will not burn on Class Day. For this reason there should be many more inexpensive editions of good books than there are at present. The Everyman Library, the Modern Library, the World's Classics, together supply the minimum want, not the reasonable requisite. The cause is that they have to rely on a general public sale as well as on collegiate demand. I believe that my colleague, Professor Charles W. Everett, once proposed that a group of university presses combine to issue at low cost a series of books, carefully

[4] The present state of affairs is well shown by a notice I received from a large publishing firm: "Here *Is* an Idea! At N—— university, an order has been placed for three hundred copies of Parrington's *Main Currents in American Thought* — one for each student in the basic course."

edited or translated by competent graduate students, for whom the task would be the fulfillment of the Ph.D. requirement. An appropriate group of such books — ten or twelve or fifteen — would normally be put into the student's hands at the beginning of each year. He would be known to have them; the teacher could demand that he read them; the text could be brought to class; the teacher could teach its proper use; and the collection would naturally form the nucleus of a personal library.

What is astonishing is the quantity of books worth reading at college age and later which cannot be bought except by luck and at second hand. The recently established "Classics Club" has done something to remedy this situation. Until it began to publish, it was for instance impossible to own or assign Samuel Butler's translation of Homer, even though it is the most readable modern version and a masterpiece of prose in its own right. I once jotted down a few titles at random that occurred to me as beyond the reach of easy purchase in English. Here they are: Coleridge's *Table Talk*, Hume's *Essays, Moral, Political, and Literary*, Beaumarchais's *Figaro* and *Barber of Seville*, Newman's *Grammar of Assent*, Mill's *Logic*, Stendhal's *Autobiography*, Shelley's *Prose Essays*, the poems of Leopardi, Pushkin, and La Fontaine; Montesquieu's *Spirit of the Laws*, Schiller's dramas, Jomini's *Art of War*, Berkeley's *Commonplace Book*, Galileo's *Two New Sciences*, Lewes's *Biographical History of Philosophy*, Diderot's art criticism. There are furthermore no readable and cheap translations of Molière, Racine, and Corneille, of Kleist and *Don Quixote*, of *Mademoiselle de Maupin*, or of Saint Augustine's *City of God*. Moreover, in this haven of Puritanism, Calvin's *Institutes* costs a fortune.

And while I am about it, I may as well submit that there is no good edition of Shakespeare. I may be wrong, but I think his works deserve to be printed as attractively as those of any other playwright. Yet no reprint that I know of fulfills the following simple specifications: average book format; single columns wide enough for a full unbroken verse; a very few notes at the bottom of the page, on words with changed meanings; a runninghead giving Act and Scene on each page; and the *names of the characters spelled out in full above each speech.* It is wearisome and ugly to see dialogue that runs *Lanc., West., Lanc.; Hot., Lady, Hot.;* and *Sic., Mess., Sic.*

III

What books are there at home? The query is certainly relevant to the reading habits of the school population. On a can of soap powder I find pasted a coupon inducing the public to start a library — twelve *impressive* books "at pin-money cost" which "your friends will admire and envy." The note of envy is certainly rather strong in all advertisements bringing books to the masses. "Snob appeal" has in fact become a recognized trade term, and it should have been in use as far back as Dr. Eliot's "Five-Foot Shelf." For in this merge the two popular expectations about reading — that it shall be a sweet and short experience, under six feet, and that it shall bring prestige. Hence all the compendiums of culture — "Seven Thousand Facts about Art" — and the short cuts to literary pleasure — "Concise Plots of the World's Great Novels: Fifty Cents."

It is easy to scorn the motives that make all this possible, but I suspect that in the long run the results are not so negligible as they seem. We must not forget in what barbarous and uncultivated condition boastful Europe left the great majority of those who built America from scratch. If when these immigrants of yesterday get the chance, they reach for the first package marked art or literature, it is because nothing and nobody has prepared them to choose better. But no motive and no generation is eternal. The family that buys the Five-Foot Shelf not to read — for it is hard work — but to dazzle their friends, will in time bring forth offspring for whom these books were intended. As John

Jay Chapman put it, "Young men are born whom nothing will satisfy except the arts and sciences." And experience teaches that these young men — and women — make their appearance in the least expected places. Lincoln was surely a most unpredictable phenomenon, self-taught with the aid of three poets and a grammar. Such men keep appearing, not necessarily of his stature, but in his tradition. One New York boy of very humble Italian extraction came to me with a tattered copy of Dante which he had been reading since the age of ten: he knew the poem far better than I. Another, whom I had detected "borrowing" from a digest of plots, was not saturated but inspired to read the works he already knew in capsule form. And he made for himself the valuable discovery that the books are nothing like the résumés — "or the movies," he added with a wistful smile.

Another time, sitting in a streetcar next to a middle-aged Negro — a chauffeur — I had the pleasant experience of finding him an excellent Shakespearean critic. He was reading a copy of the Sonnets and seeing that I also carried books, he begged leave to ask my opinion on a line he had often puzzled over. "Doesn't it seem to you," he said, "that in Sonnet 23, the line 'O, let my books be then the eloquence . . .' should be 'O, let my *looks* . . .'?" I agreed and we went on chatting most agreeably about our author.

But all such happy growths depend on the possession of at least one book. Literary taste, not to speak of talent or genius, cannot be fashioned out of whole cloth at school. It must make a beginning at the mother's knee and be nursed on the hearth. Well, what are the chances of the hearth being provided with books? A publishing friend gives me some statistics. Of all the paper used in this country, only 6 per cent constitutes the so-called "book papers." Of all so-called book papers only one sixth actually goes for books. Five sixths are used for magazines. No wonder that when an accident like war makes the book trade boom, while at the same time curtailing paper, publishers are more distraught than pleased. In normal times the concentration of books in a few hands is the rule, and we may well be astonished that there is as much circulation of ideas as we find — through rental libraries, reading groups, women's clubs, lectures, and serious magazines.

But precisely because these agencies are well-established, they exert a strong and one-sided influence. They tend toward standardization — making us all read the same book in the same week and the same kind of book from one year's end to the other. The marketing habits of publishers reflect this. They try to sell all their books to the whole American public, making a few into best sellers and the rest into different grades of what a wit once termed *flop d'estime.*

The net result is that variety, true novelty, superior quality, tend to be swamped under the good average workmanlike book in any field. Right here is the spot on which schools and colleges and libraries should exert their greatest conscious pressure. Instead of assigning the current best seller so as to court the student's interest, persuade him to pick an unknown book by an unknown author. Assure him that this is not taking a mad chance and that even if he does not like the book of your choice, he has not poisoned his system. Make him forget snob appeal by encouraging a pleasant indifference to what others are reading and gabbling about. This is not advocating contrary-mindedness, but rather the acquisition of true intellectual poise. Mob judgment is so fickle — and a mob can consist of three bohemians as well as of three academic people — that independence from it at one time may easily turn out to be an anticipation of majority feeling. In any case, what is the good of reading under social dictation and giving up real pleasure for the sake of keeping up with the Joneses?

Librarians likewise could help diversify the reading public. They ought to form *some* opinions about *some* books and not hesitate to voice them. A correspondent in the *Times* complained with good reason that in twenty years of haunting public libraries he had never once been recommended a book by the damsel behind the desk. Her role is certainly not to proselytize, but neither is it to dish out literature like ham and eggs. She should be at least as attentive to her client's needs and styles as a good saleswoman in a first-class dress shop. She knows more than many of her readers; she lives among books, and as a presumably cultivated citizen she has an obligation discreetly to make her opinions tell in the vast suffrage that determines the fate of books. Her vote should be cast, not automatically for the most popular, but for what she feels is the best. To remain alive in mind and body a democracy must compare as well as count.

But note the "as well," for no government is more firmly based on numbers than representative democracy. It is political arithmetic pure and simple, which ought to reconcile us to the presence in schooling of the third "R." I now turn to it.

5. *Let x Equal . . .*

Allusion to the general ignorance of arithmetic has . . . always been well received: whenever one member [of Parliament] describes others as know-nothings, those others cry *Hear, Hear* to the country in a transport of delight. In the meanwhile, the country is gradually arriving at the conclusion that a true joke is no joke.

— AUGUSTUS DE MORGAN

THE YOUNG LADY in the shop who has inadvertently overcharged you will excuse herself by saying that she hasn't a mathematical mind; and if you are a true gentleman — or lady — you will hasten to assure her that neither have you. Early in life, people come to think of themselves as having or not having that mysterious "mind," and until recently I do not believe that anyone dared to dispute its existence. But the belief is a superstition, and one that is largely unproductive.

In the first place, what the child and the shopgirl are talking about is not mathematics but one minor branch of it, arithmetic. In arithmetic, the operations that have to be done every day are within the mental reach of all. Whether they are correctly done or not, grasping their principle requires no special type of brains, and errors come chiefly from inattention or absent-mindedness, just as they do in spelling names or remembering addresses. It may be a comfort to be reminded that not all mathematicians can count: the late Dean Herbert Hawkes of Columbia College, who taught mathematics for thirty-five years and wrote some excellent books on the subject, could seldom hit the right answer to a mental sum the first time. Here again, routine skill and understanding are different powers.[1]

But for the ordinary person it may well be also that because of the tribal bugbear about "math," the mind stumbles more often over ciphering than over anything else. Is it a bugbear that can be traced to its den and slain? My impression is that its point of origin is the mystery created around numbers from the moment a child encounters them. It is an ever-deepening mystery, for as he grows older the pupil is asked to do more and more complicated things in increasing darkness of mind. The right answer is in the back of the book, but the right principles to explain it never seem to be in the front. At least I do not remember reading informatively about numbers until I hunted down books on the subject for my own pleasure long after school.

Then I have more than an impression — it amounts to a certainty — that algebra is made repellent by the unwillingness or inability of teachers to explain why we suddenly start using a and b, what exponents mean apart from their handling, and how the paradoxical behavior of $+$ and $-$ came into being. There is no sense of history behind the teaching, so the feeling is given that the whole system dropped down ready-made from the skies, to be used only by born jugglers. This is what paralyzes — with few exceptions — the infant, the adolescent, or the adult who is not a juggler himself.

When you add to this the fact that many ready computers who teach are both impatient and inarticulate, you have reason enough for the child's hatred of ciphering. I well remember one college instructor, said to have been a brilliant discoverer, but whose students failed with alarming regularity. He used to write

[1] It is noticeable these days in shops that have lost their trained cashiers that no one has told the substitute how to make change by addition instead of subtraction — another sign of common unfamiliarity with numbers.

on the board difficult problems in integration, and after everyone had given up he would put the chalk to his lips, make a noise like a straining gear box, and write out the correct result. How he got to it he could never explain. "Don't you see?" he would plead. We never did see. But we had his exact opposite, a rather crude and coarse barrel of a man, whom I remember with gratitude for the phrase he never tired of using at every step, "What'll this *gim-me?*" That expressed the true spirit of calculation, and to symbolize this feeling we students made up the myth that he was a successful bootlegger on the side.

The same liberating attitude about numbers is that adopted by the British mathematician Sylvanus P. Thompson in his *Calculus Made Easy*, which bears the motto "What one fool can do, another can." This maxim should be taken in conjunction with the discovery made by one of William James's students that "after all, algebra is only a form of low cunning." Quite right. The whole range of computing, unlike such arts as musical performance or the appreciation of poetry, depends upon strict system. And as every step in the system depends upon the previous one according to fixed rules, any fool — to use Thompson's endearment — can with patience do what any other can.

The hitch comes early in life when teachers say: "You just do it this way," without explaining the path from the known to the unknown nor supplying a sound reason why, for example, the way to divide one fraction by another is to invert the second and multiply. The child is expected to learn far too many details — endless measures of length or liquid that no one uses; and to do too many problems — cube roots and compound interest, and grocery-store enigmas that defy probability and weary the soul. He forgets principles all the more readily, and retains only a sort of gambler's faith that success may be achieved by blindman's buff. This no amount of later reasoning can overcome and it even casts an aura of distrust over any process of reasoning or demonstration as such.

Before school, most children are apt to count objects and to toy with the abacus fitted to their playpen. At that stage it is not hard to begin with the most interesting part of mathematics, the ultimate reaches of mathematical thought, namely Number Theory. Without using big words, numbers can be shown to be names. One, two, three, can be taught as names of classes of things by grouping objects in bunches of one's, bunches of two's, bunches of three's, and saying, "All the things that are like this we call one's," and so on. We count by comparing groups, part for part. If the child can button his coat, this idea of one-to-one relation can be pointed out, mildly, every time that he gets the lowest button fastened in the hole nearest his chin. Lastly, the advantage of predicting by addition or subtraction can be demonstrated. "How do you know that if we take away three from these nine blocks, only six will be left?" "I've learned to count in my head, so that I don't have to handle each piece." "Shall I learn to count, too?" "Yes, when you go to school" — a statement to be followed by prayer.

In school, the main thing is not to drill for accuracy at once but to show that if numbers are involved there is *always* a way of going from one fact to another next door by means that are obvious to the naked eye. This is not finally true, of course, for to achieve new discoveries in mathematics does require a special gift like any other creativeness; but there is ample time for the pupil to strike that limitation. And long before that, there should clearly be a division made between the slow and the fast computers. Half the misery in mathematics classes comes from their being together. Let Mary Jane take her time about puzzling out percentages while Tom Colin, whose father is a cashier, does them in his head and raps out the answers before the others have written the problem down. There is hardly ever an occasion in life when one has to count quickly, and certainly no quick counting can be of much use if it is habitually wrong.

The teaching of Geometry creates a special difficulty because it involves visualization, but this can be overcome by the use of paper or plaster models. Above all, detect blind memorizing and nip it before it becomes a habit. It will not teach geometry and it will create a prejudice solider than the cubes and spheres from which it sprang.

Then there is the matter of keeping up interest in made-up problems, which, by the way, ought not to be called "sums." We used to fill cisterns with pipes of various outputs, and locate trains that started from St. Petersburg at twenty kilometers an hour. More recently, I gather that airplanes and water turbines have come into play. This is good, but the "jazzing up" of the vocabulary will not overcome the worst apprehensions. The pupil knows the problems are not real, and since real problems are not suitably simple, the only interest that can be aroused is in the different kinds of difficulty raised by each type. All this should be preceded by exposition in the style of Thompson's manual. For example: "In this chapter we are going to make much use of the word *rate*. . . . Nothing . . . to do with birth-rate or death-rate, though these words suggest . . . so many births or deaths per thousand of the population. When a motor-car whizzes by us, we say: What a terrific rate! When a spendthrift is flinging about his money, we remark that the young man is living at a prodigious rate. What do we mean by *rate*? In both these cases we are making a mental comparison of something that is happening, and the length of time that it takes to happen."

How simple and comfortable! All nomenclature should be explained, not only in the formal accepted terms of the science, but in common-sense terms. Thompson, introducing the basic notions of the Calculus, begins by saying that dx means "a little bit of x" and that $\int$ means "the sum of all the little bits." He can then go on to say that formally d is called "an element of x" and $\int$ "the integral of." When he strikes an ambiguous phrase, he is careful to put in a note: "The mathematicians talk about the second order of 'magnitude' (i.e. greatness) when they really mean the second order of smallness. This is very confusing to beginners."

Nothing could be more enticing and only a fool (in the real sense) could suppose that this friendliness towards the student lowers the dignity of the science. What it actually does is replace an element of (a little bit of) hokum with an element of sense, while leaving the integrity (the sum) of wisdom unimpaired.

Of course, good teachers of college mathematics often feel the inclination to give a philosophic view of their subject, which would make it permanently enlightening, but they almost always teach under pressure of time. The students must get through so many math courses as preparation for engineering or medicine or physics. The book must be "covered." The students themselves feel the strain and are impatient of reflective thought. Colleges moreover have to repeat high school courses for the backward and the forgetful — all of which deepens the pit of ignorance. There is no inducement for the teacher to explain the rationale of analytic geometry or transfinite enumeration, the rise of infinitesimals — whose true meaning was not understood until after two hundred years; nor even so basic a thing as the poetical imagination behind the invention of zero — that doughnut hole expressing Nothing, yet seized on and set to work by having a ring put around it.

But there is still another neglected opportunity to deplore in the present teaching of college mathematics. Being one of the logical sciences, it should be taught in conjunction with informal elementary logic. The thought process which makes it inevitable that "if A is greater than B and B greater than C, then A is greater than C" is not devoid of interest even to the average student. Like M. Jourdain in Molière's play he likes to find out that he has been observing — most of the time — fixed laws of thought. And like Thomas Hobbes in middle age picking up Euclid at a bookstall, the student can be stirred into exclaiming "This can't be true!" From that moment on, he is caught for life by the fascination of the mind's ability to test its own inward workings. He wants to know how we can be sure that 2 has a square root and how probability applies to baccarat or genetics.

Curiosity about inference and deduction is in all of us, as can be seen in parlor games involving such puzzles as the one quoted about the number of leaves on any one tree. Once aroused, this interest can bear good fruit. A flair for detecting fallacies is excellent protection in a world that swarms with them. A modest familiarity with statistical analysis, symbolical representation, and the calculation of chances yields returns in many workaday situations.

Above all, the ability to feel the force of an argument apart from the substance it deals with is the strongest weapon against prejudice. Digging into the laws of thought illuminates not controversy merely, but all conscious endeavor. For in all good thinking and feeling are to be found the three great ideas underlying both logic and mathematics, namely, Generality; Form (something that can be handled when its type is recognized); and Variability. They appear in different guises fitting the subject matter but they rule thinking about art as well as politics, business as well as science.

7. *The Ivory Lab*

> I degrade Physics into an implement of culture, and this is my deliberate design.
> — JOHN TYNDALL, *Fragments of Science*

MOST of the excitement about "higher education" in the last three years has been about the teaching of history, languages, and "great books." But the most serious and pressing need in colleges today seems to me to be the teaching of science. It may appear paradoxical that I speak of a "need" which everyone believes to be adequately met, but paradox disappears when the point of view changes. From one point of view, science is taught in every American college; from another point of view, it is taught in none, or very few. Looked at in a certain light, science teaching today is the most efficient, up to date, and worldly-wise. In another light, it is backward, wasteful and "escapist." Let me explain these contrasts.

Fifty or sixty years ago, science was a new academic subject. People mistrusted its power to educate, and many of its proponents seemed as if they could never be educated themselves. The tradition of liberal studies had always included mathematics, because mathematics was supposed to train the mind; but the new physical sciences were first seen as manual arts, messy and expensive, and with no more "discipline" to them than a pair of elastic-sided boots. At the time of the fight for adding science to the curriculum, the defensive position was held by Greek and Latin, which unfortunately adopted a "scorched earth" policy. I mean that they allowed themselves to be invaded by the "scien-

tific spirit* and in trying to compete with it reduced their field
to a wasteland of verbal criticism, grammar, and philology. Literature was relegated to a second place and studying the classics
came to mean research into the uses of *utor*, *fruor*, and *fungor*.

Naturally the classics were exterminated, for science could beat
them at their own game. A young man trained in science could
on graduation get any of a hundred desirable jobs in industry. A
young "scientific" classicist could only hope to teach his own
subject to a dwindling number of students. That is what invariably comes of trying to put belles-lettres into utilitarian envelopes.
As Dean Briggs of Harvard said when the Bachelor of Science
degree was established: "It does not guarantee that the holder
knows any science, but it does guarantee that he does *not* know
any Latin." When the study of classical literature in translation
was reintroduced for freshmen at Columbia College a few years
ago, the undergraduate department of classics was surprised to
find its enrollment in beginning Greek increased 150 per cent:
they now had ten students.

But the bitter joke is not on the Classics alone. Having stepped
into Greek's vacated place, Science now occupies its position, not
with respect to size of enrollment, but with respect to educational
attitude. It is now in power and it acts disdainful, holier-than-
thou, and prudish. Someone once asked, "What is it that our men
of science are guarding like a threatened virginity?" "Oh," was
the answer, "they have a Vestal interest in their subject." Considered — somewhat unfairly — in the mass, science teachers may
be said to contribute the greatest proportion of backward-looking,
anti-intellectual, mechanic-minded members to the faculty. Characteristically, single departments of physical science have in
certain institutions tried to set up separate schools, where only
their one science would be taught for four years and rewarded
with some kind of Bachelor's degree. The intention was to monopolize the student's time, cram him full of "practical" knowledge,
and sell him to the highest bidder the moment he had clutched

his diploma and redeemed his ten-dollar deposit for apparatus.

Doubtless there is a demand for such prefabricated industrial robots and I see no reason why such schools should not function in a manner useful to the commonwealth — off the campus. But departments that once clamored for admission to university status and have had it for fifty years are unwilling to give up all the *douceurs* of the association. They would still like to profit from the university connection, to color their degree with a faint tincture of liberal teaching — perhaps they would require a year of English and a year of history and economics — and to boast that their own subject, be it chemistry or geology, is also one of the "humanities." They want to eat their cake as many times over as a cow does her cud.

A crowd of evils springs from this ambiguous mood in the present college curriculum. There is an undignified scramble for the student's time, with broad hints on the part of the scientist that the rest of the program is folderol. Repressed antagonisms divide teachers of the humanities (vague, pointless, unpractical subjects — except economics) from teachers of the real stuff represented by science. Moreover, departments of physics and chemistry require mathematical preparation in strict amount and order of time, with the result that all scheduling revolves around their claims. Since most young Americans discover their vocational bent while undergraduates, the wish to qualify for a profession is a powerful lever to make everyone study science for one or two years under these barbaric conditions. The doctor, the engineer, the research man in any science must gobble up as many courses as he can; and the man uninterested in science must "fulfill the requirement." Both are often judged on their science record, in the belief that it unmistakably reveals "real brains" or the lack of them.

The worst of all this is that neither group of students learns much about science but goes to swell the ranks of the two great classes of modern men — the single-track expert and the scientific ignoramus. Could anything more plainly demonstrate the failure of science to become a subject fit for college teaching? What makes a subject fit for the higher curriculum is surely no novelty: it is that it shall enlighten all the corners of the mind and teach its own uses. The humble three R's begin in strict utility and end up in poetry, science, and the search for the Infinite. They can and should therefore be taught indefinitely. Men have known for three thousand years that other matters of knowledge naturally divide themselves into special and general, that both are needful, but that whereas the special *add* to one's powers, the general *enhance the quality* of all of them.

At a recent educational conference, the Dean of a Midwestern university complained humorously that he was always being asked to give credits for impossible subjects — subjects that, he said, deserved to be called *in-credible*. A transfer student, for example, wanted "points" for seven hours of saw filing. Undeniably saw filing is a necessary art, but its merits as a general enhancer of power and personality stop accruing so soon after study is begun that it is not properly a branch of academic learning. The same is true of still more complex matters like shorthand, typewriting, and dress designing. Farther on in the series, it becomes harder to draw the line: stamp collecting is sub-educational but numismatics is a province of history.

Fortunately there is no doubt whatever about the place of the sciences: they *are* humanities and they belong in the college curriculum. Accordingly, they should be introduced into it *as humanities*, at the earliest possible moment. How? I have some tentative suggestions to make, but first I want to stress the danger of further delay and of the continuance of our present malpractice.

The worst danger is the creation of a large, powerful, and complacent class of college-trained uneducated men at the very heart of our industrial and political system. We may be too near to judge, but it strikes me that one of the conditions that made possible the present folly in Germany was the split among three groups: the technicians, the citizens, and the irresponsible rabble. This becomes persuasively plain if you consider the professional army caste as a group of unthinking technicians. The rabble together with the technicians can cow the citizenry; the technicians — wedded solely to their workbench — will work for any group that hires; and the rabble, worshiping "science" to the exclusion of less tangible necessaries, are perfectly willing to sacrifice the citizen. They probably think that, if necessary, "science" could manufacture German citizens — out of wolfram.

Such principles will hardly give long life and happiness to a democracy. The only hope for a democratic state is to have more citizens than anything else. Hence technicians must not be allowed to hibernate between experiments, but must become conscious, responsible, politically and morally active men. Otherwise they will find not only that representative government has slipped out of their fingers, but that they have also lost their commanding position. They will be paid slaves in the service of some rabble, high or low. Meanwhile our present stock of citizens must not simply gape at the wonders of science, but must understand enough of its principles to criticize and value the results. As for the rabble, it must be transmuted as fast as it forms, by science and morals both.

All this clearly depends on teaching our easygoing, rather credulous college boys and girls what science is. If they leave college thinking, as they usually do, that science offers a full, accurate, and literal description of man and Nature; if they think scientific research by itself yields final answers to social problems; if they think scientists are the only honest, patient, and careful workers in the world; if they think that Copernicus, Galileo, Newton, Lavoisier, and Faraday were unimaginative plodders like their own instructors; if they think theories spring from facts and that scientific authority at any time is infallible; if they think that the ability to write down symbols and read manometers is fair grounds for superiority and pride, and if they think that science steadily and automatically makes for a better world — then they have wasted their time in the science lecture room; they live in an Ivory Laboratory more isolated than the poet's tower [1] and they are a plain menace to the society they belong to. They are a menace whether they believe all this by virtue of being engaged in scientific work themselves or of being disqualified from it by felt or fancied incapacity.

I return to what might perhaps be done preventively and constructively. To begin with, a change of direction must be imparted to the teaching of science. The fact must be recognized that most students still do not make science their profession.[2] Consequently, for future lay citizens the compulsory science requirement in force nearly everywhere must be justified by a course explicitly designed for them. Such a course must not play at making physicists or biologists, but must explain the principles of the physical sciences in a coherent manner. A "survey" of all the sciences is out of the question. It would be at once superficial and bewildering. But an intelligent introduction to principles can be given. The assumptions that connect and that differentiate the sciences of matter, of living beings, and of logical relation can be taught; the meaning and the grounds of great unifying theories can be explained, and significant demonstrations and experiments can be shown to and made by the students.

Out of such a course there would surely come a changed attitude on the part of teachers and indeed a change in teaching personnel. At present, side by side with wise men and ripe

---

[1] To judge by results, it would seem that the poet climbs to the top of his tower to look out on the world and write about it. Why cavil at the building material — at once durable and attractive and requiring no upkeep?

[2] Statistics for the Middle West, based on large freshman enrollments, show that 50 per cent of those taking Chemistry 1, 60 per cent of those taking Geology 1, 73 per cent of those taking Physics 1, 75 per cent of those taking Biology 1, and 82 per cent of those taking Botany 1, never go further into the science.

teachers in the sciences, one finds many highly trained and absolutely uneducated practitioners. One also finds fanatics of the order that Dickens described in Professor Dingo, who, being caught defacing houses with his geological hammer, replied that "he knew of no building save the Temple of Science." Many university scientists openly scorn teaching and use their appointment to boil the pot of individual research. Now a life of research is a worthy one, but no amount of worthy motive justifies false pretenses and fraudulent impersonation — in this case the pretense of imparting knowledge and the impersonation of a teacher.

In the classroom, such men usually are neither civil, nor literate, nor even scientific, for their knowledge of science is purely from inside — a limitation equally bad but more misleading than the limitation of knowing it purely from outside. "What do they know of science who only science know?" They teach it as a set of rules, and speak of the profession as a "game." Drill in manual dexterity they entrust to laboratory assistants, who are only younger editions of themselves, and for whom a good notebook or speed in performing repetitious experiments is the passport to approval. There is seldom any consideration of the students as thinking minds, of the proper allocation of effort among the many interests legitimate at their time of life, nor of the philosophical implications which the words, the history, and the processes of the particular science disclose.

To offset this lamentable state of things, it must be said that two of the professions most concerned with scientific training — engineering and medicine — have lately amended their outlook and made overtures to the humanities. The medical schools have declared that cramming the student with science in college was a poor thing. He had better study other, less "practical," more formative subjects and postpone advanced chemistry and biology until medical school, where they will be taught him again in a fashion better tailored to his needs. This new policy is excellent, but it is not yet sufficiently enforced. The lesser medical schools

— and some others — do not trust their own belief in the principle; they still appeal to "practical" views and judge applicants by A's in science.

Similarly, the Society for the Promotion of Engineering Education has passed splendid resolutions approving what they call the "social-humanistic stem" — by which they mean a few branches of non-engineering study; more accurately then, the "social-humanistic faggots." But here again, engineering thought is ahead of the engineer's emotions. When it comes to the test, the student or the program is pushed around to suit engineering subject matter.

If you add to this the important fact that many young Americans choose "engineering" in the belief that this means a career of research in pure science, you may form some notion of the present anarchical mess. The would-be engineer of seventeen finds that what he really wants to work at is pure research in electricity, that is, to be a physicist. He must therefore back water, change his course, and take some new prerequisites. Meanwhile his upbringing as a man and citizen goes by the board. He is caught between two grindstones, each indifferent to the effect of its motion, just as if the boy being put through this mill were not a human being, a student of the university, and a future citizen of the nation. Who is being "practical" now?

Some would probably still maintain that the professional schools in contact with "the world" know best what is the practical view, and that the college is as ever utopian. But there is one curious fact to be added. It is that the scientific professional schools have a way of relaxing their jaws into a smile whenever the market demand for their product decreases: it is a reflex action. They fall in love with the humanities all over again and raise the amount they require for admission, until outside pressure once again lowers the floodgates and the frown succeeds the smile. This self-regulating action is a feat of engineering in itself — or shall I say of doctoring the supply for public consumption?

The question is not whether this is the easy way to go about marketing young men, but whether it is a responsible grown-up way of replenishing the professional class of society. Granted that practice is the test of all schemes and ideals, is this the most practical scheme that American ingenuity can devise? I concede that in the present state of mind of the American public, desire for vocational training takes the lead over anything else. But are the directing members of the university world to follow other people's untutored impulses or to guide and redirect them? We may well ask when we reflect that the first victims of the system are the children of the unthinking public and the public itself. For it is the oldest fallacy about schooling to suppose that it can train a man for "practical" life. Inevitably, while the plan of study is being taught, "practical life" has moved on. "They did it this way three months ago, now they do it this way." No employer who knows anything about men will value a beginner because he knows the ropes of a particular changeable routine. It would be as sensible to require that newcomers know the floor plan of the factory ahead of time.[3]

The corporations employing the largest numbers of engineers and scientific research men are on this matter way ahead of the colleges. One such firm conducted a survey last year to find out where and how its first-rate executives had been prepared. They came from the most unexpected places — including small liberal arts colleges, the teaching profession, the stage, and the Baptist ministry. It was found that the engineering schools — particularly those sensible ones that make no pretense at intellectual *cachet* —

[3] The S.P.E.E. reports: "From its very nature, engineering education operates under changing conditions which constantly challenge its processes and test its results . . . so as to adapt itself to changing needs." (*Draft of a Report*, etc. November 16, 1939, p. 1.) This is fine and good, but it holds true of every other professional subject and most academic ones. The old belief that only a few schools are in touch with the "real world" is untrue, even if the newer belief should prove true that it is best for the world to have the school conform to every change outside.

turned out a good average product, but few leaders. The company's own institutes and night courses raised the chance of foremen and district managers — but only up to a point. The survey concluded that what it wanted as material to shape future executives was graduates of liberal arts colleges, trained in history and economics, in philosophy and in good English, and likewise possessed of *an intelligent interest in science and technology*. Gentlemen, the path lies open.

II

My friend Dean Finch, of the Columbia University School of Engineering, might not agree with all I have just said, but I think he would approve of one element in my suggestions which I casually threw in. I mean the utility of history in the teaching of science. He himself is an historian of technology and offers in Columbia College a most valuable course in the subject for the use of "lay" students. What is surprising is that similar courses, accompanied by others in the history of pure science, are not given — indeed required — on every American campus.

The very idea, it must be said, is shrouded in the smoke of battle. When I mention it, some of my scientific colleagues slap me on the back and say "more power to you." They may express doubts about persuading their fellows, or finding good instructors, but they want to see it tried. Moreover they do not feel robbed when in my own teaching of nineteenth-century history I discuss Dalton and Darwin, Liebig and Faraday, Mayer and Clerk Maxwell. Though scientists, these colleagues of mine can see that to complain of general ignorance about the role of science in modern history, and to prevent historians from mentioning it, is to love monopoly above riches.

Others take the view that science has no history because every new achievement supersedes previous ones. The history of science, they feel, is nothing but biographical chitchat about scientists.

Or else they admit that it is useful to find out what the Middle Ages thought of natural science, but only in order to point the lesson of freedom from church authority and fight anew the old battle of science against religion.

This angry confusion about the history of science is dense but not impenetrable. Three things may be distinguished. First there is historical research into the beginnings of science — Greek or Arabic or Medieval. This goes on as advanced study and concerns undergraduates only in the form of broad tested conclusions. Then there is the biography of scientists, which is of immense educational importance — whatever laboratory men may say. Biography does not mean recounting Newton's imaginary embroilments with women or Lavoisier's perfectly real ones with public finance. It means finding out from the lives of great scientific creators what they worked at and how their minds functioned. How tiresome it is to hear nothing from our scientific departments but Sunday-school homilies on the gameness of Galileo, the patience of Pasteur, and the carefulness of Madame Curie. And how uninstructive! Any man who accomplishes anything in any field is as patient as he has to be, and even little boys know that glass being breakable, you have to be careful.[4]

What would be far more significant and novel, though true, would be to teach that Copernicus gambled on insufficient evidence; that Kepler was chiefly a horoscope-caster; that Faraday probably believed more wrong theories than any man alive — and turned them to good use in experiment; that Darwin, on his own admission, made awful blunders and admired the art of wriggling out of them; that T. H. Morgan's laboratory was rather messy; that Newton could not see how his own astronomy contradicted the Bible; that scientific men have suppressed and persecuted opponents of their theories, and that the best scientific

---

[4] The self-righteousness of the man of science is universal enough to sustain advertising appeals: "Like the scientist, NEWSWEEK . . . makes it its business to search out truth by continual research, relentless checking and re-checking of the facts." A grim grind!

truth can end in a rigid and mistaken orthodoxy — as happened after Newton and Darwin. The point is that science is made by man, in the light of interests, errors, and hopes, just like poetry, philosophy, and human history itself.

To say this is not to degrade science, as naïve persons might think; it is on the contrary to enhance its achievements by showing that they sprang not from patience on a monument but from genius toiling in the mud. I leave unexplained here all that accrues from studying how we came to use atoms or devise Absolute Zero or to state the Law of Conservation of Energy (including the reasons why energy is a better word than the earlier "force") or what steps led first to the abandonment and then to the later salvaging of Avogadro's hypothesis. A good scientist-historian would exhibit the assumptions and habits which affected scientific opinion at important turning points. He would unite science to other thought by discussing the nature of its evidence at various periods. And he would show the role of the pure imagination in all great scientific work. I know Bacon promised that science would level all the minds of its devotees to average size, and he is right insofar as drilling can make ordinary men into patient, careful laboratory workers. But science has not yet managed to get along without ideas, and these come only from men of special, powerful, and irreducible aptitudes. The chronological study of these men and ideas is the proper subject matter for an undergraduate course in the history of science.[5]

I know the common objection offered to all this — to an historical and a synoptic account of scientific principles in place of the "regular" science courses: it is that the substitutes would be merely talk about science and not science itself. Grant this for argument's sake. The objectors miss the point if they do not see

---

[5] Some very useful works already exist which exemplify the historical and inductive method of teaching science; among others: Ostwald's *Schule der Chemie* (translated by E. C. Ramsay), Ida Freund's *The Study of Chemical Composition* and *The Experimental Basis of Chemistry*, Norman Campbell's *Physics: The Elements*, and H. T. Pledge's *Science Since 1500*.

that talk about science has a place in the curriculum and that such talk may be good or bad, quite all right or all quite wrong, exactly like talk about art. If science is one of the humanities it must be capable of being looked at and thought about apart from direct doing — at least until we require every concertgoer to write a symphony before being allowed to take his seat at Carnegie Hall. Besides, the synoptic course I have in view would include laboratory work, and it would rest with the scientists themselves whether the students mastered enough of the operative side of true science to keep them from irresponsible talk about it. If science teachers think that a year's drudgery in physics as now given prevents silly notions in those who take it in college, they are either inobservant or illogical.

Doubtless it is bad logic they suffer from — the usual weakness of scientists . . . and of the rest of mankind, who generally want to have things both ways. Take as an example a comment made on the relation of science and history in the excellent study of Lavoisier by J. A. Cochrane. The author complains that "although Lavoisier was at the time of his death and for at least fifteen years before it one of the most eminent men in France, the general historian does not think it worth while to make any mention of him. . . . Science has undoubtedly changed the face of the world, and yet practically the only credit given to it by the historian is the Industrial Revolution . . . and even then the facts are not always accurate."

This is very sound criticism, but the scientist at once reasserts his monopoly: "No doubt the historian, having no qualifications to discuss the progress of science, feels that he had best leave it severely alone, but he can scarcely claim to trace the evolution of the modern world if he omits one of the most important factors in that evolution." [6] Which will the author have — treatment with inevitable errors or leaving the sacred objects "severely alone"? So long as we act like watchdogs over our little plots, it is obvious that we cannot have the comprehensive views that all

[6] Page vii.

profess to desire. Somebody has to take the first step — and suffer for his pains.

But it would be unfair if I gave the impression that the opposition to teaching the history of science to college students was universal or came only from certain scientists. At one great university near New York there was a thriving enterprise of this sort, popular with students and science departments alike. It was given by a young man, equally gifted in the humanities and in his chosen physical science — a budding *uomo universale*, whom fellow scientists were willing to aid, guide, and correct — if need be — on the remoter details of their science. After a few years this course built up a tradition, exerted an influence, reached a kind of perfection in the fulfillment of its aim.

With the war, changes came in staff and direction; the instructor left and the opposition rallied to abolish the course. It will scarcely be believed when I say that the prime mover in this *Putsch* was a philosopher. What inspired him, the Absolute only knows. The science course did not teach any philosophy contrary to his own; it only taught the historical fact that great men of science have employed varying philosophical assumptions to gain their ends. It taught, besides, that the several sciences do not look at the world all in the same way and that so far as science has a unified point of view, it is not exclusive of others — the ways, namely, of art, philosophy, religion, and common sense. Lastly, the course imparted a fair amount of matters of fact and showed how wrong was the man who said: "You don't have to teach the history of science to make a man understand that water is H_2O." It is precisely what you have to teach, unless you are willing to barter understanding for mere voodoo formulas.

What more could any philosophy department want? Their students were lucky enough to be taught to think. Is there any other use to make of the four years of college? The world being full of a number of things, it takes practice to think easily about the chief ones. Does philosophy pretend to monopolize cogitation because Descartes said, "Don't doubt I'm thinking!"

The fact is that philosophy has suffered emotionally, like Greek and Latin, from the triumph of science. Philosophy was a minor partner in the defeat of the classics, and that has left it laboring under the same sense of wrong, the same fancied need to be haughty — and even hoity-toity. In the '80s science said: "We bring you the answers. Philosophy will gradually be pushed out as we extend our certainty." Many philosophers agreed and looked for their retirement at the first outrush of some naked Archimedes shouting "Eureka." Other philosophers, courageously holding their ground, fought as critics of science's faulty logic or extreme arrogance, just as a few classicists kept saying, "Poison gas marks a great step forward but have you taken in the meaning of Thucydides's 'Peloponnesian War'?"

The time has now come for the three-cornered duel on the campus to cease. The classics, philosophy, and science are at once overlapping and complementary disciplines. No need even to adjust boundary differences. The students are well able to take care of seeming conflicts, and in truth profit from them, since opposition reinforces attention by heightening the drama of human thought. Science must be taught, and historically, too, or the people will perish. Philosophy likewise must have a voice in all courses throwing light on the history of ideas. It will save philosophy as a subject and save the students from caddishness and provincialism. But philosophy has other obvious collegiate duties. It must read its great masterpieces with the new generation, expound ethical and metaphysical theory, help teach logic, and do liaison work with historians, scientists, and theologians. Once in a while an original philosopher will arise, unsought, in the midst of his colleagues, and the world will know him to its own profit.

The classics, too, must enter the dance. They hold the key to the meaning of our long journey from the cave to — precisely — the laboratory. Why, one may ask, go back over those painful steps? I shall answer this presently as best I can.

8. Clio: A Muse

> History is not what you thought.
> It is what you can remember.
> All other history defeats itself.
> — *1066 and All That*

"I DIDN'T take any history in college," said the sweet girl graduate. "I took 'Social Mal' instead."

"I beg your pardon?"

"Oh, I'm sorry, that's what we called a course in Social Maladjustment that Professor X gave."

"You mean you have learned maladjustment?"

"Yes, the causes of it. You know — inhibitions, divorce, and all that sort of thing."

"I see. And now you want to take History, get a higher degree, and ultimately teach?"

That was the situation — a not uncommon one, but uncommonly difficult to meet. The young woman knew some American history on a fairly primitive level, but no history of any other part of the world except what she had picked up in newspapers. To counterbalance this, she knew that childhood frustrations were deplorable. How could she successfully do the work in an advanced history course which would take it for granted that Voltaire and Bismarck were not contemporaries? To pull her through demanded the equivalent of a reading and tutoring course which took up my weekly office hour. And the joke of it — if it is a joke to bat people around from pillar to post — is that very likely after taking her degree *in history* and being accepted by the schools as a teacher *of history*, she would be asked to give a hodgepodge course in "social science" — full of maladjustments.

History undoubtedly sounds dull compared with "social studies" in Marriage and Divorce, or with the profundities of "social science," ranging as far afield as "Africia." Accordingly, the movement to socialize history, to make it up-to-date and "practical," has now succeeded throughout the secondary schools, while in colleges and universities proposals are occasionally heard for the abolition of history "as such."

I feel I could discuss this threat more intelligently if I had the faintest idea what *as such* means in this context. Students have tried to explain it to me — in vain, though I generally learn easily from students. They tell me that history "as such" is the worst kind of "straight" history. If I understand this any better, it means date-and-fact history, featureless history, of which — alas — there is a great deal still being thrust down our children's throats in the name of Americanism. And judging from the papers, more of this same kind will be administered unless we reconsider the whole subject. I was glad recently to see Professor Packard, of Smith, going to the root of the matter by asking that we improve the quality of history teaching before legislating increased amounts of it.

History *as such* does not exist: it is always the history — the story — of something; and "straight" history can only signify that the something is cut-and-dried or trivial to the point of leaving no trace of its passage through the mind. Moreover, by its very nature history needs no "socializing." Except for a stretch at the very beginning of the record, history is the account of man in society; and that early stretch is seldom taught as history but rather as paleontology and archeology. All the rest, from the history of shipbuilding to that of baseball, is inescapably social and absolutely all-inclusive. The comings and goings of rats and lice, as Dr. Zinsser showed us, concern Clio as much as they would any good housekeeper. In fine, history being the story of mankind, and men being by definition interested in themselves, it follows that history cannot avoid being interesting.

Unfortunately, most people find it dull. The trouble is that history does not come "ready to serve" in convenient packages. It has to be studied, therefore taught, and it is just as hard to teach as any less inherently dramatic subject. To organize facts acquired in many places and project them so that they resemble life is a difficult art. Anyone who had seen the Battle of Waterloo or heard Huxley tell off Bishop Wilberforce would never forget it, nor let anyone else do so. But transferred to the page or the platform, the event flattens out like a neglected soufflé; while to the onlooker it seems that there are so many of these featureless facts in a heap that no sane man would start rummaging among them.

It is indeed futile to plunge in without some kind of container and some principle of selection. Hence the subdivision of history into military, diplomatic, or economic; into the history of costume, of ideas, or of politics. Each arbitrarily cuts off a part of human history to treat as a main theme. It so happens that politics is a fairly large portion with which others are closely connected, so it becomes the most usual container. The misfortune is that political history can be most easily reduced to a bare enumeration of dates and names. This is the form in which it is too usually taught and written; hence learned and damned by students as "straight history."

They make heroic efforts to memorize the names and dates; they provide themselves with five causes for this and ten results of that. They bulge with factors, forces, and trends. And when exhausted in the vain struggle to account for everything by such parrotlike devices, they fall back on the "climate of opinion" or on question-begging epithets.

This mad endeavor which "the system" encourages is associated in my mind with a very pleasant — and relevant — instance of its folly. My friend and colleague D. M. and I were preparing together for the Ph.D. orals. We shared rooms, and while reviewing and taking notes, would quiz each other and prod our flagging energies with fresh difficulties. One day, going over the Napoleonic Wars, I was struck by the fact that I could never remember the whole story of the Allies' treatment of Saxony in the treaties of 1815. I knew the Saxon Duke had joined Napoleon and stuck to him later than the rest, paying for his mistake. But why, how, what were the motives? I asked my partner, who as an American historian taking only a minor in European history was amiably scornful of continental affairs. I put my question.

D. M. — Don't tell me you've forgotten *that!*

J. B.　— Well, I have and what's more I can't even find it in my notes.

D. M. — How can you forget Frederick, Duke of Saxony! — the *high-minded* Duke of Saxony! Later made King by Napoleon, but that's not the point. Oh, no! Concentrate on the high-minded part. That's all you know and all you need to know. (*Looking rapidly through the textbook*) In fact, here it is — just as I said: "But the Allies did not see it in that light. The *high-minded* Frederick, having etc. etc. . . . his pledge, found himself despoiled of etc. etc. . . . square miles." A lesson to him. Got it now?

An historian is known by the adjectives he keeps, and textbook writers would become better historians if they got rid of most of theirs, or at least replaced them with more strongly felt ones.[1] The stuff of history is action, thought, chance. It should reflect this and not be treated as a moral tale until the student knows a fair quantity of facts; and even then history forbids easy moraliz-

---

[1] "Do you know Hallam?" asked Byron of a friend. "I remember being stirred by a passage where, touching on the Venetians he writes: 'Too blind to avert danger, too cowardly to withstand it, the most ancient government of Europe made not an instant's resistance; the peasants of Unterwald died upon their mountains, the nobles of Venice clung only to their lives.' This is the way in which history ought to be written, if it is wished to impress it on the memory."

ing. The facts, moreover, should draw more largely on biography, for statesmen and generals are only men, whose careers in life and in death possess atmosphere and suggest opinions. Without opinions and feelings how can a student participate in what he is being told? Impartiality is not indifference, it is the appreciation of opposite forces and clashing motives.

History being bathed in "motives," the art of teaching it consists in making the student see that these motives resemble his own, at the same time as they are subtly modified by conditions and ideas and hopes now beyond recall. That is why historical novels are so justly popular: they combine motives and local color. They may overdo the love interest in proportion to the "background," but at least the figures move by with passions we recognize and costumes we envy. In my own predicament recounted above, it was not that I found high-mindedness unbelievable — there are high-minded men even among Dukes — but that the writer himself did not believe his own adjective. He merely tossed it at me to keep me quiet, and my friend's satire on the performance was nothing else than just. Similarly with the causes and the trends: they do not exist until some historian makes them credible by furnishing examples, arguments, interpretations, and overall views. Before he can hope to arouse you or me, he must be more than "interested," he must be committed to his subject, and what is true of the printed book is all the more true of the lecture or discussion hour: the man in charge must speak as a man to his fellows about their common descent — not from the ape, but from the Pilgrim Fathers, the heroes of the French Revolution, the artists of the Renaissance, the saints of the Middle Ages, and so on back to the Medes and the Persians.

II

The student seldom inquires, but he has in addition a right to know why he should be made to find the Puritan and the Persian who lurk inside him. He thinks he has no such inmates and his mind goes out to things contemporary. That is why if left alone he chooses sociological courses on "The Family" or plunges into "scientific" social studies — which in one Far Western university turned out to mean picking apricots. The point is not that these occupations are in themselves bad for the development of youth, but that they waste time and mislead.

They waste time because the amount of wisdom to be picked up together with the apricots is slight. The knowledge of actual conditions in a cannery, the social "adjustment" to fellow workers, and the writing of reports about all this do not furnish the mind with enough principles to justify the effort. Experience is a great thing but there is always the danger that *one* experience will be taken as representing the whole truth: that is where un-co-ordinated social studies mislead. Even in "Social Mal" I suspect that certain striking conclusions of recent make are presented, and that the rest consists of facts and figures tending to show that unemployment is bad and proper housing is good. From this last point, one can safely generalize and say that under the name of social science, sociology, psychology, anthropology, and economics, many American students today are really offered one single and quite unnecessary subject, namely: Tautology.

History — by which I mean history properly taught — aims at the diametrically opposite results. It is never tautological, it is not confined to one experience or one set of experiences, it does not ape the tricks of physical science; it does not offer brisk formulas for human behavior nor pat answers to social problems. But it makes its students think maturely about all the valuable fragments of experience which may have found their way into these later and shoddier substitutes. I need not, I hope, emphasize the fact that I am now contrasting *good* history teaching with the *average* social science or sociology that frequently replaces it. I am not criticizing serious teaching in psychology nor responsible work in sociology under true masters. I have no quarrel with other independent disciplines, but only with the *Ersatz* that is put forward as fit to supplant history.

It may be objected that my aim of "thinking" about history is all very well for professional historians, but has little use for laymen. I am certainly not advocating the training of everyone as an historian,[2] but in a civilization like ours, built on records and on continuity, we are willy-nilly the past embodied. Since this is so, no one can understand himself or the institutions at his disposal without historical information. The proof of this is all around us: when we went to war, there was an explosive demand for American history. Then we found in short order that men going to fight Germany and Japan had to be taught world history. They had so long dwelt in the passing scene that they had to be brought up to date. So they were shown a film, prepared by the Army (an admirable job of combined montage and history), giving the antecedents of our struggle. And soon after that, when we planned to invade foreign territories, we found that different traditions make men different, and we had to pump our soldiers and military governors full of local lore, that is, of history.

Our original question must therefore be put differently: can we afford to be as ignorant of our inner past as we are? What history teaches is not the date of the Monroe Doctrine — that is incidental — but how such a document can come into being, why the British Navy was necessary to its effectiveness, how its meaning has changed, and what involvements of life and death may yet hang upon it. The boy fresh from a potato patch in Maine or Iowa may not know that he embodies the Monroe Doctrine, but any South American is persuaded that every North American does embody it. That is enough to affect at least two lives, for the South American also knows to a T how he himself feels

[2] I have given detailed arguments on these points in two essays, previously published: "History, Popular and Unpopular" in *The Interpretation of History*, Princeton University Press, 1942; and "History as a Liberal Art," *Journal of the History of Ideas*, January 1945.

about the Monroe Doctrine. What is our freshman to do next —
plead ignorance? Dismiss Latin America from his thoughts?
Fight for the Monroe Doctrine, or vote it down? Wouldn't it
seem rather practical to find out first what "it" is?

All this is still in the realm of the severely factual. There is,
besides the facts, a sense of history which familiar handling develops, very much akin to that by which the lumberman knows
wood and the art expert Michelangelos. When broadly based
on a good knowledge of western European history (including
that of the United States), the historical sense is a comforter and
a guide. The possessor understands his neighbors, his government,
and the limitations of mankind much better. He knows more
clearly not what is desirable, but what is possible. He becomes
"practical" in the lasting sense of being taken in neither by
panicky fears nor by second-rate Utopias. It is always some
illusion that creates disillusion, especially in the young, for whom
the only alternative to perfection is cynicism. The historical sense
is a preventive against both extremes. It is a moderator which
insists on knowing conditions before passing judgments. The
historical sense is above all political-minded. It suggests that in
the struggles of men with one another, no virtue implies the
possession of any other; that motives are mixed, and that no evil is
absolutely perverse. For these reasons, the study of history tends
to make men tolerant, without on that account weakening their
determination to follow the right: they know too well the odds
against it.

Even when history does not grip the student mind to the extent
I have shown, it induces a little humility and prevents those fits
of sudden misplaced moral indignation for which Macaulay so
roundly ridiculed the British public. A few months ago I was
present at a discussion, outside academic circles, where the American policy towards General de Gaulle was being excoriated. The
first argument was that it was a bad policy. This was of course the
very point at issue, so it was not an argument — and I am not

concerned to settle it here. What is representative of our short-comings is the second or historical argument, which was that because Lafayette had helped Washington in the eighteenth century, we must now help de Gaulle. After this had been said vehemently a couple of times, someone turned to me for my opinion. I tried to give it but I succeeded in putting it over to only one person. Not that it was very abstruse; all I said was that the two cases were not comparable; that two nations, acting under different conditions one hundred and fifty years apart, could not be likened to a pair of housewives who borrow and return a little butter from time to time.

I was not exactly lynched, but I was abused as a cynic, a logic chopper, an academic mind, and a person without generous impulses. "How can you say this and pretend to admire the Romantic poets!" exclaimed one lady, capping the climax of confusion and ignorance. Throughout the discussion, one phrase kept recurring as a joint denunciation of the policy in question and myself. The phrase was "power politics." I asked at one point what else politics could be about except power, and was stared at as if I had proposed polygamy. On thinking it over, I felt it was a sign and symbol of our modern ignorance of any kind of history that we should coin the phrase "power politics." If our alienation from concrete experience and the concrete imagination goes on, I expect that we shall soon hear of food nutrition and man-woman marriages.

III

It would seem only fair, after vaunting the merits of the historical sense, that I should give some hints for developing it. For twentieth-century Americans it requires, as I have said, a good running start from at least the end of the Middle Ages. Such a course as the Introduction to Contemporary Civilization, which has been given for twenty-five years in Columbia College, begins with the year 1200 and traces out the changes in the political, economic, and intellectual life of Europe and America to the present day. Since it is impossible to teach all the "interesting" or "valuable" things in that period, one must be content with pointing out in some detail the ebb and flow of ideas and patterns of life. The words Feudalism, Capitalism, Nationalism, Imperialism, Democracy, represent some of these tides. They are familiar enough, but under each of them belong a multitude of facts. What are these isms concretely? Who gave his life or his thought in behalf of this or that system, what groups favored the new or the old, and for what reason? What are the actual words of the doers, how were they understood, and which blinder impulses aided or retarded the change? To be informed and critical in this way about the contents of the past seven hundred years seems a worthy task for any student and any instructor.

A great encouragement to the student who attempts this is that after a while the mind holds more easily the at first chaotic mass of details. Like bricks in an arch, they wedge one another tight and stay put. It becomes indeed a pleasure to pass from one set to another without recourse to text or dates, moving freely, as it were, among the living dead. I remember discussing with students of mine not long ago Rousseau's views on science and civilization — the subject of his first work, which the group had read. It so happened that none could recall the date of publication. "That's sloppy reading, gentlemen. A man's ideas are formed by what he sees as he grows up, so the year of birth is important. Now how can we find out when this book was written?"

"Look at the title page."

"You'll forget it again — and suppose you found no date there. Some books bear no date. Why not try a little thought?"

"How can you think up a date?"

"Try this: I know that in your Humanities readings you took up Rousseau's *Confessions*. Do you remember from that work about when the writer was born?"

"Early in the eighteenth century, I guess. He says his uncle fought under Prince Eugene. I guess Rousseau was born around 1715."

"Very good; actually, it was 1712. Now, do you know from the same source whether Rousseau became a writer early in life? This essay we're discussing made him instantly famous. Was he still a youth?"

"Yes."

"How old would you put him at?"

"About thirty, thirty-five."

"You're very flattering! A youth at thirty-five: I call that nearly middle-aged for a writer. But it's right. So what is the approximate date of the piece?"

"Seventeen forty-five to '50."

"Written in '49 and published in 1750. But we're not through. You've noticed that in the essay, Rousseau argues that luxury and refinement are signs, not of progress, but of decay. If he argued it, and people were aroused to anger, they must have believed the opposite. Now whose was the newer idea — Rousseau's against luxury, or — let's say Voltaire's for it?"

"Rousseau's — no, Voltaire's."

"How do you know?"

"Well, we read in Mandeville — that's about 1730 — that vice and luxury help prosperity. He seemed to think that was a new idea. Enlightened people in the eighteenth century were rather pleased with themselves and felt that all their new gadgets were the signs of a great moral progress just around the corner."

"Understandably enough — as we in the twentieth century can feel when we fall into the same mistake. By the way, would Rousseau's essay have been reinforced or refuted if he had waited until 1756 to write it?"

"He could have added another proof against moral progress: a fresh world war broke out just then which lasted seven years and exhausted four big nations."

"I wasn't thinking of that but it's an excellent point. Even

Voltaire said Europeans had no right to call anybody else savages. But didn't anything else happen to shatter Europe between 1750 and '55?"

"I know! The Lisbon earthquake. Voltaire wrote a poem about that too, and scientists — "

I spare the reader further witnessing of a scene transcribed at the cost of any sparkle it may have had, and I rest my case for the defense of history, not on an imperfect sample of classroom discussion based on a date, but on the direction of mind that I hope it suggests. The authors of *1066 and All That* are, as usual, thoroughly right: "History is what you can remember." Make the sense of the past a function of your mind and you heighten the flavor, enrich the texture of every experience, from politics to art. It is the humanizing faculty par excellence.

9. What Once Were Frills

> Botticelli's a wine, not a cheese,
> you fool!
>   — *A Little Tour Abroad*

SOMEBODY has said that if all else fails us in the postwar world — "reconversion," markets in China, and the spread of airlines — we can always fall back on our chief home industry — music. Exaggeration aside, it is truly astonishing how dependent on sound the American people has become. One noticed it especially in the early days of the war, when habits were being broken, and people spoke of storing their record collection with the same anxiety that they might feel about parking the baby.

And steadily since, I have received letters from camps and ships casually telling me that "So-and-so has a good machine, and we listen to ——" (whatever it is). If Plato was right about art, this new zeal should change our morals. It has certainly changed our manners. A few years ago, a friend of mine asked me to pick him up at his office in the Harvard Medical School. It was after the end of term and in the deserted buildings I lost my way. Finally I heard singing and made towards it: it was a chorus of men — evidently students — rehearsing *Komm' süsser Tod* in a dissecting room.

The important fact is that they were singing Bach. Twenty-five years ago, it would have been inconceivable. Men did not go in for serious music. It was a frill. The arts were for sissies — or for professionals. We owe it partly to jazz and football since the last war that undergraduate musicians have been acclimated on the campus; and to our speed in popularizing new ways that all the arts are now enjoying an academic boom. In the best colleges nowadays — I speak of normal times — there is an artist in captivity who may be seen at stated periods actually painting, hymning, or rhyming. He is nearly always "visiting," for the popular tradition of art is flightiness, and the university does not simply respect, it enforces traditions. Whether this is good or bad for the artist, I shall suggest in my last chapter.

On their side, the students enjoy the variety of having different masters to watch and listen to, but the encounter is not so great a novelty as one might think. Quite a few undergraduates began daubing water paints as babies; at eleven they had the first public exhibition of their work, reported in the newspaper and commented on by local critics. At eighteen they have gone through several styles and can talk as man to man with anybody short of Picasso.

All this is to the good. Ease of mind, familiarity, even rudeness about art is better than the kid-glove attitude. Like most living things, art can stand an enormous amount of manhandling or it would not survive a week. It can certainly stand mishandling better than it can stand frigid respect or our old enemy, prepared hokum. So that the question for the schools now is no longer, Shall we include the arts in the curriculum but — if I may be forgiven the implication — How shall we mishandle them to the best advantage? For I believe that a true relation to art is like the slow subtle growth called Education. It takes a lifetime of self-discipline and indefatigable passion to achieve. Not everybody is willing to make this investment of effort, and even when made, it remains true, as John Jay Chapman said, that "we cannot hope to know what art is. Art is life and any expression of art becomes a new form of life."

At the present time in this country two ways of teaching art struggle for supremacy. One is the way of doing, the other the way of criticizing — sometimes also called "appreciation." Progressive schools quite logically have gone in for doing. At Black Mountain and Sarah Lawrence, Bard and Bennington, a student can devote roughly one third of his or her time to studying the practice of an art. He or she plays the violin, or sculptures, or paints, or weaves and designs clothing. A masterwork is required for graduation and there is throughout the happy feeling that academic art is no longer "academic" in the bad sense, because it has returned to the old ways of apprenticeship, once so productive.

One difficulty with this scheme is that it creates for the responsible authorities a serious dilemma regarding requirements. If Betty is "majoring" in music at Bennington, she should be taught to play the piano as well as her cousin in the New England Conservatory. In other words, there is a certain professional standard set by technical schools and market demand, which the college feels it must live up to. At the same time, Betty has been giving only one third of her time to music. It is unfair to compare her with a full-time student of the instrument. Besides, a college is *not* a conservatory and it must balance the intellectual diet of its charges: all music and no economics makes a lopsided A.B. The student of art is caught in the jaws of this machine almost as badly as the student of science.

Even worse is the fact that in trying to approach the professional standard of performance in art, it is necessary to concentrate on doing at the expense of thinking. The piano student thinks about technique and phrasing and rhythm, of course, but hardly about principles of composition or criticism. She has no time. I have met and heard music graduates of progressive colleges who could give very creditable performances. They had sureness, musicianship, and the right kind of enthusiasm. But over the teacups, after the show, they proved quite illiterate musically. They were not quite sure whether Purcell could have copied Gluck or not. They had never heard an opera, they thought we had abundant recordings of Greek music, and were convinced that "equal temperament" and "in tune" were synonymous terms.

Some might say that these things are unimportant — if the stu-dent feels a true enjoyment in playing and hearing good pieces. The rest is only conversational fodder. Or they would argue that music's the thing and details about it are for the historian or physicist — who too often has no real interest in music proper. True enough, but we must leave out of account such professional failings, for neither clan dare start throwing stones. Of all the unmusical people in the world, so many have become instructors in counterpoint and heads of conservatories that they must permit the physicist to play with his tuning fork and the historian with his special kind of notes. The academic issue must be settled otherwise, perhaps after first asking how it is possible to teach counterpoint or measure overtones and still be unmusical. Obvi-ously, it is possible because the thing that makes music an art, and not just a trick, escapes these particular men. Their attention is focused on rules and numbers, and has not been drawn to the meaning of what they work with.

Meaning in music is of course another controversial subject, into which I do not want to enter now. Let us agree that meaning is not information, that a symphony by itself does not tell us the composer's age or political complexion. It tells something else, in sound or color, which could not be better put, or put at all, in some other medium. This holds true for all the arts, and the fact serves to remind us that although I have been speaking in musical examples, I have in mind all the arts, including the dance, as they are now taught in our schools. The parallel to musical performance is, let us say, drawing from life, or composing a group dance. The parallel to the lack of musical culture in a performer is the painter's ignorance of theories and traditions, or the modern dancer's belief that a flying *brisé* is acrobatic old stuff. In short, I am inching up towards the suggestion that a knowledge of the history of art is needed to develop critical in-sight, and that critical insight is ultimately necessary for the best kind of enjoyment and performance — even and especially by the amateur.

Take a very trivial example. I noticed some years ago, and have since confirmed the fact with grade-school teachers, that children who lack musical background call "music" only what is played on the piano. Other forms of the art they call "singing" and "instruments." The harm is slight, to be sure, but the provincialism is apparent. Simply because the nineteenth century developed the piano and gorged on music written for it, the modern child equates the part with the whole. If you speak to him of music in connection with Greek tragedy, he probably visualizes Agathon or Aspasia at a keyboard. A corner of his mind is closed, through ignorance, to the varieties of artistic experience.

Now the very reason why art is worth teaching at all is that it gives men the best sense of how rich, how diverse, how miraculous are the expressions of the human spirit through the ages. The communicative power of artistic forms that are utterly unlike, and perhaps at first repellent to the beholder, shatters the provincial assumptions which nearly all of us inherit — namely, that our ways of speaking, singing, and feeling are the only really human ways, all others being outlandish and probably meaningless.

They are indeed meaningless until learned, or learned about. And if from a childish mistake about the use of the word "music" we can reach this conclusion, it follows that the history of the arts should become a part of the normal curriculum — at least during the college years.

We must remember that the college does not pretend to "educate." It can only furnish the means of later self-education. Return then to our music student who gives all her time to finger dexterity. She likes one piece and plays it, plays another by the same author, hears her teacher or her friends mention other composers, and so builds up a repertoire and a "taste" by chance contacts. But once out of college, what is to guide further choices, arouse new interests, induce comparisons, throw sudden light on hidden aspects of pieces she thinks she knows — unless she has acquired a reserve of facts and ideas on which to draw, ahead of experience?

The inquiry has practical bearing. Suppose she is visiting a friend in another city, where some organization is giving, that night, a concert devoted to Gesualdo. Shall they attend? Of course the performance may be poor, but no musically educated person would decline the opportunity, for Gesualdo's music is rare and strange. Lack of curiosity here is tantamount to lack of musical culture. It would be good, moreover, for the student to know enough harmony, and enough of the historical development of counterpoint, to know what makes Gesualdo so "modern," and to feel how "incorrect" he might sound to routine minds.

This appreciation should naturally rest on direct knowledge of actual pieces, not on opinions taken from books. For this purpose, at a certain age, a student ought to hear all the music and see all the painting and sculpture and dancing that comes his way. But in order to place and organize all these impressions, the book, coupled with a good teacher, is necessary. I might insert here the fact that at Sarah Lawrence and Bennington College this modification of pure practice by historical teaching has now become usual.[1]

The threat of historical teaching, however, makes all the skeletons in the academic closet rattle on their hooks. The very word "appreciation," which I have used without defining, affects many teachers and artists like St. Vitus' dance. There is really no cause for jigging. Everybody knows by now that appreciation does not mean gush and that it does not mean parroting conventional catchwords about art. Nor does it mean simply familiarity with names, dates, and "schools." It implies a good

---

[1] *College Music,* by the American composer Randall Thompson, is the standard account of the music question. It is at the same time a very entertaining book.

working knowledge of the latter, but as in the study of history, the names and dates are means and not ends. The objector might be reminded that according to the Greeks, Clio, Muse of History, was credited with inventing the guitar. And styles are historical facts. The student who on hearing a new record makes the intelligent mistake of confusing *by ear* C. P. E. Bach with Mozart is a better historian and musician than the memorizer of "labels" who knows — how does he? — that Beethoven's Seventh should be called the "apotheosis of the dance."

So far we are on safe ground, for it is easy to unite on negatives. But what are the positive contents of an "appreciation" course? I can best answer, I think, by referring to the work of a man who more than any other single force has made school music a real province of art in America. I refer to the late Thomas Whitney Surette, who died in 1941 aged seventy-nine. It makes one despair of human justice, by the way, to find a career like Surette's exerting so much influence and passing so unnoticed by the public at large. Even among the thousands who knew him in his professional capacity there was apparently not thought or energy enough to produce a significant obituary. But this is another point that really belongs to a later chapter.

T. W. Surette was a native of Concord, Massachusetts, where he grew up in modest surroundings, supporting and educating himself as best he could. At one time he worked as stationmaster on a branch line of the railroad, which afforded him a fair amount of paid leisure which he spent reading. His musical training he received largely from his sister, who was then a pupil of Benjamin Lang of Boston. The condition of American music fifty years ago was fairly primitive: virtuosity on the stage, inanity in the parlor and the school. Surette conceived of a mission to fulfill which should change all that. Like most great reformers he began with the aid of his family and friends. For their own pleasure and the edification of their neighbors, they played works from the classical repertoire, hitherto approached only by dilettanti, and sang folksongs in place of sentimental ditties. To bridge the gap between anyone's previous taste and the new, Surette did not hesitate to lecture, analyze, illustrate on the piano, and even refer to the poets for equivalents in their works of the elusive musical experience. He would make historical analogies and dramatize for the eye the "gesture of the spirit"[2] which the particular musical moment enshrined.

Going abroad after some years of work as organist and lecturer in Eastern colleges, museums, and adult education centers, he was engaged by Oxford University to try out his ideas on the British public, through the agency of the Extension Department. With this valuable experience he came back to this country, and without formal connection with the universities, exerted upon them a momentous influence visible to this day. Through the Harvard School of Education he reached the teachers of music, and by his recommendations of persons and programs (notably at Bryn Mawr, but elsewhere too) he gave a new direction to music in the schools. His instinct rightly told him that the only hope of permanent reform lay in the actual reshaping of the schoolmarm's habits and organs of hearing. He therefore founded in 1915 the Concord Summer School of Music, which for twenty-five years trained and retrained the teachers of the young. If in the schools of America today, boys and girls sing Brahms, Beethoven, Mozart, and Schubert;[3] if earlier still, in the kindergarten, they make up their own words and tunes as they dance; if much later, in medical school, they sing Bach chorales, practise the oboe, and arrange musical house parties, it is because Thomas Whitney Surette plowed the field and prepared the harvest.

The principles he followed are now simple to see; they are:

---

[2] This is Roger Sessions's immortal phrase about the meaning of music.

[3] See the *Home and Community Song Book*, edited by Surette and Davison, and other items in the "Concord Series." Contemporary with Surette, John Cotton Dana was pioneering in the plastic arts. For his story see the *Magazine of Art*, October 1944.

direct experience of good works and relevant information for their understanding. With these two criteria, there is no use being doctrinaire and saying, "My students steep themselves in the best and never learn a date." Or conversely, "At our place we learn the historical development from the Gregorian chant to Shostakovitch." It is apparent that no one can understand music — let alone enjoy it — if he cannot hear. The art historians are likewise finding out that canvases and buildings must be seen to be believed. So the first step in teaching the arts is to make sure that the students' senses are taking in what goes on in the work.

With regard to this basic need to perceive one often hears an extraordinary circular argument. It begins by asserting that a student cannot hear a symphony without "knowing the form," and when it is asked, How do you learn it? the answer is, You must study composition, harmony, counterpoint — with me, and out of books. In other words, only composers and performers can ever penetrate the arcana. Such teachers apparently think that if all musical analyses were banished from human record or memory tomorrow, it would be impossible to rediscover the structure of a sonata. The truth is that the real structure of a sonata can *only* be found by hearing it — even with books — and that is obviously where the beginner should start. Guided by a teacher and with the aid of a gramophone he can play the work until its composition is plain.[4] If the student has had no musical training whatever, the beginning may be one step farther back, in the perception of intervals, rhythms, and simple tunes. All good colleges now afford their regular A.B. students the opportunity to begin right there and thus salvage a misspent youth while acquiring a lifelong lease on musical pleasure. This, I repeat, is new within the last twenty years.

With ears opened, the student can then go on to discriminate one form from another; he learns to distinguish the instruments,

[4] Mr. Bernard Haggin's *Book of the Symphony* shows you an excellent way to do it by yourself.

judge performance, and discover his own temperamental prefer-
ences. He can even with a little practice learn to follow with a
score. The teacher must only see to it that when he achieves this,
mastery the student does not become an insufferable prig, for
music can go to the head as well as the heart.

Though this is not the end, it is a firm anchorage to have
found out what one likes — Whistler and the cow to the contrary
notwithstanding. For the student must be honest and stick to
"Yankee Doodle" just as long as it and nothing else satisfies him.
Notice that Mr. Surette demanded direct contact with *good*
works, not the best. The best is always in dispute, anyhow, and
it also has a way of being the "strongest" — which is usually too
strong for beginners. There is an impulse in all of us to drag
others to our level — upwards, as we think — but give them time!
I once jeopardized the esteem of a close friend by sending him
records of Grieg's "Peer Gynt" suite for his three-year-old son.
"It's wretched stuff," said the Mozart-loving father, "especially
the 'Hall of the Mountain King' which goes on and on just getting
louder." "That," I demurred, "ought to be the hit." And true
enough, a few months later I heard by mail: "Peter loves it." It
had taken no great effort to guess that my first orchestral thrill
would work on another child thirty years later.

Suppose now that our college student is developing a sensitive
ear, a musical memory, and a choice of favorite works from the
traditional repertoire. He still has the duty of rationalizing his
likes and dislikes; he must, in short, become a responsible critic.
No doubt the word "critic" will suggest carping and being finicky.
But a responsible critic is only someone who can give a fair
account of his feelings and relate them to elements in the work
before him. To do this he had better use the vocabulary appropriate to the art. It is easier to say "the coda" than "the bit
which rushes along toward the end." He must also be able to
express himself by comparisons and analogies. This is where the
history of the particular art is of use. It provides a knowledge of

actual conditions now past, which influenced creation and remain connective links among great works. If a sense of proportion is kept, it adds to our awareness when we know that Bach wrote for the services of the Protestant Church, that Gluck was inspired by Racine's reworked tragedies, or that Beethoven had a special feeling for Nature, characteristic also of his contemporaries.

I do not deny the danger of having such knowledge, particularly if it is given out in fragments. But isn't it the danger of all "little learning"? Even the scientists of the Royal Society were once upon a time divided by a critic into "Drink-deeps" and "Taste-nots." Ideally, the art student should drink deep, but there has to be a first swallow. In general, the teacher can avert more evil by his attitude than the student can encompass by his half-knowledge. If for instance the study of Mozart's career leads the young critic to generalize hastily about "eighteenth-century frivolity" and "existence *à la* Watteau," the teacher can send him at once to the damnation scene in *Don Giovanni* or the finale of the Jupiter Symphony. The critic being a judge, he is bound by the word "responsible" to take in all the evidence; and the teacher who knows his business has at hand evidence enough to swamp the brashest of beginners.

II

The college administrator in his swivel chair probably wonders what all this comes to "*in terms of* a course." At a progressive school, the difficulties are fewest, because the initial plan was to teach performance and all that need be added is a good historical introduction to the particular art. Not that a teacher for such a course is as yet easy to find, but the search is not hopeless if the college is willing to go outside the academic profession.

In a "regular" college, the chief obstacle is that the academic man is already in possession of the field and probably unsympathetic to the "unprofessional" way of teaching the arts. If he is an historian of art, he wants to train art historians; if a performer, performers — just like the scientist who only wants to propagate his kind. Perhaps he can be converted. I remember a stormy faculty meeting where a gentleman of great musical eminence declared he would not have the "freshmen wipe their feet on Bach." A philosopher got up and said they'd been doing just that to Milton for two hundred years without any damage to the bard, and with a great deal of good to themselves. The musician was a man of honor and intelligence: he retracted and is now the most active and resourceful of teachers in the Surette tradition.

With a proper staff, large enough to man small sections of twenty-five students, it is possible to offer every candidate for the A.B. degree at least three aids to self-education in the arts: an acquaintance with the rudiments of both music and the plastic arts; a sense of the development of forms and styles during, let us say, the last five hundred years in music and the last twenty-five hundred in the plastic arts; [5] and finally a familiarity with some ten or twelve carefully chosen masterpieces in each kind. All this requires a good deal of equipment — records, private gramophone booths (or earphones), lantern slides, colored prints — supplemented with trips to neighboring museums and attendance at concerts other than those of "canned music." The student must be broken in to a new kind of preparation (the gift of attention is here in request) because nothing has led him to look at a picture so as to grasp its pictorial character, nor to listen to a song repeatedly and cumulatively for its musical detail.

Especially must the teacher watch for shyness taking the form of escape. The "softer pedagogy" has made even the young aware of the existence of "blind spots," with the result that many

[5] The discrepancy is due to the fact that the plastic arts of the ancients can be studied with the aid of prints and models, whereas no music much earlier than the sixteenth century can be made readily available and intelligible.

students profess to be veritable leopards of blindness. They bring up their real or imaginary "emotional block" with a certain proud sense of being interesting and pathetic cases. Much of this is — to put it kindly — fanciful. Though the color-blind exist, the really tone-deaf are very rare and I gather from my expert colleagues that with patience all insensitivity to pitch could be overcome. And just as the color-blind can still appreciate line and form, so the moderately good ear can derive from music at least rhythm, dynamics, timbre, and melodic contour. Perception of finer shades are not to be required except from those to whom they are natural, one of the merits of art being that it admits of infinite degrees of pleasure.

The aim, in any case, is not to make picture dealers or musical stenographers, but to teach to future "educated" citizens two new and special languages — visual and auditory. Viewed as languages, the arts open out new meanings whose effect is not primarily on the reasoning mind — though it is considerable even there; the arts affect the stream of feeling; they make sensations more accurate and inward reflection richer by associations with these concrete experiences. The student who said to me that music did not so much arouse his emotions as enable him to tell one emotion from another closely akin to it, furnishes an example of what I mean.

The study of the fine arts also exerts an influence, indirectly, on articulate speech and on reading and writing. We should not be deceived by the fact that literature seems to give up its secrets more readily than music. The English critic, Herbert Read, has put his finger on a similarity truer than the difference. "I see," says Mr. Read, "no reason to suppose that because words rather than musical scales are the normal medium of communication between men, therefore the art of words, whether poetry or prose, is in any degree more accessible to ordinary men than the art of music. All art is difficult, remote, subtle; and though in the process of catharsis it may act as a release for emotions that are common to all men, yet in this process art is to many of us an unknown quantity." [6]

III

I shall say more about college courses in the arts when I come to describe the experience acquired on this score in Columbia College. I want to conclude briefly on a vast subject with a few words on the utility of forcing art upon the notice of all college students, even when it is clear that most of them will turn out to be plain citizens and not patrons of the muses. For if what Mr. Herbert Read says is wholly true, then art is a hidden treasure that only a chosen few can ever possess, and I can hear the ex-clamation "How undemocratic!" from those who object every time an unequal distribution of anything is said to exist. But one wonders more justly how folk art could ever have arisen in the midst of commonplace humanity and how, more particularly, the great collective art of architecture — in this century an American specialty — could ever have come into being.

The difficulty is that we confuse several ways of having deal-ings with art. Almost everybody is capable of taking some artistic pleasure in making things — and in destroying them. Children play with blocks and pieces of paper as if the act of arranging, select-ing, and building were natural and enjoyable. But their attention to the finished product is slight. They do not contemplate. They prefer to tear down and build again, and we ought not to be surprised if throughout history this same childish mood of destruction occurs in whole peoples, who give it vent by defacing monasteries and bombing cathedrals. We can hardly look on with unconcern but we should perhaps not be too indignant. We should recognize instead that the ruined city is the young architect's opportunity. The great fact is that the urge to create is primary; and closely wrapped up with it, the urge to destroy;

[6] *English Prose Style*, p. xii.

whereas the desire to contemplate art is secondary and usually acquired.

That is why art has to be taught to those in whom the desire is not spontaneous. When the common man enlivened existence by his own means, he probably was a fairer critic because he was himself a performer. Overlooking the village green he could "appreciate" the arts of entertainment — the dance, the tune, the song. In most civilizations, he can appreciate the city gates, the town hall, the cathedral. As long as decoration remains conventional or seems to copy nature, he can appreciate that. But he begins to lose touch and to find art remote, subtle, and highbrow, when the craftsman's aims multiply, when tradition stores up masterpiece after masterpiece, and when human lives follow many patterns instead of one. The two extremes of art could be likened to the spread between a proverb and a philosophy: both are wisdom, but one is for all to hear; the other takes patience and preparation to understand.

That preparation is like learning a language, but it is also a discipline of the emotions. The so-called untutored eye has seen many pictures reproduced on the calendars that the butcher sends at New Year's. They have given a bent to the beholder's feelings and associations, so that when he sees a Cézanne for the first time he is shocked, angry, ready to destroy. He cannot imagine any reason for painting in lumps like Cézanne, except the desire to annoy him personally.

Besides, the subject of a particular picture works directly on his emotions and he probably feels a strong desire to "create," that is to say, to alter what he sees in order to make it conform to his opinionated views. We can all remember the postage stamp issued to commemorate Whistler and based on his portrait of his mother. Some fiery creator at the Bureau of Engravings felt compelled to add a vase of flowers (always bring flowers to your mother) and rearrange the composition, which was too subtly balanced in the original. No theatrical manager or magazine editor but wants to lay violent hands on a new manuscript and remodel it. Even the Duke in *Zuleika Dobson* did not quite like the arrangement of clouds in the sky and the gods humored him.

There is moreover a directness, almost a crudity, about great art that many cannot stand. It brings life too close to the observer, who feels alternately scorched and chilled. Art may be beauty, but it is not easy beauty. It lacks the smooth contours that conventional moods and words insure. For example, in the original version of "Rock of Ages" occurs the line: —

When mine eye-strings break in death

But it was later revised to read: —

When mine eyelids close in death

which being weaker and less upsetting may be sung without thinking about it.

The study of the arts in their great manifestations is thus a gradual and deliberate accustoming of the feelings to strong sensations and precise ideas. It is a breaking down of self-will for the sake of finding out what life and its objects may really be like. And this means that most esthetic matters turn out to be moral ones in the end. Great art offers a choice — that of preferring strength to weakness, truth to softness, life to lotus-eating.

Always it is an effort and a pleasure that repays it. Not the "story" or the "message" is the thing to be mastered, but the complex structure through which that message — if there is one — is distributed. Whistler does not tell us that his mother baked noble pies, nor that he loved her dutifully. He says, "There she is, make the most of her as I have tried to do on this canvas!" Well, the way to do that is not to start rearranging the furniture, but to take her in as she is until her spell begins to work. What it will do to you cannot be predicted, but only that it will not leave you as it finds you.

The change may be slow and not wholly confined to the vessel in which the seed has been planted. It may be nurtured by the warmth of collective feeling. Who would have said twenty years ago that ballet dancing of a high order would one day be the feature of two popular musical comedies on Broadway? Isn't the ballet aristocratic, effete, silly — in fact, un-American? It is nothing of the kind as soon as the audience's mind has reoriented itself and can find in the medium, however queer, all — or as much as possible — of what is put into it.

The perception is contagious, it generates in others excitement, curiosity, and the desire to be pleased even before the nature of the pleasure is known. And that is how a people, by its capacity to warm the atmosphere like a greenhouse, fosters art. As William James said, "Real culture lives by sympathies and admirations, not by dislikes and disdains." Fostering art is not limited to maintaining a national gallery of old masters. That is only transporting art from one place to another, though perhaps with good effect. Fostering art means making opportunities for the use and the creation of art. When an engineer, such as Professor W. E. Howland of Purdue University, can conclude an article with the assertion that "every engineer would become a better one by deepening his understanding and appreciation of one or more of the fine arts,"[7] it is not waste motion to catch that future engineer in college and, by teaching him the rudiments of the "language," enable him to develop for himself the sense of what art does for a man and for a people.

[7] "Art and the Civil Engineer," *Purdue Engineer*, November 1942.

10. Tongues and Areas

"Is a Frenchman a man?"
"Yes."
"*Well*, den! Dad blame it, why
doan' he *talk* like a man? You
answer me dat!"
— JIM AND HUCKLEBERRY FINN

SHORTLY before setting foot in the United States, I tried to learn something about the country from an old guidebook which had been around the house for years. With my imperfect command of the language, one sentence near the beginning, I remember, filled me with apprehension: —

The European tongues are taught in the high schools all over the country, but the instruction is purely theoretical, and the number who can talk French, German, or Italian is very small. Tourists who wish to travel among the remoter districts of New England should be well acquainted with the language, which is the English of Elizabeth with a few local idioms.[1]

Having no idea whether I should be called upon to travel in the "remoter districts of New England," much less what was meant by the "English of Elizabeth," I pinned all my faith on this "theoretical instruction" of American youth in European tongues. I now know what it means. It means that boys and girls "take" French or Spanish or German (never Italian: the guidebook is wrong) for three, four, five years before entering college, only to discover there that they cannot read, speak, or understand it. The word for this type of instruction is not "theoretical" but "hypothetical." Its principle is "*If* it were possible to learn a

[1] *New England: A Handbook for Travellers*, James R. Osgood, Boston, 1873.

foreign language in the way I have been taught it, I should now know that language."

Various things follow. One is that Berlitz Schools do a thriving business with people who are suddenly confronted with the need to travel abroad. Another is that there is a lifelong *Sehnsucht* about foreign tongues, which quack advertisements seek to satisfy: "Astonish your friends by speaking to the waiter in French." A third is that advanced college teaching and graduate study are hampered at every turn by the students' inability to pick up and read important foreign works. Every year in my senior and graduate classes, I ask those present to write after their names on the class list the languages that they know. Most of them put down French or German or both. But when they come to choose research topics and I suggest a foreign item for their bibliography, they retract their "knowledge" with an embarrassed smile. Some of these students are at the very time "taking" the language in college and some have passed the so-called proficiency test.

There are exceptions to this generality, but most often the exceptional student turns out to have lived abroad or had relatives who speak the tongue in question. When the Army, the Navy, and the civilian war services needed native-born linguists who were also college graduates in the prime of life, they discovered that they had to set up their own language schools and cram German, Russian, Japanese, Spanish, Italian, and French into people whose previous immunity to language seemed absolute. They could "take" it forever, *it* wouldn't "take."

Everybody knows the outcome: they're all linguists now. My students send me Christmas cards in Japanese, or inform me that when they return they plan to study under my sponsorship the relations of the Third French Republic and the Tsarist regime. I see very clearly that I am going to have to learn Russian.

Characteristically, college administrators have jumped to the conclusion that the Army must have some secret "method" — held back until M-day — which the colleges ought to find out and apply. Campuses buzz with the spirit of reform, the language departments themselves being divided between the Old Guard, which defends its former "methods," and the New, whose proposals combine elements of the army training with Area studies. I shall explain what these are in a moment.

Meanwhile, the Army and Navy's victorious inoculation of the anti-linguistic American boy is not hard to account for. It was not a secret; it was mainly Concentration. The men were segregated, put in charge of foreign instructors, drilled morning, noon, and night under conditions of prisonlike rigidity. Standards were high and failures from laziness or incapacity were weeded out as fast as they showed up. A competitive game was set going, which keyed up the good minds to outdo themselves. Outside the class hours, the men would quiz each other, talk, joke, and write in the language they were learning. Two powerful motives were at work: the negative fear of not keeping up and therefore being returned to the ranks, and the positive wish for a commission and the pay that goes with it.

Clearly if these or similar motives could be brought into play in high school or college, language teaching — or for that matter the teaching of any subject — would yield astonishing results. If I did not mention as an incentive the very real desire to discharge a patriotic duty, it is because that motive already finds a parallel in the civilian's academic career. The man with the moral fervor of patriotism is likely to be the man with the moral fervor of scholarship; in both cases, the student sees himself as owing a duty to something greater than himself. This kind of ambition no system can demand; it can only use it when found.

The upshot of what I have described is that language teaching in schools is never going to reach the pitch set by army practice. That was an emergency performance, based on monopolizing the time of a few thousand men. The conditions cannot be duplicated on any peacetime campus. But some of the features of the army system are very suggestive.

First, the Army had no prejudices for or against languages, or any single one of them. The American college, on the contrary, is riddled with such prejudices. For the last twenty years, languages have been pushed to the bottom of the menu card as inferior subject matters. A cant phrase has come into use, to the effect that language must be taught only as a tool. No one has ever clearly set forth what this means, but it appeals by its aura of "practicality." Again, the requirement to study two years of a modern foreign language has been interpreted to mean French, German, and Spanish. Special permission is usually needed to meet the requirement by offering Italian, Russian, or Portuguese, even when courses in these languages are available. Lately, Far Eastern tongues have been admitted, but Polish, Modern Greek, and Czech are only occasionally tolerated.

This discrimination is absurd. If anyone wants to study a language, he should be encouraged to do so unless there is some clear reason against it. An intending physician ought to be steered into German rather than Basque; and similar considerations apply in other cases. But apart from professional needs a student should be allowed freedom, if for no other reason than that a man who knows one foreign tongue is very likely to learn others. It's the first one that's hard, because it is a wrench from all "normal" habits. As with the language of art, a strange idiom seems to go against the grain of naturalness, of human reason, of common sense. As the ruffled Englishman muttered when the conductor on a French train came through demanding *"Vos billets, s'il vous plaît, Messieurs et Mesdames"* — "Why doesn't he just say 'Tickets'?"

The ultimate educational value of knowing a foreign language is that it lets you into the workings of other human minds, like *and* unlike your own. It takes you out of your narrow local self and points out ways of seeing and feeling that cannot be perceived apart from the alien words that record the perception. The reason educated people in every country find themselves using foreign phrases in the midst of their own speech is that these expressions point to real things but are untranslatable: *gemütlich, raison d'être, dolce far niente, high life,* and so on. And if snobs ape the habit merely to show off, the imitation only proves that there is a real thing to imitate.

These locutions — whether expressive of feelings or ideas or objects — are the signs of the bigger ones, represented by a nation's literature, philosophy, or contributions to science and religion. This being so, the study of a language becomes the study of a people, and the notion of a language as a tool destroys itself: a tool is a dead, unchanging thing; a language lives. A tool is for some ulterior purpose; a language exists as a world in itself. Is the ulterior purpose perhaps to read foreign books? But the books *are* the language or a part of it. To speak to the cabman in Naples? But what he says and what you say are not "tools" with which to manufacture understanding, they are meanings — or they fail as meanings — in the instant of utterance. In short, words are not clothing for an idea, they are its incarnation.

This should give us a clue to the better teaching of language in the schools. The scholastic assumption has been that the pupil studies vocabulary and grammar, after which, like the journalist in *Pickwick* who had to write on Chinese Metaphysics and looked up first China, then Metaphysics, he "combines his information." After vocabulary and "forms" come those practice sentences about books being under the table and umbrellas belonging to every member of the family in turn.[2] So far, no meaning has raised its head anywhere. The teacher does not really speak, he repeats the inane remarks in the book; the pupils write this nonsense at home, write it on the board, chant it in unison, and hate it at sight.

As against all this, it is invariably found that a successful lan-

---

[2] Joseph Conrad called this type of language "Ollendorff" from the name of a well-known publisher of language manuals. The term deserves to live, because so many novels and other works are couched in this idiom.

guage teacher dramatizes his class hour by involving his students in the exchange of purposeful ideas. He talks to them about the day's news or the football season or their own delinquencies — something close to their life in common, yet not manufactured hokum. To do this easily and naturally, the teacher should be a native or a thoroughly fluent speaker; he ought not have to grimace to utter umlaut *ü*. He should bring to class with him foreign books, newspapers, and posters, as well as maps of the country whose language he teaches. He ought to have friends who are natives and invite them to address the group very briefly or to join in refreshments after recess. Preferably these guests should come from varying walks in life, speaking in different accents about different things. Each visit will then yield matter for weeks of argument, analysis, and criticism.

For more than any other subject, language must be learned close to its living sources. Other things can stand being made "academic" through language, but language itself is an activity which just as soon as possible should become transparent, unnoticeable, that is to say, communicative. This does not mean that the language teacher should ignore words and rules. These on the contrary become interesting from the moment one begins to see them in the perspective of their own language. Even young pupils can be made to feel the humor or incoherence of word groupings that are theoretically possible but actually contrary to idiom.[3]

All this means that speaking, reading, writing, and thinking in the alien speech must unite into a single fluency. The so-called "direct method textbooks," based on Maximilian Berlitz's innovation, aim at the same goal, but in practice fall short of it because the "directness" generally occurs only on the printed page. If the teacher knew how to be direct himself, he would need no book. We have all had in our hands these little works, which start off

---

[3] I am indebted to Mr. Enno Franzius for many of these suggestions. As a linguist, globe trotter, and teacher of languages he gives the authority of practice and successful experience to this one and only method.

"*Wie geht's heute mit dir, teurer Hans?*" and go on with chitchat, anecdotes, and pictures of Salzburg. This is chumminess misplaced. Let the teacher say "how do you do" and let the book remain what a book should be — a systematic exposition of the subject, in which the student can find what he is looking for. Nothing is more exasperating than to have to wonder whether the subjunctive was given together with a description of Bremerhaven or later, with the sad story of *Struwwelpeter*. Besides, no pupil is better off for having all the verbs given in bits, half a tense at a time.

There remains one human obstacle to cope with. The teacher must conquer the shy pupils' reluctance to make with their mouths what they feel is affected sounds. On this point, majority pressure can be gently applied. When everybody acts the fool to produce a continental "l," the few who hold out are the eccentrics. A language can only be learned by plunging into it, making mistakes, and rushing on unabashed. You simply cannot learn to skate or talk French without making yourself ridiculous. Best overlook it. It helps, of course, if the class can meet often, both in and out of the classroom. Language courses should meet daily — if not for a set exercise, then on the odd days for lunch or tea or club activities.

But the devil-may-care mood must be sustained. The club must not be a stuffy adjunct to a breezy class, which means that the directing mind must be of a different caliber from that usually encountered among language teachers. Just as it used to be said that anyone who could sign his name could teach English, so it is widely true that anyone who has lived abroad thinks himself qualified to teach a foreign language. Furthermore, the scholarly tradition of philology, which I mentioned as having strangled the classics, has left little breath in the body of modern foreign languages, and this being handed down through the routine of graduate schools saps the vigor of generation after generation of students.

Take but one aspect of this unfortunate state of fact — the choice of reading matter offered in language classes. It is true that since pupils are ill prepared in early life they cannot in college tackle the most exciting books. But they could fairly quickly be brought by the teacher to that higher level if the dead hand of tradition did not impose *Immensee* and *M. Perrichon* and *La Mariposa Blanca* as the kind of text suitable to intermediate classes. I remember a time when Gottfried Keller's *Romeo und Julia auf dem Dorfe* was painfully plowed through by sophomores: the German was difficult enough but the dialect was simply a cryptogram.

Again, the novels and tales chosen from French literature for college reading tend to be the flabbiest and cheapest by their respective authors. Of the German classics, the most remote from student interests seem to come first — Lessing's *Hamburgische Dramaturgie* or Schiller's *Wallenstein* — both admirable works but not suited to undergraduates. There seems to be throughout the choice of books an instinct for the second rate coupled with a pedantry in presenting the first rate, which together close the doors of foreign literature with the finality of a safety vault. The countries represented, moreover, are always made to seem dead civilizations, mighty only in the past. The girls in provincial costumes receive more attention than recent achievements in science, and some academically chosen century of greatness always swamps everything before and since.

Besides, the editing of the texts is clearly aimed at the man's professional colleagues and not at his student readers, while the vocabulary printed at the back is usually a gratuitous difficulty added to the original. In college, every language student ought to own two dictionaries: a translating dictionary — the smallest possible — and one wholly in the foreign tongue. He should attack every book with both aids by his side, adding a "trot" if a good one is available and recommended by his instructor. After thirty or fifty pages of despair and torture plowing through a work whose subject aroused his curiosity, he would find that he could read, at least that particular book.

Every two or three years it falls to my lot to conduct the language examinations for Ph.D. candidates in European history. I am invariably shocked at the number of mature men and women who suppose that foreign prose is basically nonsense. They must suppose this, or they would not put down English nonsense as its equivalent. Of course I know how they get into this defeatist frame of mind, but I groan at the thought that they have stewed in it since first-year high school. Once or twice these victims have had some claim on my time, which I discharged by putting them through a course of self-tuition in reading. We take a work of Ranke's and one of Michelet's, the dictionaries, and we start for an hour of intellectual misery grinding out meaning from alien vocables. The hour is only a sample. The student goes on at this pace until he or she can read at sight fluently. Fluency does not mean exactitude, sense of nuance, or even infallible recognition of unusual words: it means going with the author at a reasonable rate. New words can be guessed, shades of meaning deduced from a second reading and exactitude checked with a good translation. Scholarly work will bring its own assistance later through repetition and criticism.

What is deplorable is that this should not be a well-known technique, and that the determination to squeeze sense from a text should be so rare, even among professional translators. Every year I receive as a reviewer some current book or other in which elementary errors are committed and major misunderstandings foisted on the public. The last book published in this country by Prime Minister Edouard Herriot — *The Wellsprings of Liberty* — is a good case in point. According to the English text, he boasted of having "revived" the Estates-General of 1789. What he actually wrote was that he had made them live again, that is, for the hearers or readers of one of his speeches. This kind of error is not so inconsequential as it may seem. Through mistranslation, newspapers often give the impression that foreign statesmen can only utter foolishness or falsehoods — as when it was asserted that the French would not "admit" turning over their fleet to the Germans. This implied that they had done it, whereas the French use of "admit" signified that they would not condone the act if it were required of them.

For errors in books, publishers are partly responsible because they do not choose good translators, or perhaps cannot at the price they are willing to pay. This is only another sign of our collective indifference to words and meanings. We do not take the pains to do well what we know can be done with words, nor to insist that it be well done by those who can. But we will all "go in" for Basic because it sounds like a short cut, or rejoice in Mr. Hogben's pseudo-scientific "Interglossa" because it supposedly feeds on roots we know: "U President de United States syn duco Commisari-pe, Mr. Churchill, ge electio e regi Grati de United Kingdom, pre acte unio." [4] Why not tend those same roots more carefully in their common or garden form? If we only remembered how difficult it was for all of us to learn to speak our mother tongue, all unaided, we should not treat our investment of effort so cavalierly, we would nurse it and add to it and we would be repaid with and in interest.

II

It is plain that if we want linguists among our young, a change has got to come. And I think it is on the way because the war

[4] Quoted in *New York Times*, January 30, 1944. In the eighteenth century another learned Scotchman, Pinkerton by name, hoped to beautify English also by revision. I like his scheme better, even though it is equally needless: "I drew nearo with tha reverencé whico iz due to superior naturé; ando, az my hearto waz entirely subduen by the captivating straina I had heard, I fell downo ato hiza feet, ando weeped (. . . .) He lifted me fro the groundo; ando, taking me by the hando, Mirza, said he, I have heard thee in thya soliloquëa, follow me." (*Letters of Literature*, by Robert Heron [John Pinkerton], London, 1785, 256.)

has created a new motive. I refer to the passion for Area Studies, that is, for the study of large portions of the earth's surface in their various aspects — in plain English, cultural geography taken one region at a time.

This involves learning the language, the history, the government, and the natural resources of a people. Language comes first because it is the key to reading about the rest. The war has stirred up this new inquisitiveness because the two island empires of the West, Great Britain and the United States, discovered that their educated classes were largely ignorant of the rest of the world.[5] And just as it was Japanese bombings that made China quiver to a new sense of its unity, so it is the disappearance of Channels and Oceans that stimulates eagerness for an acquaintance with the regional blocs — Latin America, the Far East, Africa, Oceania, and the pygmy "regions" of the peanut continent, Europe.

Many colleges are already planning "institutes" or more modest "departments" to devote themselves to "teaching the great areas." Here my blood begins to curdle somewhat, not at the unknown subject, but at the preparatory jargon and "methods." It so happens that I was connected these past three years with one organization that trained civilians and mature officers in a limited number of "areas." My share was to provide in one year what introduction I could to France and her empire. The difficulties were enormous. The students naturally lacked the language, but I may say in passing that they learned more French in six months from regular French instructors working *ad hoc* than they had in eight to ten years before. The trouble came when I sought, with an able American-born colleague, to pull together into recognizable shape such disparate subjects as: the Church, the structure of government, the history of successive regimes since 1789, the political parties, economic ideals and realities, foreign policy, the schools, the newspaper press, manners and morals,

[5] "Russian Studies" were instituted in English schools after the German invasion — a trifle late.

the empire, the army and navy, charitable organizations and public health, science and technology, literature and the fine arts.

You may say, why go into all that? Well, human contacts depend on unpredictable coincidences of taste and interest. Anyone who wishes to acclimate himself to a foreign country must rely partly on his own set of tastes and traits, partly on a hospitable frame of mind that will take in whatever is offered him. The American who goes to France to drink a glass of milk at every meal has taken the wrong boat, or he who gazes at a Renaissance fountain in Verona and says "We have a better one in Toledo, Ohio," is missing the reward of the trouble he has voluntarily taken.

I remember one man in our Foreign Administration group who had absorbed everything dutifully up to the point where we struck French home and school life. He could not stomach the overworking of schoolchildren nor the institution of the *concierge*. Both, he thought, must make life unbearable and breed revolt; the first because in his view children *must* play more than they work, and the second because the idea of police reliance on janitors' reports about the citizenry reminded him of the Gestapo. At long last, the central point was got over to him: he had every right to criticize, but he must first understand; he had no right to project his feelings upon the French and think them cruel or stupid or enslaved on account of emotions which he felt and they did not.

I suppose that if the study of any region achieves this single result it will do some good. The psychology of traveling is certainly a desideratum in a world which is now less a globe than a globule. But I think language teaching ought to be able, by itself and indirectly, to bring about this proper frame of mind and maturity of feeling in future travelers. Receptiveness should result from the contrasts and comparisons carried by words, and it should be kept alive with the aid of all the illustrative material that I have urged on the attention of the teacher. I repeat: learning a foreign tongue should be learning a culture. Interest in the "area" can be employed, stimulated, and fulfilled, but I do not see the need for separate courses entitled Area Studies.

Here are some reasons why I think such courses unsuitable as a regular collegiate offering: any fragment of an Area survey belongs to some other established subject. For instance, when I "taught" France, there was a bit of French history and politics, a bit of comparative government, a bit of geography, a bit of literature, a bit of economics — none of it advanced work, I might even say, none of it high grade. It was a potpourri mixed for the occasion and justified by the emergency. Now consider the probable "improvements" the colleges will devise — they will have a series of "experts" come and lecture to the group on their specialty; or they will employ a small staff of tutors working together at a more thorough presentation in each part of the course. The former idea has been tried innumerable times in other subjects and it never works. It produces what is called a "vaudeville course," which has never taught anyone anything. The experts don't mesh, the students are bewildered and feel no central responsibility — they might as well attend a Forum.

The second scheme would work, but see what it means. It means the withdrawal from their own courses of the best men on hand. It means reshuffling subject matter so as to lay it out on a small geographical area instead of in a large and comparative chronological sequence. Even the best of teachers will be plagued by the question of how much of his whole subject is "needed" for the Area students. The synthesis will not represent the instructor's mind but the imagined needs of very diverse students. It is bad enough when a friend asks what he should pack in his suitcase for a trip abroad; when he asks how to furnish his mind, wisdom stutters and is silent.

In short, I detect a false practicality in the scheme of Area studies. I can see the appeal, and I fear it, because it is bound to attract many of our poorer students and poorer teachers. They will look upon it, innocently enough, as a release from constraints they dislike. A poor teacher trying to give European history is at least propped up by the textbook he has chosen. With any luck, the text writer knows his business and informs the mediocre instructor. But there are no textbooks in area studies and it may be a long time before a good one in each region can be written. Meanwhile we shall have the market flooded with graduates and "majors" in dozens of "areas." They will think their knowledge salable — to corporations and government agencies. All will be disappointed, I think, when it is found how flimsy that knowledge is. I may be wrong and in some ways I should like to be, for the goal is excellent and I may be jaundiced about the means by the circumstances under which I myself applied them.

Yet there was one valuable discovery made in area instruction that no one would now dispute about. The solidest thing about an area is its geography, and our people is singularly ignorant of any but its own. The war having given a boost to curiosity about places, it should be immediately capitalized. One adult education scheme by radio, inaugurated last fall, began unhesitatingly with a course in geography. A dozen good books have rolled off the presses. There is a map in the paper daily, and people are using colored ones as wall decorations for home and office. Can we keep it up, with the needful addition of related economic facts?

Certainly geography should be taught as a formal discipline right through to college and graduate school. It is not a subject for infants only, since everything that happens happens in space. Military strategy, industry, commerce, communication, political feeling, art, and science have locus and momentum. To judge and take part in them, the channels that link them through three elements must be known. And from the earliest days spent in school it would help reduce that disembodied abstract feeling about subject matter if its details could be fastened down to their point of origin. Think of the difference in the feelings clustered about the Gettysburg Address when one has attentively gone over the battlefield; or in the changed associations of the word Constantinople, after one has read Frederic Harrison's superb essay on the site.[6]

It is true that some students lack all power of visualization. When they read a detective story, they cannot keep the doors and windows straight and do not care. They would suffer in geography as they now do when compelled to take geology to fulfill the science requirement. But they could recoup their loss by comparing times and distances and linking natural resources with place names. Surprisingly enough, maps on the wall are not the best way to fix geographical data. The teacher jabs with a stick and the student remembers only the noise. It is in the study period that maps, or preferably a globe, should be used. In class the effort should go into visualizing in the mind's eye, under guidance from the instructor. There are as many ways of "thinking" yourself across land or sea as there are for establishing historical connections. Here once again the facts of language come into use, for place names crystallize history, geography, and politics into unmistakable sounds. The similarity of river names (Rhone, Rhine), the distortion of personal names (Gratianopolis, Grenoble), the changes of name for political reasons (St. Petersburg, Petrograd, Leningrad) all become charged with significance as soon as the mind shapes them into cubbyholes for retaining facts.

That is why it would be really easier to learn five related languages at once than five disparate ones in as many tries. The idea of learning language groups is in the air and may yet bring fruit.[7] Of course, there is one language — though it may be rude to mention it — which was once taught, and which is still a very good introduction to a fairly large group. I mean *L-t-n*. It was dropped like a dead thing when the Classics went under for the

[6] In *The Meaning of History*.

[7] On these projects, see my article in the *Saturday Review of Literature*, July 1, 1944.

third time, about twenty years ago. But I see no reason why it should not be revived.

At the very least, the threat should be used to make the modern languages bestir themselves in school and college. Which is the dead language, anyhow, Latin with its admirable regular structure impressible on the mind, and its roots in daily use, or the hypothetical French that no child speaks, reads, or ever hears well spoken? Traditional ways of teaching Latin might be reformed — for example, Caesar is no first-year reading subject. Try Ovid, or even Virgil. But I have said enough. I want to change the subject and modulate to the great ideas that language holds embalmed. Virgil's name is a fitting turning point, modulation incarnate.

11. The Classics off the Shelf

> "Th' Bible an' Shakspere — ï use
> thim f'r purposes iv definse . . .
> I have niver read thim," I says;
> "they shtand between me an' all
> modhern littrachoor," says I;
> "I've built thim up into a kind
> iv breakwather," says I, "an' I
> set behind it, ca'm an' contint,
> while Hall Caine rages without"
> says I.
>
> — MR. DOOLEY on Books

CLASSICS has more than one meaning. I have used the word so far to signify the Greek and Latin languages and literature — the ancient classics. But the list of books that have survived contemporary vogue or neglect is now enormously lengthened, it takes in writings of all nations, and deserves the common epithet of modern classics. The distinction between the two groups of books has in fact broken down and the lot are lumped together in phrases like "our precious heritage" and "the best that has been thought and said."

Whether it is these very phrases that chill the ordinary reader's ardor, or the books themselves, the fact is that for the public at large Mr. Dooley's position remains representative: it is even more classic than any of the works to which it applies.

But that position is not the simple one which it seems to be at first sight. I shall not spoil by analysis Mr. Dooley's precious utterance, each word of which should be weighed in the manner I prescribed on page 71. Rather I shall quote from three recent advertisements now lying before me, in the belief that all publicity bases its appeal upon some widespread public conviction. The first and largest, illustrated with the busts of poets wearing drooping laurels, covers half a page of the *New York Times*. What it promotes is a syndicate selling the Sunday Comics as "a major national medium with a circulation of fourteen million copies." The point, however, is that it begins with three short paragraphs identifying Homer, Virgil, and Horace, and then goes on: —

"These were the Big Three of the Classics. Their works endure, in libraries, and to plague students — mean little in the life of today." [1]

The second advertises a whiskey and leads up to its merits by depicting Shakespeare and an airplane, side by side with the bottle of liquor. The caption over each is "You're sure when you say — 'Shakespeare' . . . '100 Octane' " and, of course, when you call for that particular brand of Scotch. But what are you sure of about Shakespeare? Beneath a forbidding portrait of the bard you find " — sure that you're naming the supreme master of dramatic art." [2]

The third advertisement urges the reading of a popular newspaper, and it starts in abrupt epic fashion: "His family owned four books: the Bible, the works of Shakespeare, the poems of Burns, the dictionary." Then comes a brief account of the career of James J. Hill — "one of America's great success stories. And, like so many others, it is a story of success that came, in great part, out of books." [3]

Summing up our data, the classics are "withered laurels *versus* words that live"; they are the embodiment of high quality (you're sure of Shakespeare); and reading even a small handful of classics is a principle of success.

The public can believe all three things simultaneously. But where does it pick up the component parts of its creed? Shake-

[1] *New York Times*, August 13, 1943.
[2] *Ibid.*, August 13, 1944.
[3] *Ibid.*, July 7, 1941.

speare idolatry is easy to trace: it comes from school and it serves as it did Mr. Dooley, like a bulwark against all other literature. When you've said "greatest master of dramatic art," you've paid your debt, you've dropped your pinch of incense on the altar of the hall of fame. The influence of books on success is taught in the same way. It happens to be true that many great men were great readers. Lincoln, James J. Hill, John Burroughs, are near to us in many ways, and the correlation between their success and their books is taken for granted.

As for the last feeling — that the classics mean little in the life of today — it comes from precisely the same source — the school. Only whereas the first two are taken second hand on trust, the last article of faith comes from first-hand observation. The classics are taught in school as being great in virtue of their difficulty, or remoteness, or "eternal" truth — and what is held up as eternal has a way of looking as if it suited no particular time. When, some twenty years ago, the old comic magazine *Life* guaranteed anonymity and freedom from reprisals if a score of American celebrities would write in their honest opinion of Shakespeare, the replies they received and printed showed an overwhelming revolt against the tyranny of school bardolatry. Though some comments were obviously exaggerated for effect, the replies ranged from indifference to painful boredom, with many allusions to early "conditioning" against the classics.

Shakespeare is only a representative example for the English-speaking world. But everywhere the old-masters feeling is bred by the schools and resented by the pupils. Not only everywhere but at all times, as far back as the Greek and Latin golden ages, you find complaints that great literature is neglected in favor of current best sellers — except in the schools. There, only dead men tell the tales, to the detriment of both pupils and great authors. Samuel Butler has defined the canonization of books by teachers as "the meanest revenge that dullness can take upon genius," and this is so painfully true that in the life of a teacher who feels not only humble before genius but exhilarated by it, there come moments when he would gladly banish it and its works from the classroom.

This does not come from the fear that "youth will wipe its feet on Milton" but from the fact that in order to acquaint the student with a fine book the teacher must begin by taking all the savor out of it. Imagine the paradox of what might be called the Shakespearean destiny. At one moment in history, *Macbeth* is the latest thing out — a rattling good play — horror, murder, thrills, ghosts, with good poetry thrown in free. It could, should be, and was, described in Hollywood terms. Gradually it becomes last year's success, then old stuff, then quaint old stuff. More time and it rises from its ashes, but transformed into a "text." Scholars peck at it like domestic fowl. The play is "early" or "late." It exemplifies the "second manner" or the use of the supernatural. Children are made to feel guilty for failing to remember where the climax comes. In due course, the name "Shakespeare" stands for a consecrated bore, with the odd result that once in a while a good stage performance surprises everybody into feeling that "it isn't so bad after all."

Bear in mind that what I assume in this process is not bad teaching of the written classics, but just teaching, the average kind. Teaching great books differs from the handling of the other arts in this respect, that with music and painting the sensitive student can always behold the work as an entirety before him. He can make himself deaf to the teacher's lecture because it goes on to one side of the object. But in literature, history, and philosophy, there is no path to the attainment of pleasure but through first hacking and parsing and shredding the very thing that should be seen whole. One is reminded of the satirist's fancy, "I saw a woman flayed the other day and you would not suppose how much it altered her looks for the worse."

But why this preliminary destruction, dignified by the name of analysis? Because for intrinsic and historical reasons, the classics are rich fruits encased in thick and bitter rind. When an honest man tells me he took down a classic from the shelf and found it dull, I tell him he is right. If he says it was more than dull, it was exasperating, awkwardly written, roundabout, and perversely redundant, I agree with him again. I am not placating a lowbrow but recognizing an inevitable reaction. Have you seen an infant have his first taste of carrots or swallow of beer? All tastes above pap, in any realm, are acquired; and pap goes down easy because it has no taste. The acceptance of stronger sensations may be slow or rapid, but even with the first olive of the man who can tell he will become an addict, there is probably a split second of indecision.

With the classics as with food and drink, there is only one way: developing the habit of withstanding the bitterness of novelty. People who like "foreign" food of one kind will at least show readiness to try other kinds. It is a principle born of past pleasure. They are not committed to liking but to trying out. So with books, try everything once, for in numbers there is strength — of stomach. That is why earlier I recommended that children be allowed to read everything. The ravenous appetite will digest stones unharmed. Never mind the need to discriminate; it will come in its own time.

If what I say is true, then the way to improve the unhappy situation of schools-and-great-books is to read more of them, oftener, and in many different kinds. There are great books for every age and taste, but they must be fitted more or less to each child, or each group of children. The trying out must also be less heavy-handed. The high schools have made a mistake, as I see it, in devoting the senior year of English to teaching one or two plays of Shakespeare. They should read six or eight. But I am not sure I should have Shakespeare read in high school at all; anyhow I should certainly urge greater speed. This means letting "form" go and concentrating on ideas. These are always easier than words, as we saw before We must bear in mind that youth's most characteristic feeling about life is that of the man overboard who sees miles of water between himself and the shore. Can he make it? "Making it" means coping with life, alone, unhampered by parents. This means that young boys and girls will gladly take up with anyone who will talk freely of the things I mean by "ideas" — moral rules, personal traits, virtues and vices, ways of fulfilling ambitions, all the paraphernalia, in short, of the explorer who does not know what dangers the jungle will present.

It happens to be a fact that all classic works without exception deal directly or indirectly with problems of conduct. That is their great virtue for school use. Not that they teach a plain goody-goody morality, but that they show and discuss and solve dilemmas that a shipping clerk or an athlete can be made to understand. For this understanding, the discussion of any classic *must be superficial*. If you dive below the surface with your pupil you drown him. Certain teachers are always terrified of superficiality; they seem to think other teachers will scoff or that the dead author will scold. Let them remind themselves that their colleagues' profundity would strike the great author as either surface scratching or pedantry; and let them remember that for every reader there is a time when a given book is being read for the first time.

The greater the book, the less distinct will the details remain in the mind after the first reading. One freshman who was failing and whom I quizzed about his reading of *King Lear* told me that he was not uninterested, but that all he had "got out of it" was the terrible hurricane at sea, when everybody was going crazy and threatening to put their eyes out. Though he was mixing up *Lear* with *The Tempest* and was wrong in every detail, he had nevertheless grasped and combined two moments of stress having common features in them. This is not nearly enough, for better minds of the same age can derive far more from even a single reading, but it is something, and something more genuine than "correct" facts about subplots or lines with feminine endings.

I should be content to have secondary schools leave all the classics for a first reading in the college freshman year. This does not mean that I question the ability of high school teachers to do the needful thing, but only that I find their notions of what is needed far too set. Probably they are weighed down by state education laws and College Entrance examinations; in any case, they seem to me — with notable exceptions — to be trying to make young scholars in English instead of stouthearted readers. Even the latest trick that I have heard of, namely, translating Shakespeare into slang, is beside the point. It is nothing more than making a system out of what may be useful from time to time on the spur of the moment. The truth is that good reading does not come out of systems, just because each great book — if it really is great — establishes its own language, manner, and point of view. A great book is in effect a view of the universe, complete for the time being. You must get inside it to look out upon the old familiar world with the author's unfamiliar eyes.

Fortunately there are connections between one great book and another, which enable us to capitalize on our reading experience. These connections come from the fact that great men tend to read the great books of their predecessors and form what we call a "tradition." And this in turn implies that reading the classics (no specified number) is like entering a company of notables and learning their friendships and hatreds, prejudices and wisdom. Judging by the fables of all lands, men have always wanted to descend into the lower regions and converse with the great dead. Well, students can soon be made to share that desire, even if it quite literally means, for a while, Hell on earth.

II

One other neglected fact about the classics has still to be recorded. Who has kept up the tradition of reading great books? Obviously the schools. If a nation issues blacklists as Germany

did and they are enforced in schools and libraries, the new generation will not know that John Bunyan or Cervantes or Swift ever
existed. But if our schools have kept up the tradition, why is it
that in the 1940's we cannot open a periodical without finding a
discussion of the *new* "classics curriculum" at Chicago or St.
John's College, Annapolis?

The confusion is of words. Great books have always been read
in American colleges and universities, as well as in the lower
schools. But they have not always been read entire, *as books*.
The anthology of snippets taken from English or American
literature is familiar to all. In history and philosophy courses,
parts of famous works have always been assigned. They were
read by the student and he was examined on a few points. This
has been true for half a century past. Before that time, that is
before the influence of science and scientific scholarship in all
lines, the older curriculum consisted very largely of the ancient
classics.

But if we think that one hundred and fifty years ago, college
men must have been ignorant of modern subjects because they
read chiefly Greek and Latin authors, we make a serious error.
They read the ancients as sources, and learned from them an
immense amount of history, economics, sociology, anthropology,
philosophy, mythology, comparative religion, archaeology, and
military science; and this was in addition to grammar, literary
history, and the arts of rhetoric, poetry, drama, and belles-lettres.
One has only to look at the notes to a good early nineteenth-
century text of Aristophanes or Horace to see what nourishing
marrow could be squeezed out of a "dead" classic.[4] The revolution in curriculum that I described before dried up the juices
and left only the skeleton of philology.

Did the revival of interest in the whole sequence of classics
as books come, then, in the 1930's at Chicago and St. John's? I

[4] The skeptic should leaf through the *Life and Letters of Dr. Samuel
Butler* (1774-1839), edited by his grandson and namesake.

think not. In 1919, John Erskine, then Professor of English in Columbia College, was aroused by the unread state of many great works and the failure of certain types of scholarship to bring either pleasure or wisdom.[5] He instituted a course called General Honors Readings, for which he prepared a list of fifty-three great books from Homer to William James. He chose fifteen students and a second instructor, and the group began to read one book each week, meeting for discussion two or three hours on a chosen evening. The flexibility of the hour helped make the discussion at once informal and searching.

When I took the course as a student eight years later, it had grown fourfold. There were two groups of juniors and two of seniors — some sixty in all — who spent two years reading and discussing in the manner I have described an expanded list of important works. Of the eight instructors in charge, I had the good fortune to draw Mark Van Doren and Mortimer Adler (later of Chicago), the combination of whose gifts made these evening sessions an incomparable experience. About the same time, fame of the enterprise was beginning to spread. John Erskine's list had been published.[6] Unofficial reading groups were forming and finally the Director of the People's Institute, the late Everett Dean Martin, organized a number of regular ones under his auspices. These were taught by some of the Columbia instructors as well as others. With an interruption of three years (1929–1932) spent in reorganizing upper college work, John Erskine's original course has continued at the summit of the Columbia College liberal arts offering.

Now what is the variation introduced by Professor Adler at Chicago and by his colleagues at St. John's? The books are the same, the respect for their integrity as books is the same; but their place in the scheme of things is conceived differently. It is characteristic of the difference that Erskine first chose fifty-three

[5] See his volume *The Moral Obligation to Be Intelligent.*
[6] Columbia University Press, 1924.

books — not any fifty-three, but not the best or the only fifty-three. The preface to the published bibliography makes it clear that hundreds of other titles could have been added or substituted. The choice reflected practical considerations as well as the mood of a man, a place, and an age. It followed that these books did not constitute a curriculum in themselves.

At St. John's, on the contrary, the hundred and ten on the catalogue list comprise the four years' reading in every subject matter given. Mathematics and Science, Languages and Literature, History, Philosophy, and Political Theory, are taught principally through these books, using the Erskinian seminar method, but supplementing it with formal lectures, laboratory work, and tutorials in language and mathematics. This is an ingenious and attractive idea, which, if well handled, was bound to pique the curiosity of the American public. For by relying altogether on books that relatively few people want to read, it combined the mystery of a homeopathic dose with the impressive size of a regular prescription. And since the medicine was exhibited with a statement that American liberal education was quite sick (not to mention the fact that it was not the parents, but the boys, who were to do the actual swallowing) the prescription caught the fancy, crystallized opinion, and has on the whole done much good, by drawing attention to its contents as nothing else could have done.

I believe nevertheless that it is not a cure, nor even a safe course to follow. The great-books curriculum is an overreach, an excessive stretching of Erskine's excellent scheme beyond what it can be expected to do. It is a return to the practice used when the *ancient* classics served, as I showed, to introduce men to their own culture. This is no longer possible because modern culture has become specialized and each specialty, even when broadly conceived, requires the direct study of its current output.

To illustrate, the St. John's readings in history are based on six historians — Herodotus, Thucydides, Plutarch, Tacitus, Vico, and Gibbon. A dozen and a half other political writers are added, whose works touch more or less on medieval and modern history — in all twenty-four books that are very rich in substance and diverse in direction. I could wish that every student had the time to read these very books at least once in his college career. But to give the student a coherent idea of modern history from these books alone is more like a wager than a reasonable enterprise.

Even if read without previous preparation, certain of these books will yield information and experience; and I agree that some such readings should be required — as they are in Columbia College — during the freshman year. But to read these same works as sources for a knowledge of history would demand much more time than can be spared from other studies. It would require, too, the reading of many other books of commentary on particular points. The difference I point out in the use of the classics is roughly that between reading *Treasure Island* for the pleasure and profit it may bring, and using it as a chart and manual for finding buried gold. There is not enough time in four years, and perhaps there is not enough knowledge in any faculty, to make the classics *textbooks* as well as simple texts; I overlook many other professional problems which any teacher would at once encounter and be hard put to it to solve. In science and mathematics the difficulties must be insuperable; in language, the notion of learning Greek so as to read Euclid, and French so as to read Molière, is plausible but unsound, given the absence of a previously developed *Sprachgefühl*. And equally grievous is the lack in the present St. John's program of any first-hand introduction to the fine arts: reading esthetic theory is no substitute and may well be a deterrent.

The whole impracticality of the plan could be summed up in this way: St. John's tries to do in college what the educated man should be expected to do for himself ten or fifteen years after his graduation. By then he should have the power to take any great book, enjoy it, go back to it, and distribute its substance among the prepared receptacles in his mind, his college training having given him the taste and the technique. No one disputes this, and I maintain that it should be done by combining the study of subjects as subjects with the reading of books as books. My next chapter will supply a few details as to how it can be accomplished while fitting a young man to become a doctor, a lawyer, a man of business, an architect, or a pure scientist. I repeat, however, that the country should be grateful to St. John's College for having tried and publicized a system so clearly suggested by Erskine's initiative that sooner or later it was bound to challenge attempt.

III

There is at least one more doubt to be quelled about the great books. In saying that the college graduate ten years out *ought* to be able to take down Homer or Machiavelli again with pleasure (remember that ideally he came to own a small library of inexpensive good books) I must be held accountable for the "ought." Many people who value culture with a capital C think of it as to be gained once for all — *before* graduation. One can hardly blame them for thinking so: haven't they been told often enough by public speakers that it's a *permanent* possession? It is and it isn't. Acquire the taste for reading and you will keep on even if it means learning Braille. But the desire must be fed; culture requires cultivation.

Not a few of the students who apply to me for admission to the present form of Erskine's reading course give me as a reason that they want "the background" and will have no other chance to "get it," because they are about to study medicine or engineering. Their idea is, we "give it" and they "get it." But what is it that changes hands in this way? Background is the wrong word altogether. What is acquired is a common set of symbols, almost a separate language. I open today's paper and I see over a story of naval action: "David-Goliath Fight by Foe at Sea Fails."

Immediately, I infer that some small enemy flotilla fought a larger force of ours. The image was instantaneous, and would have suggested more — namely the foe's victory — had not the writer added that it failed.

A common body of stories, phrases, and beliefs accompanies every high civilization that we know of. The Christian stories of apostles and saints nurtured medieval Europe, and after the breakup of Christendom the Protestant Bible served the same ends for English-speaking peoples. Bunyan and Lincoln show what power was stored in that collection of literary and historical works known as the Scriptures, when it was really a common possession. We have lost something in neglecting it, just as we lost something in rejecting the ancient classics. We lost immediacy of understanding, a common sympathy with truth and fact. Perhaps nothing could better illustrate the subtlety and strength of the bond we lost than the story Hazlitt tells of his addressing a fashionable audience about Dr. Johnson. He was speaking of Johnson's great heart and charity to the unfortunate; and he recounted how, finding a drunken prostitute lying in Fleet Street late at night, Johnson carried her on his broad back to the address she managed to give him. The audience, unable to face the image of a famous lexicographer doing such a thing, broke out into titters and expostulations. Whereupon Hazlitt simply said: "I remind you, ladies and gentlemen, of the parable of the Good Samaritan."

It is clear that no amount of explaining, arguing, or demonstrating would have produced the abashed silence which that allusion commanded. It was direct communication; the note that Hazlitt struck sounded in every mind in the same way and it instantly crystallized and put into order every irrelevant emotion. That, if I may so put it, is what "background" does for you. Even today, without Bible or classics, everyone possesses some kind of tradition which he uses without knowing it. The man who should look blank at mention of George Washington and the cherry tree, or who had never heard of Babe Ruth, or who thought that Shakespeare was an admiral, would get along badly even in very lowbrow circles. He might be excused as a foreigner but he would be expected to catch on as soon as he could. This does not mean that culture is for keeping up with the Joneses; it is for talking to your fellow man — talking more quickly and fully than is possible through plodding description.

In college and after, it so happens that the fund of ideas which it is needful to possess originated in great minds — those who devised our laws, invented our science, taught us how to think, showed us how to behave. They speak in highly individual voices, yet rely on the force of a common group of symbols and myths — the culture of the West. The elements of it are of course not found exclusively in the classics; they are in every kind of book and mind, just as David and Goliath turned up in the paper. But it is the classics we read, because there the dose is concentrated and prepared with art; so concentrated that it creates the repelling exterior I began by admitting.

The one thing to be said for encouraging the frightened reader is that if he perseveres, if he lends his mind attentively to whoever it may be — Goethe or Descartes — it will be returned to him, not as good as, but better than new. The classics are packed, dense, thick, ugly, but when truly read they are also full of wit, knowledge, and beauty. And the adventurer who risks an evening upon one of his choice will find, like the banker who discovered *Hamlet* in middle age, that "there aren't ten men in Boston who could do as well."

"Truly read" — there's the rub. Because of the rough outside and the packed contents, most classics invite the use of fancy tricks to get inside them — culture by burglary. There is in truth only one way to read, which is to begin at the beginning. Usually the text has an Introduction, which is supposed to serve as a cold chisel to force an entry, a shoehorn to get a foothold. But like so many other routine devices, most introductions are not written

for the students but for the writer's colleagues. Perhaps an introduction cannot be written at large. The teacher who knows a
particular group of men or women can say: Look for these things,
don't be misled by these other things. But even here he must
soon stop, because he is like a man giving directions over unknown
territory: they make no sense until you are on the spot.

Worse still is the offer of a "method" applicable to all books.
I have already expressed myself on that score, and I tried to show
in describing a Colloquium [7] how instruction ought to fit the
book, the participants, and the occasion. It is my impression that
with the St. John's curriculum goes a system — I am afraid I have
heard it called "an approach" — designed for all books. It prescribes that the reader look for the "dialectic" of a work — its
inner oppositions and balance. This is supposed to generate the
"form" and to enable the student to judge how "perfect" it is.
By this method, so I have been assured by one enthusiastic student, it is possible to detect that there is a scene missing in
Hamlet, one in which the Prince of Denmark would arrange to
have himself kidnaped by the pirates: it would balance something or other and satisfy our reason. I fear that my reason is
better satisfied with the play as it is than with the method used
upon it. I shall be told that the way of reading I prefer is loose,
lacks rigor. I would reply that the systematic way strikes me like
rigor mortis. I am not concerned to have students judges of perfection. Their verdict means nothing. All great books are imperfect, having been written by fallible men, ignorant of dialectic;
and all great books are perfect, having in them the quintessence
of passionate thought.

A teacher who wants to read a series of books with his students
will be well advised to show a kind of willing discipleship shifting ground from book to book. He must be a Christian moralist
with Dante, a skeptic with Lucretius, and a pantheist with Goethe.
Not that he must convert and reconvert his class every Wednes-

[7] Page 41.

day evening to some new creed; but if he wants the readers to lend their minds, he must himself be able to do it. Some students *may* be converted afresh each week; the experience is in itself educational and fulfills the command: try all things, hold fast that which is good. Since it may be trying, in another sense, for the teacher to run the gauntlet of world systems from paganism to science, the addition of a second instructor justifies itself. Each man can once in a while attack the classic of the evening and help dramatize the ever-present conflict between adherents and opponents of each living world view.

Above all, if the classics are indeed one form of the ideas we still live by, there should be no artificially promoted heroes or gangs of heroes. The answer I took down at an oral examination shows the evil: "Aristotle wrote on everything that interested him. He seemed to believe himself an authority on all of them. Fortunately for us, he was." This last afterthought was to mitigate the doubt expressed in the second remark and conciliate the Aristotelian in our midst. This is bad. Let the teacher openly avow his Aristotelianism, persuade us of its soundness, but never enforce it by the arts of cajolery and coercion that come so easily to the holder of a chair.

Finally, though the books delight us when we once know them well, they must not beguile us — readers or teachers — into the error of finding in them the record of a golden age. The Greeks, alas! have done as much harm as good by allowing themselves to be lumped together and worshiped en masse. Seen close to and separately, they were not all beautiful or good or gifted. They were not serene or "adjusted." They did not live in twilight marble splendors, nor in a fresh young dawn alive with nymphs. Don't talk to me about the Greeks: read them! And when you read them, be careful to call what you find by its right name. There are people who, if they read Homer without having heard the phrase "Achilles sulking in his tent," would refuse to call it sulking. "No Greek could sulk."

That I am not exaggerating this pious blindness toward the Greeks (for others, the chosen epoch is the Middle Ages or the Renaissance) was shown by an indignant protest once made at a Faculty meeting against a certain course. The objector taught one section of it but reproved his colleagues. "Why," he said, "one student I talked to told me that the Greeks in Homer were mainly interested in women and booty!" "Mainly" is quite right, and it is this very fact which assures us that mankind has not changed in the intervening three thousand years. More than that, it is the basis for beginning to feel that Homer talks about people we can come to know. I say the *beginning;* to stop there would be falsification. Homer himself is interested in many things: Hector's fatherly love, the horrors of violent death, Vulcan's skill in working metal, the color of the sea, or the anger of the gods. We relate these things to our own experience because we start from a common humanity. If the freshman, therefore, had grasped this main thread, he was on the right road to understanding Homer, and any other honest book, and himself as well.

12. Columbia College, Columbia University

Oh that mine enemy had
founded a college!
— *Job*, revised

I HAVE DONE with specifications for subject matters. If in so
doing, I have had to generalize critically about certain practices,
in order to set in relief what I felt were more desirable ways,
it should not be inferred that all the evils I spoke of were concentrated in any one place or kind of institution. And now that
I am going on to discuss institutional arrangements, let me begin
by saying that in normal times it is possible to obtain in this
country a thoroughly satisfactory college training. As with the
evil, so with the good. There is not one choice spot where wisdom holds an exclusive salon. There are several varieties of the
good and they may be had in every kind of natural setting or
architecture. The small country college, the state university, the
small-town big place, the big-town big place, the progressive, the
old-fashioned, and the middling, all provide, under favorable conditions, a type of instruction which easily matches that given
abroad, and which certainly surpasses the instruction given in the
same places fifty years ago.

What is to be deplored is that the facts about any institution,
facts which no one tries to conceal, should nevertheless remain
hidden from parents interested in educating their sons and daugh-
ters. This is one great difference between higher learning here
and abroad. Educated Europeans know their schools. They hear
of it at once when Bovril College, Oxbridge, loses its best tutors.
The heads not only of universities but of preparatory schools are,

by virtue of their office, national figures. They are accordingly subjected to a public scrutiny that is valuable to them, to their schools, and to the country.

Over here, it is not uncommon to find a reputation outlast the grounds for it — good or bad — by twenty to thirty years. I am thinking of two sizable neighboring institutions, one of which is generally considered a "serious" place and the other rather a country club. It so happens that the academic eminence of the first has somewhat declined, though not dangerously, and that — what is more important — the second has emerged in every respect superior to the first. "How do you know that?" One knows it chiefly by comparing the teaching staffs in each branch, and by observing on the spot the practical arrangements in use as well as the products of the system.

Similarly, given the absence of serious interest on the part of the public, it is possible for an institution to publicize changes of plan or "new" features without any chance of verification by those most interested. Almost anything passes for "new" and there is no checkup on the extent to which plans become facts. One can imagine, for instance, a university quite sincerely making much of its devotion to the principle of teaching, and yet continuing the bargain-counter method of holding huge classes without adequate supervision of individual work. Practical reasons may forbid it, but that is not the point: the point is that the student or his parent is led to think he is going to be taught personally, whereas he finds that he is lectured at, graded, and "put through" impersonally.[1]

Let me take an actual case of the reverse ignorance, though it affects what may at first seem a trivial point. Everybody has heard of a place called Columbia. The name is in the papers, the institution is in New York, and every novelist who wishes to "locate"

---

[1] Some universities have Visiting Committees composed of graduates taken from the laity. This seems to me an excellent and necessary device to keep academic authorities from mistaking a blueprint for a going concern.

a metropolitan character makes him either an instructor or a student "at Columbia."

These fictional persons add to the general impression of size, so that new acquaintances who find that I teach "at Columbia" ask me without a smile whether I ever get to know my students; seeing that I lecture to thousands at a time. When I reply that most of my teaching is done in classes of twenty-five and that I am in fact attached to one of the smallest of men's colleges in the East, they can only stare and suspect me of irony. I explain to them that there is a part of Columbia University called Columbia College, founded nearly two centuries ago and consisting of one thousand seven hundred and fifty male undergraduates, taught by a faculty of about one hundred and thirty. For the space of five minutes they believe me. At the end of that time, their mind snaps back and they burst out with one invariable question, which is: "How is it that with thirty thousand students to choose from, your football team is always so poor?" At this point, I either explain again, or I do not.

Does it matter, after all, whether the public knows that the enrollment figures in Columbia's undergraduate college are less than those of Harvard, Princeton, or Yale? [2] It does in one sense, namely that if it is impossible to get over this first hurdle and take it as cleared for good, it is certainly impossible to explain a scheme of instruction which, with all its shortcomings, *is* a going concern and has steadily and noticeably influenced practice elsewhere.

[2] It might save breath if I had small cards printed with the following statistics: —

	Enrollment Fall of 1940
Harvard	3,561 men
Yale	2,375 men
Chicago	3,512 men and women
Princeton	2,405 men
Wisconsin (College of Letters and Science)	6,142 men and women
COLUMBIA COLLEGE -	1,672 men

I have already spoken of John Erskine's reading course in great books, after which others have been patterned, and the latest offspring of which is the radio program, "Invitation to Learning." There may be good enough reasons why Erskine has not yet received due credit for his innovation of 1919, but it is obvious that no one can begin to grasp what that idea was if one's imagination pictures him at that time discussing Dante informally with thirty thousand students of all ages and sexes.

Perhaps I am unduly sensitive on the point; if so, it is not because I have an abstract dislike of large numbers. If I had, I should never have done any radio broadcasting. My reason is rather that I believe in hand-to-hand, mind-to-mind encounters as an indispensable part of teaching, and the undying *idée fixe* of the public concerning that nonexistent thing "Columbia" puts me in the mood of the British undergraduate who, being a member of an unfashionable College at Oxford, got into the habit of supplying the right response: "I'm from Wadham — Oh!" I could paraphrase it: "Men only — one, seven, five, o!"

Oddly enough — and this is why I dwell on its true character — Columbia College is highly representative of modern instruction throughout the country. Whether it be the Honors programs, the many introductions to the history of civilization and to the humanities, the abandonment of loose electives, or the interdepartmental devices for staffing small classes and reading groups, they all owe something to the ideas of the late Dean H. E. Hawkes and his associates in Columbia College. Yet it seems to be only at that college that these separate improvements have been fitted together into an established whole, and the sense of the innovation accepted in its fullness. This has come about partly because the college is small enough to permit flexible arrangements, partly because the resistance of older traditions of teaching has been amicably overcome during a period of twenty years.

Still using Columbia College as an epitome of changes now well entrenched in many places, I should say that "modernism" in the

American college began towards the end of the First World War. At Columbia the need to explain war aims generated a course known as An Introduction to Contemporary Civilization in the West, compulsory for all freshmen. A year later, in 1919, came Erskine's reading course, for selected juniors and seniors. Ten years after that, the Contemporary Civilization course was extended to cover two years, and very soon after it was supplemented by two new courses, also obligatory and also covering two years — one in the Humanities and one in the Sciences.

The sense of the plan can be seen at once by starting, not from the college, but from the world. What are the broad divisions of thought and action in that world? There are three and only three: we live in a world saturated with science, in a world beset by political and economic problems, in a world that mirrors its life in literature, philosophy, religion, and the fine arts. In all reason, a college can but follow this threefold pattern. To this extent, the problem of "What shall we teach?" is nonexistent. This is what we must teach. To quote the present Dean of Columbia College on the teaching of science, social science, and the humanities, "Any one of them without the other two gives a lopsided, incomplete, dangerously ignorant product. A false specialization that chooses to neglect even one of these fields is like a three-legged stool with only two legs." [3]

If this is true, it would seem logical to ask that all freshmen and sophomores in the liberal arts should be required to take courses introducing them to these three matters of ancient and modern learning. In the Columbia Introduction to Contemporary Civilization they are shown the historical development of the modern world since 1200. By studying the institutions, ideas, and ways of making a living prevalent during that period, they are prepared to go on with courses in economics, government, philosophy, and history. The second year of this Introduction con-

[3] "The Making of Leadership" by Harry James Carman, *Saturday Review of Literature,* September 15, 1944.

centrates on America and ends with an analysis of the world about us, its politics and its economic structure.

In a parallel Humanities course, the students must read books, hear music, and see pictures. The books, ranging from Homer to Goethe, are read in their entirety, include fiction, history, poetry, and philosophy, and take up the whole of the freshman year. The sophomore year serves to introduce music and the plastic arts, with a choice for the student to take more hours of the one than the other. But both he must have. I indicated above the kind of instruction that is possible and profitable in the arts.

Finally, the freshman must make acquaintance with the physical and logical sciences. He can do so in two ways. If his bent is scientific to begin with, he can choose the mathematics and other sciences that suit his purpose. But if he is to remain a layman, he must take the two-year introduction to scientific concepts and techniques. The first year includes geology, astronomy, physics, and chemistry; the second, biology, botany, mathematics, and logic. Needless to say, the course does not "cover" these vast subjects: it describes their contents and viewpoints and relates them. In the present state of quasi-universal ignorance of science, it is a great thing to have liberal-arts students learn accurately what biology is concerned with, how the biologist leans on the chemist and the geologist, and what a cell or a syllogism is for.

The first two years, then, take the student and show him a mirror of the world. He not only fills his head with fair pictures of reality, but he can begin to think with tolerable good sense about what he himself wishes to do, both in his next two college years and later on. Any part of this program, suitably altered to fit local needs, is undoubtedly good in itself, as adaptations of the Columbia College scheme have repeatedly proved. It is moreover generally acknowledged that teaching individuals is better than lecturing masses; and the recognition of intellect through Honors work has proceeded apace.[4] But there is a virtue peculiar to the

[4] Swarthmore and Princeton have made interesting innovations; Harvard

full introduction, obtainable only from the deliberate and protracted hand shaking with all the muses in turn, for in teaching the whole is more than the sum of its parts.

To be sure, this initial dose of instruction sounds formidable. It taxes the powers of both students and instructors but it produces genuine students capable of really advanced work. But before sketching the character of this advanced work, I want to point out the drawbacks and difficulties of the introductory stage; drawbacks and difficulties that must be cheerfully faced and fought, if the whole arrangement is to be kept from turning into hokum.

The chief need and the hardest to fill is a good staff, willing to work like dogs with small discussion groups. They must be well-informed, active, interested in students, conscientious in their preparation, and committed to the idea of interdepartmental work.[5] The next biggest difficulty is to make the three main required courses fit into the time available. For of necessity, freshmen and sophomores have other demands made upon them as well. They must write English prose, continue a foreign language, and they should, if possible, engage in extracurricular activities and acquire some physical skill.

As things stand, modern languages and English prose undoubtedly suffer. Both are dealt with by asking "proficiency" rather than by following courses. The student writes English or learns German until he can pass the set examination. Usually he has to take one or two courses in the language to pass it. But it is bad to put foreign languages on the footing of a nuisance to be got rid of; and it is equally bad to make the writing of English an

---

has gone farthest with its tutorial system, and Toronto should be given credit for early and tenacious attachment to the idea.

[5] In Columbia College, instructors in Contemporary Civilization are drawn from the departments of history, economics, government, and philosophy; instructors in Humanities (first year) from English, philosophy, history, Greek and Latin, and modern languages; (second year) from music and fine arts.

isolated performance which is also to cease after "passing." It will take work and thought — and they have begun to be applied — to iron out these major blemishes. It is perhaps only fair to add that other plans in force elsewhere reveal the same weakness in languages and composition. Again, the techniques for teaching music and the plastic arts to every kind of mind are still in their infancy. Trial has been followed by error and this by trial again. Some improvement is noticeable, substantial enough to suggest that the right road has at last been struck. But success here also depends on gifted teachers.

Finally, the third conflict of desires comes from the situation of the scientific and engineering students. Their specialized preparation, as now outlined by the professional schools, demands a large allotment of time to science courses. These must come in a set sequence and naturally require much laboratory and outside work. Hardship cases are frequent and have to be dealt with as they come. But the situation is fundamentally unstable and something must topple over: either the basic, required *collegiate* preparation will be seriously breached, or the basic required *vocational* preparation will have to yield. This is true generally over the country, and the curriculum I describe only reflects it more vividly because it has gone farther than most in prescribing the work of the first two years. It is surely not fair to subject young men to the drawing-and-quartering of incompatible demands. It verges on the immoral to compel a choice between education and professional competence, and if the American college cannot reconcile them it will deserve all the hard words that normally accompany superannuated institutions to the grave.

Two things strike me as possible: either the engineering and pure science vocations will choose to follow the lead of medicine and law and reduce their demands on undergraduate time; or, keeping the requirements the same, they will recast their courses. I tread on mined ground in saying this, but I should not be surprised if an overhauling of lecture contents and laboratory manuals could not be made to yield precious time. No doubt some of the acceleration done during the war emergency went much too far: I heard of a Qualitative Chemistry course being given by lecture alone; but an occasional upsetting of the apple cart may show administrators that the regular way is not necessarily immutable. One can understand, even honor, men so devoted to science that they put it before all other things, but it is poor political arithmetic to go on to say, like most scientists, that science should share the student's time half and half — one half for science, one half for all the rest. I say poor *political* arithmetic, because under this assumption the future American Citizen, the voter, the democrat, the parent of later generations, will be quite simply a half man.

II

To the point where I have taken him, the undergraduate has not yet heard a lecture — unless he has replaced the Introduction to the Sciences by specialized courses. Nor has he taken part in a seminar or colloquium. In his junior and senior years, he will probably experience both.[6] He will be put in charge of a senior adviser, who will act in concert with his previous counselor, to whom he was assigned as a freshman on the basis of professional plans. The senior adviser's task is to fit the resources of the College — and of the University, for the upperclass man may with permission take graduate work — to the individual interests and purposes of the man in his charge.

This will probably mean the choice of a dominant interest in one branch of study, accompanied by two lesser interests. A student once compared this to Aristotle's golden mean and when I asked him what he meant, he said, "One virtue flanked by two

[6] In a seminar, each of ten or twelve students does individual research or reading, and reports before the group, who question and criticize. In a colloquium, all the students prepare the same readings and discuss them.

vices." In the main subject, the student will take one or two courses plus a seminar — such as the junior or the senior seminar in economics. There he will do research and reading and receive training designed either to top off his preparation or to lead to graduate work. The lesser subjects usually bear some relation to the main one. An economist may take statistics and political theory; an historian will be advised to choose philosophy and English literature. The permutations are endless, and indeed, the student is not to be thought of as "an historian" or "an economist." He is still the raw material for an educated man. But the tradition of "going on to an M.A." is so strong in the American college population that it is advisable to make of the senior year the working half of a universal joint.

Interestingly enough, at Columbia College the unspecialized "Colloquium on Great Books" [7] — the Erskine course — seems to draw steadily from all ranks of special interest. Future doctors seem to favor it especially, thinking perhaps that bedside books go with the bedside manner. Mathematicians come and dispute over Berkeley; poets endure Adam Smith so as to rhapsodize over Milton and Hardy; and engineers express the hope that they will imbibe style and the sense of beauty from viewing so many masterpieces in different tongues and genres.

In connection with this reading course, a long and careful attempt has been made to teach writing on the principles I indicated earlier. Each Colloquium student writes one short paper each month on a topic of his own choosing and dealing with any aspect of the readings or discussions. The paper is submitted in duplicate; it is fully annotated by the two instructors in charge, and returned for later reference or immediate rewriting. After three papers, most students begin to think, talk, and write in less boyish fashion, and after six of them, half the class can write with

[7] The list from which the books are drawn is edited by Alan W. Brown and published by the American Library Association under the title "Classics of the Western World." Chicago, 1943.

a sureness of touch affording pleasure to both author and reader.

It remains to say a word about lecture courses. They are of two kinds: courses given by members of the College Faculty exclusively for college students, and courses open to graduate and undergraduate students alike. The virtue of the latter kind is that it offers college men the opportunity of studying with well-known authorities in the field of their choice, even when these men are attached primarily to the Graduate School. Conversely, certain College teachers offer courses for Graduate students. Thus another artificial gap in the ladder of learning is bridged over, and the truth recognized that the unceasing aim of teaching should be to let the instruction fit the class.

In all lecture courses, however, the undergraduate contingent is responsible for more written work than the graduates, and for one additional hour, spent with the lecturer for the purpose of thrashing out left-over difficulties. How well this third hour is handled, how closely the written work is checked, how suitably the three or four lecturers that each student hears supplement or contradict one another — these are matters left to chance, and perhaps not to be regulated without loss of desirable freedom.

The Columbia College curriculum is anything but perfect. As in all working machinery breakdowns occur, parts wear out and have to be replaced. "Efficient" teaching is an absurd aim, though doubtless "effective" teaching is not. In any case, perfectionism in education is a false idol which too often induces paralysis or meddlesome bustling about. The particular form which weaknesses in language and composition study take in the Columbia College scheme, I have stated. Other failures, personal ones, are only too evident at the end of each term, and with them comes the sense that it takes two to fail, just as it takes two to teach. Diversity of aims, temperaments, and opportunities, which makes for various kinds of success, also allows mishaps that in gloomy moods seem preventable. But risks of this sort are not to be conjured away by system. The strength of this specimen institution seems to me to reside in two things: one, it teaches in close co-ordination the three live subject matters in modern life — science, social science, and the humanities; and two, it does not undertake to "process" men for the sake of any single virtue.

Columbia College does prescribe a much greater part of the four-year course than do other institutions. But the required work is concentrated in two years and its contents are designed to help the student choose wisely in his upper years. The unrestricted right to shop among electives may look like freedom, but it may actually be confining, as a student from the Middle West con-fessed when I asked what his preparation in history had been. "I was going to be a minister, so I took Pre-Theological Rural Sociology." Custom tailoring is excellent for the human form, but in collegiate teaching it can soon become patchwork. Besides, its appearance of perfect adaptation is deceptive. There is no such thing as a separate sociology for rural ministers. The title betrays the touch of the salesman, doubtless well meant, but more con-genial to the catalogue maker than to the teacher.

13. Deans within Deans

> "Is the Bean dizzy?"
> — Heard from a committee-
> man at the end of a long
> day

Who does write the Catalogue in an American college? Programs and schedules and courses are formally passed upon by the Faculties; actually they are shaped by the Deans and Directors. These usually work with the aid of committees drawn from the teaching staff, but Deans are in so many ways independent that there exist in most places two unequal bodies of opinion on most matters — the Faculty and the Administration.

Nothing so strikes the foreign observer with surprise as the size and power of American collegiate administration. The best offices in the best building, the rows and rows of filing cabinets, the serried ranks of secretaries and stenographers, make the European feel that he has wandered by mistake into some annex of a large business concern. The thick carpets, the hush and polish of the surroundings, cannot form part of an academy. The foreigner is used to a distinctive shabbiness, to hollowed steps and an inky smell, without which no school, college, or university seems genuine, be the place England, Germany, Italy, or France.

On the continent, at least, the whole of university administration is embodied in a superior janitor who gives out information, enters names, and in some cases collects fees against a receipt. Beyond sits a Rector in a handsome room, but — if I may make an Irish bull — he is never there. In short, continental universities run themselves. Their constituent faculties make the few necessary decisions. The state appoints the teachers and jointly with

Tradition regulates the programs — the students all taking care of their own records, attendance, and responsibilities.[1]

American institutions dealing as they do with younger people, and furnishing far more numerous services, have to be run by a separate body of diversely specialized managers known collectively as the administration. The Director of Admissions admits, the Registrar registers, the Bursar imburses, and a galaxy of Deans decide. There is a Dean of Men, a Dean of Women, a Dean of Studies, and Freshman Deans in droves. In a large university, there are as many deans and executive heads as there are schools and departments. Their relations to one another are intricate and periodic; in fact, "galaxy" is too loose a term: it is a planetarium of deans with the President of the University as a central sun. One can see eclipses, inner systems, and oppositions. But usually more sympathy obtains among fellow administrators than between them and the teaching personnel. If it came to a pitched battle, I feel sure that the more compact executive troops, animated by a single purpose, besides being better fed and self-disciplined, could rout the more numerous but disorderly rabble that teaches.

Not that it would be easy to find a clear-cut issue for war. The difference of views that exists is ill-defined and more permanent than deep-lying. Most deans are beloved of their Faculty, especially when neither dean nor teacher is in his own seat of authority, and the good steady friction that shows the wheels are gripping doesn't come from a single cause. True, the difference of income is important: a dean usually earns two or three times as much as a teacher in mid-career. But this has an obverse side: if the dean is drawn from the faculty, he comes to feel like a deserter and guilty about it, for he has ceased to teach, to keep

[1] For example, instead of a vast office full of clerks and machinery to register marks, the European university student has a small booklet in which every instructor enters the grade of the examination just passed. A single small transcript is filed — again, with the Janitor.

up with his subject, and to remember what those things were like. He has become an overworked harassed arbitrator, housekeeper, public orator, and employer of men.

This last function also has its share in separating him from his faculty — either he has power to hire and fire, or his recommendation to the President and Trustees has the same effect, or possessing no real power (it being lodged in autonomous departments) he has to pretend that his faculty *is* his faculty. In all three cases, he is plagued by awkward personal relations. Contrast these with the continental practice of licensing all teachers, with appointments guaranteed by the state, independent tenure, and promotion by seniority, and you see at once why to the foreign observer the atmosphere of the American university suggests a business concern.

In smaller colleges, the functions I have ascribed to the Dean are exercised by the President, the Dean standing to him or her as a special assistant in charge of curriculum, perhaps, or of students. More usually, the President is wholly an "outside" man. His task is to "handle" the Trustees, the public, and the money. He makes speeches and contacts, and signs diplomas. If after his term of office he has secured for the college a new gymnasium or library, he is held in as high esteem as if he had contributed an idea or an atmosphere.

So much for the executive branch. In almost all places, large or small, there are standing Committees of the Faculty, set up to legislate. Their purview is infinite: courses, students admitted, infractions of the rules, scholarships, buildings and grounds, library acquisitions — there is no subject under the sun which has not at some time or other been the *raison d'être* of an academic committee. In general, the more "enlightened," "progressive," and "democratic" the college is, the more committees there are — and the less the life of a teacher is worth living.

I have sat on a committee so democratic that the chairman, who had received a publisher's circular offering a new syllabus in the social studies, read the letter aloud and asked for a vote to obtain a sample copy. At the other end of the scale, committees meet not to debate over fifty cents' worth of printed matter, but to settle the great imponderables, such as how to insure in wartime the survival of permanent human values. I am told that on one such occasion a blunt logician pointed out that if the human values were really permanent the college might let them shift for themselves. This broke up the meeting, but there is no reason to believe that the other committeemen were properly grateful.

For addiction to meetings is the teacher's professional disease. One can see why. The weakness comes from the nervous strain of teaching, coupled with the burden of a professional conscience. The morning classes once done, a teacher would find it good to do nothing and say nothing for an hour or two. But the day is only half over. If no students turn up for consultation, the only proper thing would be to read or write: there is always a piece in either kind to be worked on. Yet truly, freshness and inspiration are lacking and — a glance at the desk calendar — "there's a meeting on (Thank God!). It is important, it must be done, it counts as work."

And just because the mind is tired, the meeting is bound to be long and tedious, and probably all to do again next week at the same hour. With three committees to attend each week, a teacher may properly be said to be going around in vicious circles.

I shall not go so far as to suggest abolishing committees. Abolish every other one and see what happens. Also, choose chairmen who have a manly conception of what "democracy" is. It does not mean letting everyone speak for as long as he likes on any theme that offers; it means settling questions after a full exchange of relevant views. Relevance suggests the rule: no gavel, no chairman. The best committee I ever sat on, not from my own partial point of view, but according to the consensus of its members, was run by a man of the old school, granitic in look and manner, who after the first meeting was privately accounted a brute. But he was a just brute and he got the best sense of the meeting that our collective noddles could supply. He worked hard and so did we, and by his skill in making us toe the true line, we sped to a finish in short order; our report, drafted by him in three pages, could be understood at sight. Could not men of business, who are only one degree less efficient than teachers, also ponder this technique for their conferences?

There is of course some connection between old-fashioned ways and expeditiousness, so perhaps my one instance has no value. The "old school" had stiffer manners — our chairman did not hesitate to address us as "Gentlemen" whenever he wanted our attention. In the looser modern style, by which everybody is John and Henry, the goal seems to be not so much to transact business as to stagnate in friendly feelings. These apparently forbid one to contradict, to argue concisely, or to recall any speaker to the point. Under these conditions, if the minutes of the meeting show any sign of consecutiveness, it is because the secretary has a good head and writes them up at home.

As for meetings of a whole faculty, they are closely comparable with the sessions of Congress — some good and some bad, no oratory left, much reliance on committee reports; with the Dean acting as the Chief Executive who wins or loses on the proposals in his "message." There is relatively little caucus work except on rare constitutional questions. Campus politics is of course fact not fiction, but it takes rather the form of personal influence upon the executive power than moving assemblies to decisive votes.

I must modify this last point to take in certain colleges which have a two-party tradition. Liberals and Conservatives go on fighting, not over the ordinary meaning of these terms, but on local issues that split the old guard from the new. Faculty meetings are trials of strength. A newcomer has to choose between the parties and his choice determines whom he lunches and plays bridge with and what part of town he must dwell in — not to mention his chances of advancement. Teachers, as I said before, are as passionate as the rest of mankind and are entitled to enjoy the great human pastime of politics. And they know how to flavor it with gossip as well as anybody else.

Oddly enough, though politics is tolerable on the campus, and indeed inevitable since real interests are at stake, democracy is not. A few institutions, chiefly among state and city colleges, have adopted a system by which the members of a department vote for one another's promotions. The result is a fearful and constant tension, productive of all the practices elsewhere condemned as corrupt — logrolling, coercion, delation, and sycophancy.[2] It would take a philosopher-king to rule such a roost, not that teachers sink lower than other men when tempted, but that their fall from grace infects their merits more directly. A teacher ought not to be constantly thinking about his status, his salary, his deserts, and his chances. He ought not, certainly, to associate these thoughts with the sight of his colleagues or his boss. Though the academic grove is not the Garden of Eden, it ought to be laid out so as to guarantee a reasonable freedom. And this matters to the students as well as the staff, since the young are not only quick to sense strain and friction, but are entitled, during teaching hours, to their instructors' undivided attention.

II

Before coming back to the choice of a good teaching staff, I must make here a necessary digression about freedom — the special kind known as academic freedom. This is the principle appealed to when Professor Z has publicly advocated the nationalizing of peanut stands and the President's desk is flooded with complaints from parents and Trustees. The situation becomes really bad when a wealthy or powerful man, an alumnus or the uncle of a

[2] In one famous Southern university the Faculty elect their President. The occasion must be infrequent enough to keep it from creating factions, and yet must afford a highly desirable kind of representation.

freshman on probation, chooses to give himself a little publicity by denouncing the university in his home-town paper. At that point, the university turns into a "hotbed" — one radical being enough to heat a whole suite of beds — and it is found upon investigation that the students are indeed asked to read the *Communist Manifesto* in some history or economics class.

This damaging fact is news to the President; the Dean vaguely remembers that it was true even in his day on the faculty; and both agree that steps must be taken — measures, such steps as the situation may require — in other words, give the public the impression that Professor Z has been fired. Unfortunately, this cannot be done in pantomime and when it is done in earnest, the students, half the faculty, the Civil Liberties Union, and any number of other organizations jump with delight and defiance into the fray. Publishers rush up to the marked man with signed contracts and he is temporarily the campus Hampden, with dauntless breast withstanding the little tyrants in his field.

From time to time, of course, the battle for academic freedom has none of these comic-opera features. It has the grimness of an execution by the secret police. A teacher is dropped, silently, callously, with the clear intent of an unfrocking and of an attainder against his dependents. The cause is by no means always political; it is sometimes religious, sometimes "moral," almost always bigoted. Against this there is no redress, for it occurs usually too low in the world of educational institutions, it concerns too small a post, and it can command no publicity. The victim is indeed fortunate if he belongs to an association of teachers that will look into his pitiable case.

Even in the more common instances I first described, the newspaper account and the facts vary widely. Rights and wrongs are seldom evenly divided between the two camps. And behind the scenes, or rather, on the spot, the facts may look different. Yet a distinction can be made between two types of professional "radicalism." I am here assuming, by the way, that "radicalism"

is defined by the community. In a bone-dry county, to propose
the legalization of wine and beer would be as radical as in an
"enlightened" city to propose government ownership of banks.
This being so, three questions may be asked: Has the teacher the
right to express his opinion on the mooted subject in the classroom? Has he the right to express it outside? And finally, has he
the right to use class time to convert students to his opinion?

Everyone would (or should) admit, in answer to the last
question, that he has no such right, and that on the contrary the
students, who are perhaps compelled to listen to him, have every
right to complain if they are preached at instead of instructed.
I have personally known men who thought it fair to indoctrinate
the captive freshman, and yet called it a violation of academic
freedom when they were cautioned or restrained. Needless to say,
academic freedom implies no such opportunity: it is even a
question whether it confers the right to be systematically boring.

When we tackle the other two questions, we tread on more
delicate ground, because the teacher's "opinion" may mean one
of two things — his views on a part of his subject, or his views
on some matter which he may feel strongly but know only as an
amateur.

Regarding what he says as an authority, his freedom should be
absolutely unimpaired, no matter who disapproves and for what
reason. The teacher may say that Shakespeare's works were
written by Mary Queen of Scots, if he so chooses: a university
must always remember that the new truth almost invariably
sounds crazy, and crazier in proportion to its greatness. It would
be idiocy to keep recounting the stories of Copernicus, Galileo,
and Pasteur, and forget that the next time the innovator will seem
as hopelessly wrong and perverse as these men seemed. The cost
of this freedom may be a good deal of crackpot error, but nothing
good goes unpaid for: this is the price.

With respect to subjects outside his field, the teacher has,
not academic freedom, but academic responsibility; that is, he
may on demand or of his own accord tell his students what he

thinks of Psychical Research, or the British Empire, or the Brooklyn Dodgers. If he touches subjects more sensitive still, he is bound to observe the same tact that he would in good society. Standing on a raised platform six inches high does not give the right to insult religious beliefs nor to outrage moral convictions, however bigoted these may appear to an opponent. Students, on their side, have no right to publish what is said in class, or they kill its informality. The teacher's sense of fitness naturally involves judging what is and what is not germane to the discussion. I should add from experience that what makes the greatest difference in all these matters of propriety is tone. The teacher can say almost anything, provided he is really saying what he means and not fighting some secret war of the feelings against a particular student or class.

The same formula covers the teacher's outside utterances. He must respect his own status and that of his college, but outside the classroom he has the full freedom to express himself on all matters that any citizen has. Only, he must make it clear to his hearers or readers when he is speaking as a citizen and when as a University expert on some special branch. Within these limits, inside and outside academic halls, the university leaves the teacher free, so that it may itself remain free, like the editors of a periodical or the master of ceremonies at a public gathering.

All this wisdom, by the way, I produce at second hand. I mean that having witnessed the political tempests of the thirties on several campuses, I followed up conflicting statements of academic freedom until I ran into the classic and definitive one by A. Lawrence Lowell, which I have roughly summarized here. It was issued during the First World War, chiefly, I believe, in defense of Professor Laski's teaching at Harvard. Set down in eight short pages, it should be reprinted and hung above every President's or Dean's desk, for it is as practical as it is definitive.[3]

[3] It can be read in President Lowell's *At War with Academic Traditions in America* and again in the Appendix to *What a University President Has Learned*

III

Since fortunately there is in America no nationwide control of teachers and teaching posts and consequently no automatic assignment of teachers, executive officers — whether Presidents, Deans, or Heads of Departments — must appoint them. The American tradition varies as between privately endowed and tax-supported colleges but generally upholds the free choice of teachers. This works some hardships — those of unequal treatment — but mobility and variety are enhanced. Most of the hardships are not even inherent in the scheme but rather in the state of mind of college administrators. Without pretending that there is a single such state of mind, and allowing for administrative quirks or genius, it remains true that certain habits prevail at certain times, which constitute the "regular way of doing things," particularly when the thing to be done remains ever the same.

Colleges and universities annually face the need to make two kinds of choice: young men must be hired, for elementary work as well as for insuring the continuity of the several departments; and distinguished men, for advanced work and immediate prestige. The latter are easily singled out by their reputation among their fellows, and the only caution a Dean must observe is that he shall not appoint a man so near the end of his powers that he will "retire on salary" and serve the students not at all. Hiring him in these conditions is only an expensive kind of advertising, that may also demoralize the working members of the newcomer's department.

In choosing young men, colleges tend to follow two opposite rules: they take their own graduates or they take anybody but their own. The arguments are evenly matched — one, that colleges know their own product best and think it best trained; two, that filling the ranks exclusively from their own people soon produces "inbreeding." It is not always clear what kind of Jukes or

Kallikaks are expected to issue from an inbred staff, but the feeling is strong that the danger exists.

Both rules, it seems to me, work against the only good rule, which is to judge cases as fully as possible on their merits, and to choose not classes of men but individuals. After all, temperamental differences are greater and cut deeper than academic training. Perhaps the average product of Littleburgh College is uniform, but then don't take the average product. No staff is better — I won't say than the men who compose it, for that is a truism — but better than the range of differences that the men represent.

This is where deans — using the term generically — have a hard time. By necessity they love peace and hate trouble. But by professional duty, they ought always to prefer facing trouble and resolving it if the effort required means getting a variegated faculty. Peace may mean only routine and suspended animation of the soul; trouble may express intellectual vitality and positive accomplishments.

It is extraordinary how many diverse kinds of men and women make desirable teachers, and I hope I did not suggest a "type" when earlier I discoursed at large on the profession. Remember you need lecturers and discussers and tutors. They can differ in endless, unpredictable ways. You can take the halt, the lame, the blind; men with speech defects or men who cannot be heard above a whisper; gross and repulsive men (at first) like my blessed mathematics instructor; men who are lazy and slow, who are bright and unstable, or incorrigible *enfants terribles;* you can even risk some who are deficient in learning, and join them to form an admirable as well as an induplicable faculty. This is possible because the students also display a variety of human traits and cannot all be reached and moved by the same spells.

The important thing is to be sure you are hiring a teacher and not a wolf wrapped in a sheepskin. But it is also wise to bear in mind that any one teacher need only affect 10 per cent of the enrolled student body to be worth his price. If a man regularly exerts a positive influence on thirty-five out of a graduating class of three hundred and fifty — I am thinking of an actual case — it makes no difference whether the remaining three hundred and fifteen loathe the sight of him. Having such a man on the staff demands some care in scheduling. Let those who dislike him drop his course; and obviously also, don't fill all teaching positions with similar eccentrics. But the life of mind requires the two components of mind and life. If a teacher has both, he may be forgiven many faults.

I went so far as to say that in some cases deficient learning might itself be acceptable. I recall one teacher, a Scotchman who had made his way from dire poverty to academic standing, and who made up for his humble origin by mastering as many foreign languages as he could. He took pardonable pride in his knowledge and was an admirable teacher. Among other peculiarities he had a set of gestures with which he unconsciously scanned conjugations, so that during class a glance at his left arm sawing the air would tell the student that he should be using the imperfect tense instead of the future. But occasionally our linguist overreached himself. One day the phrase *hoi polloi* came into the discussion and after giving its meaning, he announced that it was a Hawaiian expression. One of the students remarked that he had always thought it was Greek. To which, imperturbable, the dominie replied: "Right! It comes to us *from* the Greek *through* the Hawaiian!"

A large university must maintain, in addition to instructors, a certain number of men whose worth lies in productive research rather than in teaching. They must be used accordingly and not, for instance, let loose upon freshmen in the most difficult introductory course. As supervisor of the curriculum, the Dean must think like a well-known physician who was trying out a special diet on a group of patients. It suddenly struck him that it was not enough to have the hospital send up the right dishes: how much went back untasted to the kitchen? The Faculty's "program" goes into effect only if it is actually taught; and plainly, the administration is there to administer it.

As for securing teachers who are meant to teach, it should not, in theory, be difficult to find out their qualifications before hiring. The applicant submits a complete scholastic record with letters of recommendation, and he is usually available for interview. In some colleges he runs the gauntlet of an Appointments committee. I have sat on both sides of such inquisitions and I feel they could be improved.

To begin with, the occasion is falsely considered to be embarrassing; the result is that the interview consists either in small talk or in an exchange of views on "fundamentals that exist." In the one case the administrator learns nothing except that Mr. X has or has not a ready flow of repartee; in the other, the candidate commits himself to positions that either damn him or overvalue him — or more often that mean nothing at all. One person I know was asked whether she thought she could "challenge" students. She could think of nothing to say except, "So as to get the password back?" and this unbecoming levity cost her the post. Clearly, the only proper topic for such an interview is subject matter. Let the candidate say what courses he would like to teach, in what way, with what books, and so on. If he has himself written books or articles, draw him out on these — never was such a golden opportunity to talk shop! Only, the interviewer should have sufficient breadth of interest to gauge the quality of what he is told.

Since many do not feel competent to do this, they have recourse to questionnaires — a series of them if need be. This is tantamount to abdication. The executive mind is supposed to judge, not to devise tricks by which judgment can be avoided. No counting of Yeses and Noes will give certainty in place of doubt. Besides, question makers always look for perfection: the last man appointed, though good, turned out to have human failings; so the next man must be a paragon. Just examine a few requirements, taken from an actual questionnaire, six pages long and composed of fifty-eight questions and criteria. According to this "efficient" executive, the applicant must be "the kind of person college students take to with enthusiasm and in whom his faculty colleagues have confidence; in brief, a strong and warm personality." He must have "intellectual ability of a recognized high order . . . ; the ability to participate congenially in the social life of the community . . . public speaking ability, so as to discuss his work with alumni and other groups. . . . Excellent health and physical vigor. . . . If a candidate is married, his wife must also possess the characteristics described . . . under [social ability]." In another part of this self-portrait which the candidate must fearlessly limn, it is suggested that his educational philosophy must be such as to induce him, if he has children, to place them in the college's experimental school. A man who could step forward confident of meeting this institution's demands ought to be able to name his own salary, or else should be rejected for megalomania. The whole thing is a farce and an imposition, particularly on the young and poor.

The use of letters of recommendation suffers from the same vices. Since administrators want giants of intellect and strength, everyone has got into the habit of writing only the nice things, even when the statement is confidential and goes direct to the employer. The writer knows he is pushing a good man, so his conscience is clear, but he knows also that to hint a fault here and there will prejudice his protégé's chances as against holders of less candid letters. So that every teacher who has not actually robbed a bank is endorsed in the most unconditional manner for every available position. This being so, letters are discounted by their recipients — the deans — who are thus left in the same old necessity of forming judgments and deciding on the right choice of persons in the good old way.

IV

I say "persons" because I am also thinking of students. And here in some ways the business becomes graver still. With entrance examinations on the decline, the interview and the school ratings of personality assume a decisive importance. Naturally no system worked by human hands will insure justice, and the examination in subjects was a hardship for many; but there is a special kind of cant produced by the newer way, which I confess I particularly dislike.

It amounts to a sort of demand for subtle flattery of the questioner or the institution on the part of the candidate. What happens is not easily described; it must be felt. But I think everyone would admit that to ask a young person to say why he chose Littleburgh College before all other places is not fair. And many other "innocent" inquiries are of that character right up to the professional schools. "Why do you want to become a doctor?" The fact of having applied should be enough. No human being at any age should be asked to display worthy motives on command. Actions come from mixed motives, in the first place, and what people consider worthy to say is by no means a sure test of worth. I recently heard of an intending theological student who declared that he wished to become a scholar in Biblical study. Unfortunately for him, the authorities of his Seminary had recently decided that what the church needed was pastors and missionaries; so that without even waiting for his purpose to mature or change, he was made to feel the impropriety of his "selfish" choice. He had missed the first trick: just think of the impropriety of calling your soul your own! At seventeen, this lesson is more cruel than a flogging. Officialdom does not always recognize how harsh a front it presents, even when outwardly smiling, because it forgets what it is to be young, inexperienced, and constitutionally honest. The upshot is that in many serious matters — of admission, of scholarship grants, of grades and honors — the advantage goes to the precocious worldling who has found out "the ropes," or the instinctive hypocrite.

Side by side with the love of interviews, the passion for fuzzy psychologizing has led to the use of tests and questionnaires for choosing and "guiding" students into and through college. The child hoping to enter college writes for a week — her autobiography, her tastes, her hopes, her fears; she is asked about her parents, her friends, her brothers and sisters. Her mother must also write. The child is so completely turned inside out that it is a wonder she can still look like a freshman. Indeed she is more like an escaped convict, because while she has been doing a Bashkirtseff on her soul, her boarding school has reported all her quirks, failings, and misdemeanors. That vase she broke pursues her to the grave and her tantrums reverberate down the corridors of time. It is curious that in the very age when criminology has learned that a fresh start calls for a new environment, with people taking for granted the reformed pirate's honesty, "modern" education has turned the freshman into an old lag. "Have you read Form A and Form B on Sally?" asks the dean of studies of a new teacher. "No." "Well, I'll get them for you, so you can size her up." Sally's only hope is that the new teacher will keep the file shut and his mind open.[4]

Meantime the dean has not only read and absorbed but remembered the whole dossier. Twice a year, on the strength of this knowledge, Sally or John will be academically reviewed, and if need be interviewed, by this same dean or his assistant. In most small places, the dean makes a point of knowing each student by name, of being accessible at all times, of being "the good old Dean" — a feat which the undergraduates value more highly than

[4] My point of view on these matters is not absolute. Parents should of course exercise judgment in giving or withholding personal information about their children: a chronic disease or peculiarity of mind should unquestionably be reported to the school authorities, and *they* should exercise judgment in making use of the knowledge.

anything else. I have heard it said that in the larger centers in the Midwest, with seven thousand new freshmen each year, a dean arranges to give each of them three minutes of heart-to-heart talk so as to establish firm relations with them before the end of the crucial year. All this is routine personnel work, which must be done in addition to settling disciplinary cases, financial problems, special programs, and the indescribable demands of parents.

It must be apparent that with such heavy duties to be discharged, the life of a conscientious administrator is not a bed of roses. It makes as much of a draft on wisdom as any other part of the teaching profession, but calls for it day in and day out, in small change. Seeing this, many teachers who would have the requisite gifts decline the offer to serve when it comes. They voluntarily give up the tripled salary and the honorable limelight, for the sake of continuing equal toil of a less distraught and impermanent character. As a composer-teacher once put it: "They wanted to make me a musical statesman, but I want to remain a musical citizen." This means that there has necessarily grown up a class of professional administrators, not members of the faculty, but academic middlemen who find university life congenial and students interesting, but who would just as readily manage a brewery or a bank for all the attachment that they feel towards learning.

This only aggravates the personnel situation in all its branches.[5] Like businessmen, the managers rely more and more on paper work, filing devices, and punched cards. Casual hearsay of an "objective" sort serves them in place of judgment — I heard one administrator refer admiringly to a candidate for a position as a

[5] To take only one instance, a director of student activities who is in no sense an educated man should not rank higher and earn more than officers of instruction who are his superiors in every other way. Yet on many campuses the uniform eminence of administration as such brings about this topsy-turvy relation.

"two-textbook man." I did not dare ask whether this great double barrel had written two books or only owned them.

Going by signs means, again, that real quality near at hand passes unnoticed or even arouses unconscious dislike. It is too "intellectual," or too independent. The constant appeal is not to ability but to "the spert of cowopperation." With such Deans or Directors, the "good fellows" on the faculty are at a premium. There is unconscious encouragement of the self-advertisers, who turn out more Progress Reports than actual work. The good teacher is the one who constantly uses his students as guinea pigs for some "study" or other. "First-semester sophomores with respect to retention of theoretical materials" sounds to such a Dean most interesting and most important. If the teacher aims at higher scholarship than this, he must write short articles at short intervals and send reprints to "the office" for good effect. Like other "material" they will be judged by physical and not intellectual weight. That is the logical outcome of the indirect measure of quality, when once the direct sense of it has been lost. Oddly enough, the fittest symbol of this loss in America today is the Ph.D.

14. *The Ph.D. Octopus*

> The dazzled reader of the list,
> the parent or student, says to
> himself, "This must be a terribly
> distinguished crowd — their titles
> shine like the stars in the firma-
> ment; Ph.D.'s, S.D.'s, and Litt.D.'s
> bespangle the page as if they
> were sprinkled over it from a
> pepper caster."
>   — WILLIAM JAMES, *The*
>   *Ph.D. Octopus*

THE PH.D. DEGREE has become the union card of the American college teacher. From the time when William James first raised his voice against the three-letter fetish to the day when A. Lawrence Lowell established the Society of Fellows at Harvard in defiance of the need for degree-hunting, the number of doctorates obtained in course has doubled and redoubled. In the last fifteen years, forty thousand Ph.D.'s were made. Between 1910 and 1940 the number of institutions granting annually more than a dozen doctorates in one subject — history — rose from four to 25, which resulted in a total increase for the same period from 98 to 718.

A young man on the educational market without a Ph.D. must endeavor to look as if he were working for one, because even Junior Colleges and State Teachers' Colleges will take nothing less in a member of their staff. At the same time, with overexpansion at the top the possession of the degree is no longer a special distinction; it is taken for granted, as is shown by the fact that one seldom speaks of the dissertation that earned it. Few administrators choosing a prospective teacher have ever been known to read the work before appointing its author; they merely want to know it exists. It takes on an average five or six years of study and one thousand dollars in fees to obtain a Ph.D. If the granting institution requires the publication of the thesis it costs the candidate an additional thousand dollars. He has then paid his initiation fee into the most expensive and least luxurious club in the world.

The meaning of all this has not changed since the turn of the century when James warned against the spreading and sucking tentacles of the octopus. In his warning article, he gives the instance of a man, trained in Harvard in philosophy, who was hired elsewhere to teach English literature provided he could at once obtain a Ph.D. Everyone concerned admitted that the demand was purely for show, purely sprung from the desire of the smaller college to have on its catalogue nothing but doctors of philosophy. This rule fulfills three purposes — it expresses snobbish feeling, it measures competitive power, and it passes on to the degree-granting institution the task of judging intellectual and scholarly aptitudes.

The doctorate of course shows nothing about teaching ability. After seeing degree holders and reading their theses, it is hard to say what the title shows. As a ritual, it is one of those unlucky importations from Europe — largely due to the influence of Daniel Coit Gilman of Johns Hopkins — that at one time gave the United States the feeling that it had academically come of age and could hold its head up with Göttingen and Oxford and the Sorbonne. Oxford defies generalities, but the continental universities, being held to greater uniformity of standards, can invest a degree with much more meaning. Even so, in France and elsewhere, a doctorate is not by itself a passport to teaching. A further examination is required which consists in the delivery of an impromptu yet formal lecture upon an assigned subject. This may be a mechanical device, but at least it fits the conditions for which it is prescribed.

In this country, one can divide doctorates into three groups —

those taken in science, those in the humanities, and those in "education." The first and last named compete in annual output, usually some five hundred in each kind every normal year. The doctorates in science constitute the most justifiable sort: they represent good sound experimental work, possibly not earthshaking, but invariably new, and instructive at least to the doer. On the contrary, doctorates in education cover such a wide range of indefinite subject matter that they have been repeatedly and deservedly ridiculed. I shall return to this sore subject in a moment. The most pressing case for consideration is that of Ph.D.'s in the humanities — that is, in the main subjects of the liberal-arts curriculum. There the situation is anarchical and the practices demoralizing.

Follow a typical instance. A young man of parts decides in college that he wants to write and teach history. His instructors encourage him and on his graduation award him a fellowship. He studies for one year, writes an essay, and is now a Master of Arts. With this degree, and after obtaining several licenses requiring complex examinations, he can if he wishes teach in the public schools. But he does not wish to; he prefers collegiate teaching. He ignores the licenses, but must go on to the Ph.D. His department renews his fellowship and he finishes his courses, but he still has the dreaded "Orals" to pass and a book to write. What next? He must choose a topic for his thesis. In many fields, however, doable topics are exhausted, or he must go abroad and spend long years scratching up materials. Time presses; both he and his department want him to do "a quick one," with sources available at home. It is probable that he will study "American opinion" on something or other — Charles Dickens or Columbus's landing. The subject does not interest him, but it must be done; the book is not needed, but it must be written; the country needs teachers and teachers must have Ph.D.'s.[1]

[1] This must not be interpreted to mean that all important subjects have been covered. But important subjects call for practised scholars, experience

Meantime the future doctor of philosophy is of an age when other young men begin to earn a living. How is he to support himself? If he is of a suitable caliber, the department in which he works will appoint him instructor, on the understanding that he will continue his graduate work. This is the first mishap. It looks like an understanding but it breeds an inevitable misunderstanding. The salary is given as a subsidy towards doctoral work, yet it must be earned by carrying on the duties of a teacher. The young man is expected to give an elementary course to two or three separate groups of students, or else he is loaded up with "third hours," [2] and all the clerical work that that entails. He probably acts as reader of examinations for an older colleague besides, and as the latest comer he very likely becomes the departmental maid-of-all-work in little things.

Being hopeful and ambitious, he wants to do everything to perfection. He prepares carefully and teaches like one possessed. In short, he means to "polish up the handle of the big front door." This is all a mistake. A real friend would take him aside and say: "Young man, you are on the wrong track. Bluff through your classes, discourage students from coming around to talk to you, neglect the office files that you keep in apple-pie order, and grade Professor Lummox's papers by counting 'eeny, meeny, miney, mo,' starting with the one on top. And use the time thus saved to bone up for your orals and to start writing your book. Stop occasionally to do a short article on a side issue of your subject; get it published and distribute it broadcast like leaflets to passers-by."

"But, why neglect my teaching? It's my chosen profession. And why injure the college, the students, and the department while rushing through an immature doctorate?"

---

of life, and years of study. The German Doctoral dissertation, for kindred reasons, has in the past half century become a seventy- or one-hundred-page essay, usually of little worth.

[2] See above.

"Because with the Ph.D. you have a value, or rather a price tag. Your articles will advertise you. With luck you may be re-appointed right here, *with tenure*. Whereas if you merely teach conscientiously, even brilliantly, you will not be reappointed and you will *not* have your Ph.D. to go out and bargain with."

This argument is as unanswerable as decapitation. Some few of the factors on which it rests are occasionally modified by cir-cumstances. For example, it is possible that the young instructor will not be fired at the end of one or two or three years, but reminded to hurry up and finish his Ph.D. preparation. This is not a better but a worse plight than the other. For as the instruc-tor takes on years and experience he comes to look upon his post as real and self-renewing. He marries, forms friendships, and develops minor influence in the college. It becomes harder and crueler to dislodge him. But the more he works at teaching, the less does "The Book" progress. Colleagues begin to feel awkward inquiring about it and the tug of war between the instructor and the Elder Statesmen continues as an undercurrent of guilty feel-ings on both sides: "You must" — "I won't."

Add to this the fact that instructors' salaries are meager, while opportunities exist to eke it out, with evening courses, summer sessions, hack work, or textbook writing, and you see why the Ph.D. gets stuck on the ways. Ph.D.'s "in progress" thus form an enormous shadow behind the mass of Ph.D.'s annually awarded; a shadow which casts a chill over too large a province of higher education.[3]

The first and worst result is that teaching suffers. Students feel neglected and are neglected; they hate and despise their "section men," who return the compliment. The second is that scholarship suffers. Books and articles written under such conditions can scarcely be called labors of love, and in many young men an

[3] Canvassing the situation in a departmental report some years ago, Carlton J. H. Hayes inquired: "Are we preparing Ph.D.'s for this life or for the life beyond the grave?"

inner block develops that prevents all future productiveness with the pen. Lastly, departments are split into Elder Statesmen and Young Whippersnappers, to the detriment of morale and good will. This deprives an institution of all the enthusiasm, freshness, and vigor which young men can give — in default of ripe wisdom — and it creates an administrative dilemma on which somebody is bound to be impaled.

At some places, the staff of instructors does not advance, retreat, or budge. Instructors aged forty-five and fifty are found treading the mill at the point where they began ("Can't promote a man who hasn't his degree"). At other places occurs a kind of sabbatical shake-up — the young men, sometime in their thirties, are swept out, after half a dozen years' service and on a year's notice. They find other posts, good, bad, or indifferent, but never forget the cruel Alma Mater that took their best years and made them start anew in mid-career. Certain administrators, thinking that the trouble was with the hierarchy of ranks — instructor, assistant professor, associate professor, professor — have abolished the grade where the greatest congestion seemed to come, the idea being to serve unmistakable notice to young men of the impermanence of their position.[4] Elsewhere, on the contrary, a new title — lecturer or associate — was created outside the regular line for able teachers who were to be neither dropped nor promoted. They are lodged in this vermiform appendix and expected to keep fresh and sweet there, while their contemporaries rise to chairs and full professorships.

All this is mere fiddling with the difficulty. I doubt whether any obvious solution exists, but it ought to be clear that playing with titles and adopting ostrichlike policies will only irritate the soreness. The real evil to uproot has not begun to be sufficiently

[4] The eight-year plan at Harvard (three yearly appointments plus a final five-year term) and a similar scheme at Yale do at least make the instructor's future plain to him. It is too soon to pass upon the general results of these new rules.

recognized: it is that the present hiring of junior officers combines and confuses two distinct aims. The first is the matter of licensing or certifying college teachers, and the question to ask is, "Does the Ph.D. degree do this?" The second is that of coping with great numbers. Eastern American universities have grown so rapidly in the last fifty years, and Western ones have undertaken such stupendous mass instruction, that there must necessarily be in each department many more beginners than can be kept for later promotion.

It is not in itself bad to put young men on probation so as to choose the best. What is bad is to wrap up the fact in the pretense of promoting scholarship. The testing period should be an admitted fact and a definite limit of time set to it. Of course, one modern habit stands in the way, which I have already mentioned in connection with committee work — I mean the dislike of plain speaking. Most of the heartburnings in the academic world come from somebody's yielding to the temptation to be nice at the wrong time. Arrangements should more often be set down in writing, and more strictly adhered to by both sides. Tell the young what to expect: they need it more than most.

This means also that while on the job, they should be told clearly what that job is and it should be seen to that the job is a manageable one. I shall show later why writing a first book and learning to teach are almost always incompatible occupations; and attempting both under a superior's eye adds to the strain. Moreover, doubt sometimes arises as to whose commands must be obeyed. In one university I know of, a beginner has to consider three separate but overlapping authorities as his boss. They compete for his time as scholar and teacher, and he is bound to dissatisfy at least one of them. On being talked over he invariably turns out to "be a disappointment," to have "belied his promise," and unless an older man with faith fights for him, he ultimately goes.

If we follow him after his dismissal — for argument's sake —

the prevailing system still beclouds his future. He leaves a first-rate institution to go to an inferior one. What is he expected to do? The new place hired him chiefly to teach and to teach more classes than he is used to. But unless he wishes to stay in that pre-sumable backwater, he must do something else — engage in re-search, write books and articles, address learned societies. So that here again he is riding two horses, cheating one more set of students, and striving to achieve what may not be within his gifts.

And this brings us back to the Ph.D. The octopus has the young teacher in its grip and does not let him go. More literally, the American university system is built on the two false premises that all teachers must add to the existing stock of knowledge by research, and that all self-respecting institutions fulfill their role only by employing productive scholars.[5] Sometimes false premises are happily neutralized by bad logic. But no such luck has be-fallen the American university. If teaching is unimportant and scholarship all-important, then it is logical to make the Ph.D. the prerequisite that it is. But in that case, parents and students must be reconciled to indifferent teaching as the rule, and men choosing the academic career must either give up hope of ad-vancement or be master-jugglers in their early years, at the cost of other goods of life — health, friendship, and contemplation.

Defenders of the system as it is often say that good teaching is inseparable from research and that the man who ceases study-ing at twenty-five is a dried-out and dull teacher ten years later. These are two statements that only seem to be the same. Of course the teacher must keep reading and thinking abreast of his time, but this does not mean that he must write and publish. The confusion hides a further absurd assumption, which is that when a man writes a scholarly book that reaches a dozen special-ists he adds immeasurably to the world's knowledge; whereas if he imparts his thought and his reading to one hundred and fifty

[5] The progressive colleges have valiantly and successfully set their faces against this belief.

students every year, he is wasting his time and leaving the world in darkness. One is tempted to ask what blinkered pedant ever launched the notion that students in coming to college secede from the human race and may therefore be safely left out when knowledge is being broadcast. A distinguished physician of my acquaintance, who attended one of our leading university colleges, told me that while there he was made to feel superfluous, a nuisance to be got rid of, an encumbrance to serious scholarship. He did not know what good advanced teaching was like until he entered medical school.

This is a touchstone for the significant difference: in medical school, the instructors devote themselves heart and soul to making other doctors; but in college, the research scholar clearly cannot hope to make everyone into a scholar like himself.[6] He should use his knowledge to help make enlightened citizens. But he considers this beneath him; so he goes through the routine of blindly scattering the facts in his field, leaving the seeds untended, and being pleased with himself notwithstanding. This he does unless he happens to be committed to teaching as an art and willing to accept the consequences — injurious to himself — of that commitment.

II

The reader may think I have forgotten the thousands of Ph.D.'s in education: surely *they* must be committed to teaching; what becomes of them? They are for the most part in the public schools as principals, superintendents, supervisors; in teachers' colleges and university Schools of Education as instructors; and in a hundred and one institutes, foundations, and bureaus as researchers digging down tirelessly to the very antipodes of educational

[6] The Institute for Advanced Study at Princeton, N. J., was founded in 1930 to enable scholars to pursue special studies with distinguished masters, free from the thought of credits and degrees. Their work lies beyond the range of the graduate school and answers the need of ultimate specialization.

theory and practice. With a few exceptions, most of these certified persons are committed not so much to teaching as to
"methods."

"Methods" is a world in itself. Methods sustain the weary and
comfort the poor in mind: for methods have all been worked
out and tested. There is a method for supervising schools and
another for being a principal. Every subject matter taught has
its special method. Even janitorial method can be learned, and
the method of teaching janitorial method also. Methods grow like
fleas on one another ad infinitum. Whenever I hear of an instructor who is an "exponent" of methods, I see him at once as
a small figure perched up to the right of a number, and I only
wonder whether that is Number One — or zero.

Any layman would consider that no one can say or do much
about "methods" in any field until that field has been mastered
by the methodologist. But that is only the layman's innocence.
By racking his wits and the dictionary, an educator can devise
methods for subjects he does not know and for subjects that have
no matter in them. Consult the textbooks: although they are
almost as large as medical and law books, they seldom do more
than pad out statistical matters of fact, such as the number of
primary schools in a given state, or the enrollments for the year
before. The medium in which these facts are awash is educators'
lingo of the sort I have quoted. Certain words recur until they
are scrubbed clean of any meaning — "fields, areas, problems,
objectives, projects, experiment, values, valuation, re-evaluation"
and, when at a loss, "society, social value, societal value, and
frames of reference." Since education as a field — I mean area —
is nothing if not scientific, re-evaluation is its highest goal. And
since it is *not* scientific in any intelligible sense . . . the reader
can draw his own inference.

Meanwhile observe the soothing effects obtainable from sheer
language. I have before me the syllabus of an education seminar
designed to teach young men and women who will be teachers

something important and advanced about their craft. I quote at random: —

In answering the questions posed in Topic I we have opened up questions broader than your own purely personal motives, important as they are. We shall now wish to deal more systematically with each subject-matter area by considering such questions as the following: —

1. What values are claimed for your major study?
2. Why teach it at all?
3. What role should it play in education and society?
4. What conflicts of opinion do you find . . . concerning such role?
5. How long has your major been a recognized field of study in high school and college and what arguments were used to help it achieve that status?

Five questions evolved from one, which was not worth asking in the first place.

Then it goes on, fuguelike, "We shall have to ask these questions specifically of each of the major areas of liberal arts study as classified below. As we consider each of these areas of knowledge, you will feel special responsibility for study and discussion within your own field, but you will also want to see what relationships you can among the various fields." I skip the rest: the whole "course" could be given in fifteen minutes of casual conversation between an older and a younger man, both interested in the same subject.

Let no one ask me when "fields" became "areas." I only know that I was present, through an error, at a secret conclave where a powerful educator revolutionized methods by proposing that "we no longer speak of subdivisions of fields as 'units' but rather as 'nuclei.'"

What is remarkable about "methods" is not that discourse about them can go on so long without substance, but that in the midst of the vacuum certain fine minds have been able to survive, to think, and to make their mark in a most useful fashion as trainers and inspirers of teachers. Whether they are happy in their invidious and Ovidian exile, I shall not undertake to say. Rather, I am struck by the fact that even the most complacent of methodologists seem from time to time to have qualms. I do not mean their perpetual and pretended "re-evaluations" of what they do. I mean their steady nudging and winking at "real life" and their endless talk about invading that undiscovered country. For instance, a new experimental project commends itself in a circular because it "aims to develop students toward effective maturity through purposeful, constructive, and intelligent living in a place where activities are real, not dramatized."

This doubtless persuades many a parent, but think of the appalling confession implicit in that short sentence. This project being an offshoot of an established training school for teachers, its novelty implies that hitherto there has been no effective maturity, no purpose, no constructiveness, no intelligence; that suspended animation has replaced "living"; and artificial activities real ones, all in a manner now repudiated as "dramatized." Since in good times new outposts of "method" are continually being planted here and there, the worth of the previous ones can be gauged by the claims made for the latest. Or rather, the whole business may be dismissed as well-meant and self-deceiving ballyhoo. The war has reduced but not stopped it. I find that a "new experiment, called the 'experience curriculum,' is being tried out on one hundred and twenty pupils in a high school near New York. Nine areas of experience have been outlined . . . Teachers will meet daily to plan projects . . . and [how could they help it?] Parents give consent." [7]

The hold which "methods" have on the public schools results from an otherwise excellent idea. Local school boards, in their regard for learning and self-improvement, offer substantial increases in salary to teachers who will spend time taking addi-

[7] *New York Times*, June 13, 1944.

tional credits towards an M.A. or Ph.D.[8] These teachers throng the now numerous teachers' colleges, and become converts and carriers of the methodological message. It is the line of least resistance: no one is personally to blame; the best motives are at work; it is a case of the evil that good men do.

If I trace it all back to the Ph.D. mania, my reason can perhaps be best understood by an analogy. Suppose that instead of having to do research, and write books, and talk jargon, all teachers, and teachers of teachers, had to paint in oils. We would certainly spur a few unwitting geniuses to rival Rembrandt, but pretty soon the standards of firm outline, strong color, and modeled form would disappear, and to permit the large numbers of normally useful but untalented people to "get through," the authorities would come to accept any daub of color on canvas, any salad dressing with oil in it, as equivalent to a painting. Oil spreads and stains easily, and in a few years every teacher would bear the marks of it.

This is roughly what has happened through the inhuman scheme of requiring degrees and scholarly competence from every teacher. It ought not to have to be said that no specialized skill implies the possession of any other, that the ability to discover new knowledge is extremely rare, and the power to put it into writing rarer still. Compared with this, the ability to teach is relatively widespread and ought to be used to the full. And this emphatically does not mean that a born teacher should be asked to theorize intelligently about his art. We know how seldom a musician or a painter can explain what he is doing; usually artists are not even capable of deriving any help from general theories, however sound. So with the teacher: his native gifts can be developed; he can be shown and cautioned and guided — by other

---

[8] My godson sends me the student magazine of his school, where I find this news item: "Our new teacher, Mr. M., was born in Omaha, studied there, then went to A.B. College to become a teacher, taking a course known as 'Education.'"

practising teachers; but he is only made into a pathetic fraud by being crammed with nuclei and made to run around in areas looking for relationships.

If, on the one hand, scholarship had been looked upon as a special form of creation, and on the other teaching had been recognized as an art, the confusion would never have occurred. By equating them both with science, we have only diluted scholarship, spoiled natural teachers, and given birth to the most cephalopod of pseudo-sciences. James was inspired when he spoke of an octopus: that describes its flabbiness, its ubiquity, and the squirting of ink which is its main reflex. When I broach the subject of the intellectual life in my last chapter, I shall make a few tentative suggestions for rescuing the many diverse gifts I now see going to waste. Meanwhile there is another ink bath in store for us, an adjunct of "methods," but which is also an integral part of teaching, namely, tests and examinations.

15. Your I.Q. or Your Life

> The final result would indicate
> that maladjustments during the
> engagement period tend to lead
> to the divorce courts after mar-
> riage. The principal result of
> these studies is the establishment
> of the tests themselves.
> — Report on the Burgess "Mar-
> riage Forecast," *Chicago
> Sun*, March 23, 1944

"Examinations make us pale" sing the boys in a translation of
an old medieval student song. The lads probably do not know
when they are well off. They hear that many colleges now run
without examinations and as youngsters emerging from twelve
years of quizzing, they cheer inwardly. What they do not know
is that once admitted to college they will undergo a "battery of
tests" — that is the accepted phrase — they will be mown down
by it, and classified accordingly. At entrance, probably, the student comes tagged with an I.Q. picked up somewhere, like vacci-
nation. The college gives him another rating by means of the
Thorndike Test, which is a rather sensible general-information and
aptitude test; and in truly sensible places the score obtained on it
is treated very casually, as an index of merely probable success in
studies. Later, in the freshman year, the battery begins its work.
Someone in the Psychology Department is studying hunger in
young North American males — so two hundred guinea pigs paying fees starve under supervision. The study shows that the majority became irritable after three days and fell on hamburgers
when released.

But the vocational experts are also at work and they administer a test of a beautiful simplicity. You check off on a printed form the things you like to do, read, see, and talk about. Answers are counted up by groups, and since the cunning designers have given the same list to five hundred successful persons in each of fifteen professions, by comparing the degree of similitude among answers, it is possible to discover whether you are more like a farmer than a real-estate man of equal eminence. Sometimes the student is allowed to see the list of notables originally taken as a "control group," and the young poet or musician finds that he has been "measured" against syndicated versifiers and tin-pan-alley composers.

Of course no validity is claimed for the test. I have yet to find a test which its maker backs heart and soul as performing what it seems to perform. The usual formula is that the results show high correlation with some other test, or with Phi Beta Kappa lists or with *Who's Who*. In other words, persons in one college are, *as a group*, very much like persons in other colleges or in the professions, or in honorary societies. But the impression given to the taker of the test is that he has been individually rated and given "scientific" advice about his vocation. Being a naïve youth, he still thinks his choice of vocation as individual a matter as his prescription for eyeglasses, and he finds no more comfort in the generality of the test result than he would in a pair of lenses ground according to an "average" prescription.

But the tests continue to rain down: they measure the depth of information pumped into him, they try to predict medical, legal, engineering aptitude, they delve into emotions, characterize social and other background, classify political "temperament," in short, attempt to decant personality into small bottles. I recall visiting a friend shortly after he was made Dean of a respectable country college. He showed me "the plant" and explained the system. In his office, I looked at files and records, and noticed that on the back of the card bearing each student's name, address, and marks, there were stamped a number of symbols, like this: —

CON	COO	OPT	FAM	SEX	WOR	NER	PHY
40	20	31	22	60	55	62	31

"Is it fair for me to ask what this means?" I inquired. My friend laughed. "I can't answer you. It's a relic from my predecessor. He received a grant of money from a foundation if he would allow the student body to be tested, for the better guidance of deans. The thing was done by a visiting psychologist. Now he's gone and nobody seems to know how to interpret the records." The secret was as tantalizing as the cipher in Poe's *Gold Bug*, but all we could "deduce" was that COO and SEX seemed to diverge very strangely in amount.

Doubtless this test was a variant of the original free-association test, by which when the tester says "Black" and you say "White" — or something else — the time and the nature of the response become of diagnostic value. Free association is also stimulated by ink blots, passages of fiction, and pictures. One "research" organization administers this and other tests to adults who feel they are miscast in their present job and want advice. They are not given precise directions, but are told that they are "subjective" or "objective" and that certain professions go best with each type. The distinction really comes down to the famous — and less pretentious — one made by Gelett Burgess between Bromides and Sulphites.[1] But this would-be human engineering (a phrase in actual use) goes on to measure separate aptitudes; it finds a type which it calls the Too-Many-Aptitude Person; and in testing its own tests, it takes alarm at any sign of high correlation between one aptitude and another, for that must imply a single aptitude branching into a seeming difference.

[1] *Are You a Bromide? or, The Sulphitic Theory*. New York, 1906. "The Bromide does his thinking by syndicate. He follows the main-traveled roads, he goes with the crowd. In a word, they all think and talk alike — one may predicate their opinion upon any given subject. They follow custom and costume, they obey the Law of Averages." (Pages 17–18.)

I restate these beliefs in some detail because they bear on the school situation and on our intellectual life at large. Apparently since "science" has taken over testing, no one any longer believes in Intelligence. The reason seems to be that the first intelligence tests proved useless; so refuge has to be taken in the weasel idea of aptitudes. The difference between the two is that an aptitude is a single quality that stands behind special skill, whereas Intelligence must necessarily be regarded as a central powerhouse that sends out current into any performance. The very nature of intelligence is adaptability, and it is this general quality which modern schools, modern tests, and modern life systematically neglect in favor of robot "aptitudes."

The excuse for doing so is slight but real. In the first place, an industrial world thinks it wants only a pinch of intelligence to season a great plateful of mechanical aptitudes.[2] In the second place, though intelligence is and always will exist as a general power, it appears nowhere in full perfection. The man who can solve differential equations probably hits his thumb with the hammer at every stroke. Physical and emotional barriers keep intellect from shining like a bright light in all directions. Hence psychologists, noting the dark bands of inetrference, imagine separate entities which they name aptitudes. They ought perhaps to remember how widely "gifted" most children are, both physically and mentally, and although observers may later find versatility reduced, they should still assume a center of unspecialized mental force.

Teachers should not only assume it but work on it, for it

[2] It should perhaps be said that in certain exceptional cases, usually cases of abnormality, the tests show that a watchful eye should be kept on a particular student. But a college that maintains a good counseling system and teaches freshmen in small classes would get the same information from its staff without the test. Minnesota tried out the tests on a really heroic scale and concluded that their interpretation for use required men of great insight giving their whole time to the task — which is what the tests were supposed to make unnecessary.

atrophies if unused. Darwin has told us how his taste for poetry passed away as he specialized, and everyone can note in himself the loss of comparable powers. We may be reconciled to it as a sacrifice for greater ends, but we must not forget that they are *powers*, no less than sources of pleasure. Every college should therefore be dedicated to Intellect — not in the sense of pedantry, or verbalism, or highbrow superiority, but in the sense of Mind, free and restless in its desire to experience, comprehend, and use reality.

If that is desirable, then tests of the kind I have described should go. They are an insult to Intelligence, except when played with as parlor games. And something else must go at the same time; I mean the *form* of such tests. Every man of education ought to take a solemn vow that he will never "check" anything on a printed list. Students should not be asked to pass so-called objective examinations, which are the kind composed of mimeographed questions to be marked Yes or No, or to be solved by matching the right name with a definition.

I have kept track for some ten years of the effect of such tests upon the upper half of each class. The best men go down one grade and the next best go up. It is not hard to see why. The second-rate do well in school and in life because of their ability to grasp what is accepted and conventional, the "ropes" of the subject. They become pillars of society and I have no quarrel with them. But first-rate men are rarer and equally indispensable. They see into situations quickly, and with the fresh, clear eye of Intelligence, and they must be encouraged to continue. To them, a ready-made question is an obstacle. It paralyzes thought by cutting off all connections but one. Or else it sets them thinking and doubting whether *in that form* any of the possible answers really fits. Their minds have finer adjustments, more imagination, which the test deliberately penalizes as encumbrances.[3]

[3] On looking over a regular section of the Thorndike Test, I find this type of question: "Below are blank spaces marked with the initial letter *h*.

This basic difficulty occurs no matter how carefully the questions are drafted and how extensive their coverage. I sat and worked on a committee that prepared objective questions in history for the so-called Graduate Record Examination, which is now widely used to test college seniors' readiness for graduate work. In committee, it was revealing to see how a question that seemed "foolproof" and "obvious" to two or three men, thoroughly trained in their field, struck others of the same caliber as "ambiguous" or "misleading." Add modifiers and you make the question so unwieldy that it can hardly be grasped at one reading; simplify and you reduce it to bare common fact. Neither extreme, moreover, brings anything *out* of the student's mind; yet the power to relate, to *think up*, to see into, is what distinguishes the first rank from the second in all walks of life. The results of the Graduate examination no doubt correlate very satisfactorily with other indices, but they scarcely give data for the most needful kind of diagnosis. Nor have they ever been tried on the masters of the profession, which would be the test of tests, provided running comments were allowed. When one courageous man proposed just this at an institution that thrives on endless testing, the idea was dismissed as a joke in poor taste. One can understand why some satirist, disbelieving in the integrity of teachers, defined the type as "a kind of moral mermaid."

In some progressive schools all tests have been abolished. This might look like a solution, were it not that examinations are a necessary and important part of instruction. In saying this I am not arguing from the practical need to give students marks. I refer to the student's need to learn how to jump hurdles. When I say this to a class that has just groaned and stamped its feet at the

---

Opposite are ordinary words like *leather*. Write in the blank spaces the name of something made of leather and beginning with *h*, such as *harness*." My eye goes to the third word, which is *water* and I am stuck: I can think of *hydraulic*, *hot tea*, and even "*hice*," but of no proper answer. Since the test is against time, the mental gears are very likely to jam for good.

announcement of a test, there usually arises a spokesman of the Shattered Nerve brigade. He offers to tell me all I want to know, if only it can be done orally and not on paper. I accept and usually find that my bodily presence does not help him organize his knowledge, whatever may be the effect on his nerve. The fact is that the examination-shy are like fence-shy horses: they have been trained badly or not at all.

Examinations are not things that happen in school. They are a recurring feature of life, whether in the form of decisive interviews to pass, of important letters to write, or life-and-death diagnoses to make, or meetings to address, or girls to propose to. In most of these crises, you cannot bring your notes with you and must not leave your wits behind. The habit of passing examinations is therefore one to acquire early and to keep exercising even when there is a possibility of getting around it.

In the lower schools, one has, or used to have, the excellent practice of daily recitation. The pupil stands up and speaks before the class. Excess of it is dull, but used in moderation it is the proper start of a training which should end with frequent oral examinations and public speaking in college.[4] Is it not evident that every doctor, lawyer, teacher, engineer, architect, business executive, should be able to think on his feet and talk about his subject? I should except only dentists, whose crowning merit is golden silence.

Written examinations should produce brief impromptu essays on questions fairly fully outlined by the examiner. At the end of

[4] Much might be written on the status of public speaking in our colleges, some of which maintain elaborate courses for teaching the subject in a thoroughly educational fashion. Yet it seems to appeal to but few students, doubtless because of old unhappy associations with debating and oratorical contests. Two separate things seem to be needed: one, a compulsory course, carrying no academic credit, for students with bad voices and vulgar speech habits. Girls especially should be forced to lower pitch, loosen the throat, and untwist their lips, so that a roomful of them should no longer sound like an aviary on fire. Second, an elective course for students whose future profession requires the ability to speak coherently and pleasantly.

a course, examination questions might well be taken from a list previously handed to the student. The list resumes the whole course and the choice of two or three questions from it removes the hazard of grading answers which the student avers he "just didn't happen to remember." If possible the written examination should be short — two hours at the most — and the questions should fill it more than full; the aim being to test the student's knack of outlining essentials, subordinating detail, and keeping a sense of proportion. Minds so drilled will be less likely later on to tell long pointless stories, but such a training will take place only if the examiner makes clear what he expects and why.

Four written tests a year should be enough if supplemented with orals every time some natural sequence of subjects is completed. At present, most colleges consider the end of a semester to be the closing of an era in the student's development.[5] He is through with that. The past is sacrosanct and no one inquires into it. Very occasionally there is imposed a cumulative "exit" examination at the end of the four years, a useful device, but an unfair one if the student has never met an oral test before, a foolish one if he must neglect his last months' work in order to cram, an inadequate one if it is confined to his major subject. College subjects intercommunicate at many points and should be tested orally by a group of well-selected examiners. This last is important, because much of the candidate's nervousness comes usually from the questioner's own shilly-shallying; and also because it is possible to quiz a person for an hour (too long by half for a college student) without eliciting any very conclusive information.

Yet there is the necessity of concluding by giving marks. These used to be numbers, on the basis of ten or a hundred. More generally now, they are letter-grades, A, B, C, and F, ornamented

[5] Harvard has a well-worked-out system of departmental and divisional examinations, both oral and written, which is applied in the student's third and fourth years.

with plus and minus signs to signify intermediate levels. I need not point out — or rather, current abuses compel me to point out — that a marking system should be as far as possible uniform. Marks are a convention, a language agreed upon and therefore to be respected. Differences of judgment are inevitable but they must not be affectations, as when a teacher announces that *for him*, B+ is the highest grade. How would he like his creditors to say that for *them*, a five-dollar bill is worth only four? It is absurd to say that marks are unimportant and that real students should disregard them. Cruel nonsense! If marks are important enough to make the Dean expel a man from college, they are important, very important, to the man running that risk — not to mention their linkage with Phi Beta Kappa, honors, scholarships, and even with the silly harangue of the man who set a ceiling at B+. I put in the same class the markers who decide ahead of time how many A's, B's, and C's they will give, regardless of the quality of the men before them.[6]

As might be expected, the progressive schools will have nothing to do with marks. Most of them repudiate examinations. The teacher being a daily observer of his relatively few students is supposed to know how well they are doing, and anyhow, not to judge them with one another, but each in relation to the fulfillment of initial talents. He is said to measure "growth." What he knows, he is asked to consign to elaborate reports written in his own words. This sounds plausible but it is in reality quite mad. For there are only two possibilities: either the teacher writes "Satisfactory," "Good steady work," "Excellent performance" — which is a simple evasion of the letter-grade system; or else he turns into an amateur novelist. He writes, that is, a character

[6] This is statistics misunderstood; in France, logic misunderstood works the same kind of injustice. If five men are tied for a "First" in mathematics, the next man, with a score one point less than the top, gets a "Sixth" and since ratings matter tremendously, he is penalized out of proportion to his ignorance.

sketch of John or Nellie. And in this sketch he struggles with shadows; he explains the inexplicable. The student's "growth" has been retarded by this emotion and pushed forward by that. Her work shows too theoretical an interest, or relies too much on immediate perceptions; it is out of focus. . . . With what? For whom? How do you know? The teacher has really lost his footing by abandoning the idea of a common standard. He may write half a page of vague and accidentally true description, but how is the student to fit it in with another teacher's half page? Ordinarily, the day after reports are sent out, every office hour is taken up by interpreting their language to the students — and it winds up with "You're doing all right" or "You'd better work a little harder."

Supplementing this fictional effort, there is filed also a printed form asking the teacher for particular answers about the student's work. This is to enable the progressive school to hold intelligible converse about its pupils with institutions distrustful of free-hand portraits. The printed form calls for comparisons with other students and with standards in force elsewhere. The answers are given by ticking off "Below average," "Average," "Good," "Superior," and so on. But some forms are worse than others. I have one at hand, issued by an art school, which consists of ten sheets of different colors, all asking such questions as these bearing on the student's Taste: —

Does its character arise from aptitude or need or focus of consciousness based on experience?
Is it constant or fluctuating?
How is it related to contemporary social configuration of accepted taste?

Needless to add, the responsible progressive colleges have never gone so far as this, but "reports" are still one of their weak points. They do not say what students, parents, other colleges, want to know; the students contribute nothing to them in the form of work written under standard conditions; and it is not a rare occurrence for the faculty to suspend classes for a week so that each instructor may compose in the sweat of his face a series of twenty or thirty "profiles" which have not the merit of being either scandalous or true.

The facts support a conclusion, with a moral. The conclusion is that unless we recognize Intelligence as the general quality I tried to define, we shall all bog down in a morass of ill-defined virtues, aptitudes, and accomplishments. The only yardstick fit to measure an Intelligence with is another Intelligence. Written and oral work supply a basis for making that judgment common to all those who want or need to be rated. If it is argued that this is not "objective" or "scientific," I reply that objectivity applies, as its name suggests, to objects; and that science cannot help us classify the things we care about when we enter the realm of mind. When it attempts classification, it achieves something other than it intended. And in any case, science is not to be invoked merely by using words like "focus" and "configuration." Letter or number grades do not yield perfect justice, it is true, but neither do they put fantastic, bombinating ideas into people's heads. Wherefore the moral is: half a loaf . . .

16. The Human Boy

Oh running stream of sparkling
joy
To be a soaring human boy!
— THE REVEREND MR. CHAD-
BAND, in *Bleak House*

ALL BOYS are human, even when there is reason to suspect the contrary. I mean that they are a fair sampling of humanity, with the right proportion of cheats, liars, dolts, heroes, and geniuses. A teacher finds it important to remember this fact, for two reasons. One is that by common usage we say "human" when we mean only the agreeable traits of man, with a sprinkling of not-too-disagreeable faults. This makes us unjust to boys who are not sufficiently boyish. The other is that schools always try to run like a model republic in which virtue serves as air to breathe, cement to hold the fabric together, and whitewash to cover all blemishes.

Having only passed through and never taught in the lower schools, I am not fit to judge whether that virtuous atmosphere is valuable or only unavoidable. I can see that we have taken a great step forward since the days of Thwackum, "whose meditations were full of birch," and the older times of the rowdy medieval university. We have substituted moral suasion and a code of conduct for flogging and fisticuffs. This is especially to the credit of American teaching, for in England one still hears of canings, and on the continent there are occasional outbreaks of "disciplinary" sadism.[1]

But I wonder if we do not carry too far the pretense embodied

[1] See G. B. Shaw's *Sham Education* in his *Collected Works*.

in the song about school days and Golden Rule days. There are penetrating remarks on the point in the amusing little book that Mr. Chanler Chapman published a few years ago under the title *The Wrong Attitude*. The title of course refers to the thing that was the matter with him when at school, but he shows that some of the wrongness was due to impossible expectations — to wrong attitudes, that is, among his teachers.[2]

Certain it is that in college, all moral hokum should cease. The institution should of course mete out justice as fairly as it can. I do not advocate turning college into a replica of the catch-as-catch-can business world, which would be as false and mischievous as the "Experience Curriculum" laid out in nine "areas." But the ideal of ethical conduct should go with a recognition of what boys and girls and men and women do actually feel. It is absurd for a teacher to make believe, for example, that students are in college solely to pass courses, and that they are moved exclusively by zest for learning. Nothing tends to create a wider chasm between person and person, between subject matter and life, than the teacher's blindness to the common impulses of students and the suppression of his own towards them. For most of the time that blindness is deliberate; it is put on as the Right Attitude, and since it is false, it breeds falseness. Instead of seeing that the freshman who has not handed in his paper when it was due was prevented by Saturday's football game or dance, and that this is both intelligible and healthy, the instructor forces the boy to seek more elevated excuses, and makes him, in short, a liar or a prig. Again, by remarks casual or considered, teachers will suggest that they are "above" normal feelings and failings — above political bias, interest in prize fighting, desire for pretty clothes, yearning

---

[2] "More bilge is talked and written," says Mr. Chapman, "about this character-building side of school life than any other . . . most of the character building is done by the boys themselves. . . . Wise masters know this and content themselves with giving their lessons in classrooms . . . and merely conducting themselves like honest, sentient adults, if they are lucky enough to be those rare creatures." (Page 47.)

for praise, or attraction by the other sex: a faculty recruited solely from wooden Indians.

This kind of impression is of course much more likely to be conveyed if the staff only lectures at stated times and restricts office hours to academic business. For in a tutorial or discussion group the teacher would have to be very much on guard to keep his or her personality inaccessible. If the college has a staff of intelligent and experienced teachers, as many of them as may be should act as student advisers, and in that capacity they must naturally become approachable or lose all opportunities to give guidance.

But in all these freer contacts there is danger as well as opportunity. The normal American student has a strong urge to make friends with his teacher, and the teacher a strong one to seek popularity by becoming even more familiar and easygoing than friendship demands. Some boys choose a country college precisely because they think the faculty can be trapped, like big game, in its domestic haunts. Indeed in certain places it is stipulated in the terms of appointment that the faculty member shall be available to students at all reasonable hours. This is most unreasonable; it is bad for the faculty, and it amounts to a misunderstanding of what boys actually need.

Let me say bluntly, as I do not hesitate to do when my students broach the subject, that friendship between an instructor and a student is impossible. This does not mean that the two should remain strangers; there can exist cordial, easy relations, tinged perhaps with a certain kind of affection; but friendship, not. For friendship has strict prerequisites, among them, freedom of choice and equality of status. Neither of these can exist in the teacher-student relation. The absence of equality may horrify the sentimental but it is a fact nevertheless. Consider only a few of the things a teacher must do — he must judge work done, decide passing or failing, order tasks, reprove mistakes, discipline conduct, and *deal impartially with all similar cases*. These, I submit, are not the acts of a friend, even if — as equality would demand — the student were allowed reciprocal privileges.

I shall go further and say that it is not good for a teacher to associate steadily with students. Real reciprocity is here again out of the question; differences of age, temperament, purpose and background, are so many hidden reefs over which even conversation founders. This does not mean that it is not delightful once in a while to accept a dinner invitation from a group of students who are friends among themselves, or to join "the gang" in a sandwich and glass of beer after a seminar. And the talk over the beer need not be in the least stiff or scholastic. Simple manners go farthest, provided they are genuine, and they best protect the very delicate adjustment between student and teacher on which the latter's efficacy depends.

Even in the most promising of instances, which are few and far between, students are interesting only as students — I would say "as cases," were it not that medical usage has led the laity to attach to the word a false notion of detachment and pure science. This is not so: the "case" is defined as the state of the patient. Hence it is an absorbing, ever-changing human problem and not merely a mechanical puzzle. Depending on circumstance, the problem takes in more or less of the patient's social background, more or less of his unique personality, and this excludes only what does not bear on improving him. The same is true in teaching — and the comparison, by the way, explains why it is equally bad to teach and to doctor in the bosom of the family. Too many irrelevant feelings and incompatible relations enter in. To be sure, some persons are less aware of these crisscrossings than others, else one would not see so many love affairs developing between men teachers and their women students, but in spite of the success and frequency of these involvements, I cannot look upon them as belonging to the ideal relation of teacher and taught. Not to mention that it is bad for love-making to combine it with a desire to improve and be improved.

For improvement in some form is surely the goal of associating young minds with trained ones in what the Navy Department calls "regular contact hours." Self-improvement is certainly the motive for the student's hunting down of his instructor. The boy wants to draw the older man out on subjects that necessarily beset youth at college — politics, sex, career, family. Or he wants a sympathetic listener for his own peculiar story; he wants good advice from someone other than a parent or a friend. The family physician sometimes serves, but more rarely than before the days of busy specialization; and the father confessor is available to only a few. So the teacher hears it all — the quarrels with contemporaries, the disappointments and injustices in campus affairs, the girls that charm but leave insatiate, and most persistently, the vision of the good life clearly seen but lying inaccessible on a pathless height.

There is no use pretending that all this does not go straight to one's heart. If ever another's life palpitates visibly before one's eyes, it is at this time, when the consciousness of what living means has just dawned and no thick shell has yet grown over it to protect or suppress it. The spectacle is in itself so touching, its details often so moving, that sentimentalists and cynics among adults take advantage of it to indulge their vices of mind. The sentimentalist eggs on the flow of feeling to wallow in it helplessly; the cynic — equally upset — dismisses the manifestation as "a stage" and the trouble as "adolescent."

Meanwhile, the "stage" is a reality and adolescence remains one of the four seasons of life. It is the season of storms and its shipwrecks are genuine calamities. Unless the causes are foreseen and dealt with, both firmly and tenderly, the disasters are wept over in vain, too late. It is at college, among boys who are barely young men, that the first winnowing by the unseen hand occurs. It is at this time that they feel ignorance and the desire to know, despair and the desire to act — all with a vividness and an urgency unbelievably powerful and explosive. It is just because these forces are as yet raw and unchanneled that young men can be taught; and for the same reason, that with bad luck or bad handling the same forces destroy from within: boys take to drink, commit suicide and murder, plot wild schemes to recoup money or other losses, burn inwardly with shame, injustice, or contempt, stare dishonor in the face, or feverishly nurse mad, hopeless, and sometimes meaningless ambitions.

Not unnaturally, the teacher who has these glimpses of the demonic in the confidences that are brought to him may be unnerved. Often he is the youngest man on the staff. He inspires trust by the recentness of his student days and the fact that he has crossed the bar and been stamped with the professional seal of guarantee. Yet inexperienced himself, how is he to deal with so many chaotic revelations? What advice can he give, with what assurance, and how far can he engage his responsibility? Perhaps he should have thought of that before becoming a teacher. As every mariner must expect that his first voyage as captain will be signalized by a typhoon, so with a teacher *in loco parentis*. That is the normal risk. Besides, he can apply to older friends, though taking care to maintain professional secrecy; and he can regain poise by reminding himself of certain truths. In the first place, he cannot act for another, or even feel. He can only think, and convey calm and comfort. What any boy needs most to be told is that he is not alone in his distress; that cases similar to his are known to history, and that the victims have lived to tell the tale. You would suppose that college men would help one another by just this kind of talk. But they do not. Boys may live and play together and yet remain like a handful of small shot in a bowl — hard, round, impenetrable — and, if shot could feel, lonely. Since in real trouble the family is "no use," the teacher is the only man who can be counted on to reassert that we are members one of another; and since this belief depends on a subtle sympathy which cannot be commanded, it is best to let college men freely follow their affinities and take as advisers men they trust.

For the same reason, the teacher should not turn over a hard case to the Dean of Men or the official psychiatrist until it is clearly beyond him and pathological in degree. Until then, he can do a great deal with very little outward show of activity, simply by being what he is and where he is. It is astonishing how much the teacher learns unconsciously from instructing a student, which the psychiatrist may find out only after repeated interviews, and then always in a context of ministration to mental ills. The great virtue of the teacher is that he is *not* a psychiatrist, does *not* want to find out anything, and though aiming at general improvement, is *not* bent on reforming, curing, or "adjusting." He is only trying to get his subject matter taught, and he takes up personal trouble as an accident that happens to interfere with the main course of the student life.

This ultimate fact, too often forgotten by Progressive Education, suggests a second rule of thumb, which is that all dealings with those taught should to a certain degree be contradictory — by no means all kindness. The customer is always right, perhaps, but not so the student. In matters wholly scholastic, reproof and encouragement must be administered together. "This is the worst paper I have read in a long time, Mr. Scott, it is unbelievably bad; it's inaccurate and slovenly. But tell me what was the matter? Your previous work was rather good. One or two phrases in this very paper show me what you could do. Did the readings prove too much for you — or was it the Junior Prom?"

It seems elementary that one cannot require a performance from a man while denying to his face that he has the power to do it. This is true at least of mental effort, so I am not taken with the football-coach method of stinging rebukes that are supposed to arouse disproof in the form of heroic deeds. At the end of a thoughtful life, William James believed he had found what philosophers most wanted: it was praise. And young men, who are not philosophers, want the same thing or the opportunity to earn it. Setting them tasks they can do, or a little beyond what they can do, is not enough. They must be persuaded that they can leap the fence; and to persuade without coddling, all that is usually necessary is to have the creature recognize that it has legs to jump with, namely, the means already acquired to be used for the new effort.

If as so often happens, the academic failure is due to some non-academic cause, the same technique of blowing hot and cold simultaneously must be tried. The last thing desired by the youth who goes to his teacher in trouble, and often in self-pity, is to have his mentor weep with him. After he has been told that his case is not unique, he wants to hear not an echo of his fears, but the clipped voice of duty. He wants to know what elements in his own make-up he can use to build a defense against the enemy. Nothing in fact is more enheartening to a student than to find his teacher uncompromisingly opposed to some trait in that student's character, or to some desire he has just expressed.

Since choice of conduct is often a choice between two kinds of person, either of which the chooser will become by the proposed action, the youth wants to hear a description of what he will be if he does the one thing or the other. Nor does he want any tampering with the scale of worldly estimates. The boy who supports himself by delivering milk at 5 A.M., or by acting as night chauffeur to a detective, really prefers to be told that milk-fed babes and women taken in adultery are not substitutes for mathematics. The "personal problem" must never degenerate into an honorific distinction, or else the greatest source of personal strength is neglected in favor of temporary help. Temporary help must remain in the practical realm: money must be found, or the schedule lightened, or more manageable employment secured. But the greater issues must not be confused, at the risk of debasing character, particularly when the question is one of wisdom on which the teacher is asked his opinion. In giving it, the teacher does not require heroism, which would be absurd, but he tells the truth, refusing to give pretty names to ugly things.

This is clear enough when the trouble simply pits education against lack of money. But the same principle holds throughout, though gradually more difficult to apply. The blind boys tend to think their achievement so remarkable that they should earn Phi Beta Kappa with B's when others need A's. The crippled, the one-lunged, the foreign-born with imperfect knowledge of English, must similarly be kept from warping, from indemnifying themselves at the expense of the very currency of praise or honor which they seek. It may be hard for a young teacher to believe, but the claims of humanity and of subject matter are almost always identical. Respect for the human being in front of you, and self-respect on his part, both come out of a joint regard for the subject that brings you together. Partiality and pity are fatal, either for treating the immediate trouble or for the future relations between teacher and pupil. Here again, the bending of the rules must only affect practical details — an extension of time, a special examination, extra hours of tutoring missed — anything of this kind, and nothing that damages the prize worked for. And of course, the meaning of this hard leniency must be pointed out as a lesson in itself.

It follows that in really catastrophic cases it is far better to suspend scholastic work than to tamper with it. I have told boys who said they were so desperately in love as to be able to think of nothing else, that they should cut classes and take off six weeks as a burnt offering to Eros, rather than parade their obsession to no purpose. "Call it spirit fever and we'll see what can be done afterwards to make up for lost time." They usually returned in three weeks to write essays that can only be called "dynamic."

Sometimes, on the contrary, the continuity of work is the best help. The tragic situation of the boy whose parent is a confirmed alcoholic must be all talked out in three or four sessions during which some order is brought into the chaos of emotions. Then a moratorium is declared on discussions and a special task set — possibly the reading of fiction or philosophy or even classical psychology. There is only one promise to exact, which is, "Keep me posted and don't do anything rash before seeing me: I shan't argue against it, I only want to be informed." The particular case I am thinking of took two years to work itself out, in the midst of complications which written down would make a very implausible tale; but they were worked out by the sufferer himself. The help required only a listener who knew how to put questions so that the narrator could not deceive himself, and who occasionally pointed out the obvious in matters of fact, feeling, or human relations.

Platitudes? Yes, it is only the platitudes that nobody will believe, and boys have heard so many irrelevant ones from infancy that they are the hardest things to make credible. This is particularly true when the boy's own parents are in question. The typical situation is that Richard wants to take more courses in Fine Arts, whereas Dad insists on Elementary Accounting or Business Law. *Ipso facto*, Dad is a man of narrow outlook and stunted feeling, whom Richard loves dearly but would prefer utterly unlike his present self. Depending on the facts, one must strive to change Richard's ideas either about his father or about himself; sometimes about both. With their native perfectionism, reinforced by too virtuous schools, young men do not readily see that human characters are like pudding stone and not ever made up of choice features only. So Dad's "narrow outlook" must be shown as closely linked with his business ability which sent Richard to an expensive college, provided him with good clothes and a good time, and which is merely trying to perpetuate itself by suggesting "practical" courses.

Such courses may in fact be out of place, and if Dad's conversion is to be made by remote control, intelligent and intelligible arguments must be supplied to Richard. And first he must be made to face his own limitations and obligations in as manly a manner as possible. His illusions about the life of leisure of the artist or the teacher must be dispelled, and some vein of real ambition discovered, whether marketable or not.

Most difficult of all is the attempt to convey a just measuring stick for the relative values of money on the one hand and intangible goods on the other. "Should I go on with my music and turn down Uncle Jonathan's offer to put me through Law School?" Or again: "I'm engaged since Tuesday: should we get married right after graduation or wait four or five years until I've made my way?" The questions are impossible enough to be comic and one would burst out laughing if it were not for the grave young look that accompanies them and all that one can guess at unseen — the mother and father, the girl hugging an engagement ring, and another pair of anxious parents not knowing whether to be pleased or sorry. Meanwhile the Law and the Muse look on, unconcerned which of them will receive the new recruit. This is the cool touch of common life and it is no time for any urging or pushing down either of the branching roads. The teacher can only make sure that the signs are read aright and add a brief blessing.

II

Nor is advice or "education" possible about another subject uppermost in the minds of college youth — the subject of sex. Nowadays freedom to discuss it has been won, but it has hardly been instructively used. Perhaps there is no way in which such instruction can be given. We hear much about what parents should do in this regard but in reality they can do little or nothing after the first burst of the child's curiosity concerning the newborn baby. Adolescence is difficult enough as it is without stirring up needlessly complicated emotions, and even later, the parent is the last person to deal with the difficulty: remember Hamlet at thirty. As for schools, I do not know what generalization, if any, might be made about the private preparatory and public institutions. What is clear is that the college courses in Hygiene are quite useless.

For one thing, they are always on the margin of the program, taught usually by "Gym" instructors, and too often by means of lectures in large auditoriums. Now it is a fact of nature that you cannot talk about sexual matters to five hundred undergraduates at a time. You can entertain them in this way and they will assist — too readily — in turning the business into a farce; but they will go away just as ignorant and bedeviled as before.

Some of the causes for this failure to teach what is ostensibly being taught are beyond the school's purview: they are rooted in social feelings and conventions as yet unshaken by any liberalizing influences. We see the effects in the delinquency and other grave mishaps that overtake youth in wartime.[8] It is not even an abstract and outside "society" that is to blame; the young themselves find their hearts and minds difficult to steer in harness through the years of approaching manhood. Many of them rush into early marriage as an easy solution to a problem they think obsessing but not complex, and this in turn leads to more harassment ten years later — at worst incompatibility and divorce, at best children and low incomes.

It is plain that in recollecting the experiences of many of my students I am only drawing attention to a real puzzle, not pretending to have made the least step toward a generally applicable solution. Certain static truths nevertheless emerge. One is that undergraduates want to talk about sex among themselves in the regular midnight talk fests known as "bull sessions," and with their teachers in tête-à-tête. The latter conversations have some view of verifying, of sifting the data acquired in the former. For

[8] It is small comfort to recall that the post-Napoleonic era saw a precisely similar wave of adolescent violence, delinquency, and morbidity.

this laudable purpose, among others, many college houses and dormitories maintain resident counselors, preferably younger men. It is a good plan also to make available an open shelf of books treating of the relevant subjects. A conversation with the counselor is much easier for the student if he can relate his inquiries to something he has read. The talk remains sufficiently casual, "scientific," and can remove a great many misapprehensions — which show, by the way, that the little-boy sophistication communicated behind the barn is more fantastic than harmful, and usually so suspect to its possessor that he dare make no use of it.

The great difficulty occurs right there, after half-knowledge has been corrected and modern science has said her last word in Greek terms supplemented with truly horrifying diagrams. The student now wants positive advice, wants inspiration and encouragement, indeed, a full backing for the spirit of adventure which is his birthright. He gets a shock on finding that his mentor leaves him the whole of the responsibility and contents himself with repeating cautions now irritatingly familiar through book and precept.

The youth is in fact lucky if he has been taken by the hand as far as this. In the present state of public ambiguity, and with the overhanging sense of guilt that most undergraduates retain in spite of enlightenment, the teacher can do no more. He ought not, even in a better state of affairs, to have to do more. But to his distress he often finds that the scientific knowledge he has given, though useful in its place, has only added another dead load on the student's psyche. He discovers for example that the same venturesome youth who desired aid and relief from personal responsibility is shocked in class at reading Rabelais and Rousseau. The young man will accept neither plain recognition of sexual feelings nor joy and jollity about them. Rather, he seems to want surcease from desire at no expense of human emotion; or again, he tries to invest his instincts with some sort of grave moral beauty — in the one case, desensitization; in the other, protective hokum.

It might seem as if what happened next were no concern of the teacher's or the school's. Unfortunately, the student is not a collection of separate functions, but a live man, acted on through all his senses, and modified by the events of his physical body as well as of his intangible mind. The college, however helpless, can no more overlook the resulting quality of character than the public can be indifferent to its consequences in action. But the true way is yet to find.

III

"What people want, you see, is excitement." The late President Lowell was talking to me about education, not long before his death, as we were watching a party of young boys and girls playing Christmas games. The more one thinks about teaching, the more his conclusion takes on the character of a first principle. It illuminates not only the topic I have just discussed but the reason for giving what I called dramatic form to the communication of knowledge. More than that, it serves to explain a good many things too often dismissed as "college-boy stuff" — as if any permanent manifestation of young manhood could be dismissed. If one looks at what goes on in college halls besides classes, it is clear that what is wanted is an outlet for the gregarious, the political, and the would-be-adult instincts of youth.[4] This the American college provides better than any other institution in the world, with the possible exception of Oxford and Cambridge, and it is a merit, not a fault.

I refer, of course, to the elaborate organization of extracurricular

[4] If I interpret it correctly, I disagree with a statement in an excellent *Harvard Report on the Training of Secondary School Teachers*, 1942, p. 68. "Whatever a trained mind may be," says the report, "it is certainly not a mind that demands of the world a constant opportunity for emotional outlets." The word "constant" is fairly absolute and yet I think this denial of a demand which is in fact *constantly* being made, and by the best minds, is psychologically unsound and politically dangerous.

activities. And most important is athletics. When history students of mine begin to reflect about the revolutions in nineteenth-century Europe, they often ask me why the men in universities were always rushing to the barricades. One answer is that they did not play football. Likewise, the German students carved one another's faces with swords partly because there were no track meets and wrestling teams. We can verify this from our own past by noting the steady decline of student rowdyism ever since the time when intercollegiate athletics were organized. One university president — not Mr. Lowell — once boasted in my presence that in his day, men at his college would relieve the tedium of studies by blocking traffic on the main street, mobbing a horsecar and overturning it in its own tracks. The blood of the younger generation seemed to him pale and devitalized, for all that remained of the tradition was the midnight howling party at examination time, punctuated with streamers of toilet paper flung from campus windows. Again the discrepancy can be accounted for by sports and related activities.

The gain seems to me evident. No modern town could endure the traffic pranks of former days. And yet the "spirit of youth on the city streets" could no more be permanently bottled up now than it was then. Accordingly, I do not share the common view that athletics as such is the curse of the American university. It is better than the dueling mania, the organized drunkenness, and the other social or political substitutes current abroad, just as it is better than the hazing and vandalism that were normal over here until thirty years ago.

It is true that many of our modern students are football mad; that too much time is spent in support of public contests for the benefit of outsiders; and that corrupt academic practices often result from our chosen form of excitement. Still, the situation has greatly improved since the 1920's, and even with all the nonsense that we see and hear in the name of competitive sports, the probability is that it is the right kind of nonsense — just as prize fighting is the right kind of "brutality" as against bear-baiting, bullfights, and the Roman circus. We must not be perfectionists, and if intercollegiate sports yield still a little more ground to the growing taste for intramural, "duffer" sports, much will have been gained.

As against this conviction, a colleague looking over my shoulder reminds me that in many places, the majority of the students would be dumbfounded if they were told that they attended college primarily in order to study. They go, he tells me, for gregarious reasons, with their crowd from high school or prep school; they go to follow the fortunes of the team; they go to join fraternities and sororities; to "make contacts" — future business connections — and also to meet that "not impossible she." I confess that these strike me as thoroughly good motives for youths of sixteen or seventeen to act upon; good, that is, on one general condition, which is that they be real motives and of reasonable intensity. The boy who thinks his career will be made if he only gets into the right fraternity is more to be pitied than censured, and there is usually a stupid father or older brother at the source of his superstition.

Similarly, the student of either sex who is crazy about all members of the other indiscriminately is also a "case" of unbalanced judgment that must be watched, precisely like the sports addict who lives wholly on statistics and biographies relating to his favorite game. But we must remember two things — one, that indulging such fads early in life is the best way of outgrowing them: wild oats for wild oafs is frequently the best cure, and college is the proper place for feeding, forgetting, or shedding certain childish passions. The fraternity boys who called on an acquaintance of mine at a country university and begged him not to give one of them a high grade because the taint of intellect would de-grade their club, ought to be made to feel as caddish as they in fact were. Besides which, the system that intermingles scholastic ratings with clannish snobbery ought to be revised in the direction of mutual independence. Anyhow, not every child matures at the same rate and I have known delightful awakenings to the "true meaning of life" take place within the last six weeks of the senior year. It is always a little absurd and even suspect, but sometimes the longest ripening gives the richest fruit, and the "finished" gentleman of twenty is usually finished in too many senses of the word.

The second truth to hold on to in assessing student folly is that we enter the world as little lunatics and leave it with only an outward artificial skin hiding our real condition. This is not misanthropy on my part but self-knowledge, checked with observation. I cast my mind back on the Christmas scene I alluded to and I see again a child of eight or nine, taking no part in the game, but jumping up and down by himself from sheer excitement, his face happy and red and his fingers clutching the air — a pleasure for all to see — though not exactly the image of Aristotle's contemplative man.

This perfectly sane and normal boy was of course acting irrationally. He could have given no clear account of his behavior. He will get over it, you think? I wonder. Let him grow up into a stockbroker, a politician, a publisher, or a warrior, and what will he be able to offer in justification of his doings except that these professions are conventionally recognized and, in part, useful by the way? The clutching excitement, the foolish aims, the anxious desires, the childish disappointments that he feels now at eight, he will still experience at eighty — provided he knows how to look into himself honestly. And a summing up of his moments of reason by a fair observer would not give a very impressive total. I am therefore not greatly distressed if at eighteen he yells himself hoarse over a near-touchdown and loses his head over a girl with green eyes and pink hair. The one requirement is that he balance his lunacy with a modicum of usefulness to himself and to others.

That the desire to be useful is very great in college youth can be shown by pointing to those nonacademic activities which are also nonathletic. To run newspapers and fraternity houses, hold debates and give plays, manage lecture series on social problems, form leagues and represent the country's political parties on the campus — to play at being grown-up, in short — is a normal wish. It is likewise excellent training in a variety of standard accomplishments as well as in dealing with one's fellows. For to learn to read the man sitting next to you in class is as important as learning to read the book before your eyes. The one leads into the other, since politics, psychology, and all the humanities have man as their subject.

To be sure, the intrigues of campus factions sometimes exceed proper limits and have to be controlled by older heads, but it is at least as necessary to experience them in the flesh, on a small scale, as to conjure them up out of Machiavelli. For many boys, moreover, college is the first spot where they are not balked and baffled by the thick influence of self-righteous "virtue," and the new freedom goes to their heads. Even so, it is better to exceed the limit in college than on the stock market, and the lessons that can thus be learned are more numerous and subtle than first appears. I remember, years ago, a boy of good parts whose chief aim in life was to be a universal philanthropist. Many of his schemes were excellent and he had the energy of ten men. But he lacked self-control and by dint of turning up in everybody's path with helpful suggestions he made himself thoroughly unpopular with his contemporaries. Paragraphs appeared in the paper, satires in the magazines, whispers in the atmosphere. He reported these things to me without understanding in the slightest the cause of his persecution, and goodness so radiated from him that I was unable to dim it with the suggestion that a little neglect of the world's troubles on his part would make everyone happier.

Finally, I hit upon the idea of telling him that he was unwittingly depriving his fellows of a constitutional right. This brought him up short. "Why, what right do you mean?" — "The right to dislike you. Here you are, thrusting your good offices upon everyone, and preventing them from being indifferent to you or even hostile: it isn't fair. You try to purchase their good will, against their own will." He left in a state of considerable shock but gradually his ardor lessened sufficiently to make him more sociable and no less useful.

The reforming instinct is of course at the bottom of much so-called student radicalism. But this bugbear of a word covers so many things that I must wind up my inexhaustible subject by pointing to a few. Trustees of colleges are especially worried by radical youth and they inquire about it of Faculty members with such a hunted look that I am always tempted to say, "There, there, don't you be frightened any more, we haven't had a radical undergraduate since Alexander Hamilton."

Without question a young man who is not a radical about something is a pretty poor risk for education. The relevant question to ask is, What does this young man's radicalism express? In general, if it is doctrinaire, if he has learned all the answers to the world's problems out of a book or from a wise guy outside, the worth of his beliefs is slight, both to him and to society. The cut-and-dried patter must first be got out of him before his mind will give a clear tone. It is true that the reasons for the early adoption of ready-made beliefs often deserve sympathy. Poverty, injustice, a sense of wrong connected with a physical or other defect, are predisposing causes. In other instances it may be great intellectual curiosity coupled with a yearning for absolute truth. This is why students — though the Trustees do not trust it — can go so easily from the doctrine of Karl Marx to the doctrine of Saint Thomas. By means of these systems, converts can act out their dissent from the regular way and secure the comforts of a vast intellectual edifice.

But dissent of a different type remains the really fruitful element in undergraduate thought; though here again quality is important. Dissent from the teacher because he is an authority is meaningless, but the defiant conviction that it is no atrocious crime to be a young man, *born later*, with a different world impressed on the mind, with the consciousness of untried powers and unlimited courage — that form of dissent is without doubt the one quality to nurture when found and to shield if need be against all literal conformity. For what it fulfills is the solitary truth rattling through the empty periods of the Commencement orator when he says: "Young men, the future is in your hands."

Imagine a generation of young men who did not think they could govern better than their fathers, who did not want to revolutionize the world with new inventions or make T. S. Eliot's laurels fade! If they do not believe they can do this, who will tell them? Certainly not the institutions that rightfully nurse a Tradition. But a tradition lives by being added to, and it is the young who must make the effort of creation. It is irrelevant to suggest that this ambition moves thousands of hearts every year and ends in workaday routine and indolence. That is to look only at the husks. As long as we cannot prophesy who will turn out a winner, we have no right to question initiative and self-dedication.

As a matter of fact, the near totality of undergraduates have a spring of freshness and inventiveness somewhere in them. They unconsciously prove how sensible democracy is by showing the observer how widespread originality and talent are. What makes talent scarce later is the difficulty of bringing it into play once duties and commitments and fears clamp down on the individual. In college, these seem still remote, and in flash after flash, the teacher gets glimpses of the freedom and mobility of mind, the healthy damning of consequences, upon which all really great success is built. One is reminded of it during every world war — which brings out winning generals aged twenty-six — and after every war — which brings out mature artists even younger. Excitement animating good brains does it, and there is truth in one of these very flashes from a student with whom I was discussing the eighteenth-century view of Reason. "No," he said, "they were wrong. There is no such thing as their Reason — or if there is, it isn't what makes the world progress."

"Why not?"

"Because it's only a cerebral sort of wisdom."

17. The Subjection of Women

> It was a consuming vexation to my father that my mother never asked the meaning of a thing she did not understand.
> — *Life and Opinions of Tristram Shandy, Gent.*

TIME WAS when the war of the sexes in education was marked by a clear division among accomplishments. Greek and Latin, Mathematics and Philosophy, on one side; Italian and French, Art and Music, on the other, were the respective secondary sexual characters of politely finished males and females. Equal rights have changed all that. Women learn everything that their brothers do; they become scholars and scientists, and what W. S. Gilbert satirized in *Princess Ida* as "the maddest folly going," namely, a women's college, is now the proper crown for any hilltop — particularly if a neighboring one is occupied by an institution for men. In the state universities, of course, collegiate coeducation simply continues the uniform instruction given to both sexes from the first grade onwards.

It is still open to doubt, however, whether what we now find normal really answers the question, What is a proper education for women? I believe that the main preoccupations of our world give a full reply to the parallel question about men. But that same world is still undecided about women. Perhaps it is risky to say it so directly, for feminism still counts numberless adherents in fighting trim, but simple observation shows that although women are capable of everything — that men do, the greater number of women trained in colleges do not enter business or the professions.[1]

The opportunity to do so is there, however, and it is a great improvement on the former exclusion and exclusivism. Women show talents in all branches of learning which are as much worth developing for the good of the state as the corresponding gifts in men. After teaching a roughly equal number of men and women, I am certain that the best mind in each group was fully the equal of the other. The question is not of powers but of uses; and not of collegiate achievements but of postgraduate careers. What happens to the girl with a diploma? As a famous feminist college president said in the days when man feared the "unwomanly woman," "Why, they marry over and over again."

Nothing could be more reassuring, but what kind of wives and lives are the result? Five years out, where has all the philosophy and English literature and mathematics gone to? Some may think the question unfair, since the men of the same class might not show much zest for collegiate subjects either. But I think there is a difference, which comes from the old division of labor between men and women. The men's intellectual interests may have narrowed, but in most cases they have fused into their professional interest — broadly speaking — into scientific, social, or purely intellectual forms. Few college men give up thinking altogether, at least for the first ten years or so. What, meanwhile, has happened to the young college women? Some have deliberately topped off college with shorthand and typewriting in case of need. Others are engaged in various types of semi-responsible office work. A few are real executives or specialists. The majority have married and devote their entire time to the household, that is, the kitchen and the baby. Of these, the most energetic may work for the League of Women Voters, or some such benevolent

[1] Some of the facts have been ably discussed by Rogert G. Foster and Pauline P. Wilson in their book: *Women after College: A Study of the Effectiveness of Their Education.*

organization. But usually their college training never comes into play; indeed they are probably handicapped by four years of leisure and learning for the battle of life over crib and stove.

All this calls for sympathy rather than satire, and for the placing of responsibility where it belongs. As with the sexual education of boys, the proper goal for women's college work is not something that can be decided by academic fiat. It is something that the world at large controls by its attitudes and demands — for the most part quite callously and carelessly. Though some women's colleges have ignored, and others have tried to please "the market," their efforts have equally failed to establish a norm. Nor have the young women themselves, who are the fittest judges in the case, been able to reach a settled conclusion. Too many conflicting forces act upon them: they do not know — they cannot know — whether they will marry or work for wages or do both together. As the world goes, none of these choices confers a predictable status, and none, as I have said, uses or requires any special education. Rather, education adds to the indignity of being considered, as most women are, half-skilled replaceable labor with no future. Employers dread the sudden appearance, one Monday morning, of an engagement ring or of a notice that Mrs. X is leaving to become a mother. Even if a woman intends to continue working under these conditions, she cannot be said to have a career nor to be really making use of her mind.

Of course the conditions of housework are possibly even more anti-intellectual. Whereas the very essence of thought is continuity, the very essence of domestic life is interruption. If a young woman dared disconnect the doorbell, smash the phone, and gag the baby, she might be able to read a book or think a thought; but with a duty towards everybody but herself, her mind necessarily reverts to the feral state. It is not a matter of intelligence or good will or even energy, but of hourly preoccupation. Robinson Crusoe would have a better chance of remaining cultivated alone on his island than a young married woman of modest income in a three-room flat within a stone's throw of museums, concerts, and public libraries.

Even without the responsibility of children, the case is hard. As a very promising Ph.D. candidate told me the other day, "I must get started on my book before my husband returns from the Army, because I'll never have another chance to do a piece of work in absolute independence again." This is not quite accurate: she will have another chance — when it's too late. At forty-five or fifty, when the brood is ready to fly the nest and comforts permit, she will have a great deal of time on her hands, and begin to try to develop "interests." She will join a woman's club and attend lectures. But it will be too late, for reasons I shall go into at greater length in my next chapter.

Anyone, therefore, who thinks honestly about the matter must at least wonder whether the four years at Pomegranate College, the five thousand dollars, and the conducted field trips to slum and factory, were not time and money misspent. The query has nothing to do with feminism or anti-feminism, nor with the sex of the inquirer: obviously the question must come from either a man or a woman, and the answer also. But the facts are, I hope, sexless. To me the fact of main significance is that when Women's Rights were won and women's colleges established, they were organized as exact counterparts of men's colleges. In this regard, the subjection of women is still complete, though modified in form. They still prove their equality by striving for identity — in ways of learning, in subjects taught, in academic ritual.[2] And unhappily, women chose a pattern from a bad period — one of imitation of Europe, of overinsistence on "scientific scholarship," of teaching by lecture and laboratory drill. Throughout, women wanted to show that they were not so much the equals of men

[2] When men's colleges accelerated their courses to hasten readiness for armed service, the women followed suit and disorganized much good work, though without any marked necessity or even desire to enter the Women's Auxiliary branches.

as their duplicates. A few of the results were good and are not to be gainsaid, but they seem incidental to the scheme rather than intrinsic. Leaving aside worldwide reform, what can be done from within the college to ameliorate the lot of the American girl?

To begin with, it would not seem unreasonable to make some kind of differentiation between those who are going to be specialists and those who are going to be housewives. Perhaps this already occurs automatically in favor of the specialists. Women technicians seem to pile up credits in biology, chemistry, and statistics, guided by the same instincts that move their male cousins. And the young woman whose whole soul is in economic research needs rather to be restrained than pushed into the specialization she craves and is bound to reach.

But subtracting all the George Eliots and Madame Curies leaves an overwhelming majority lacking purpose and escaping coherent instruction. Certain subjects, like music or designing, attract a fair minority of that rank-and-file contingent. Another group takes to nursery-school training, home economics, and "social mal." But these choices seem in many cases pseudo-vocational or would-be womanly, rather than intended for cultivation. The rest take English literature. I exaggerate, of course, but my intention is clear: literature is agreeable, and casually absorbed, it forces no issue. The whole of the woman's curriculum, even in good places with strict requirements, has no intelligible shape. It is in the transitional state that the men's institutions went through after the heyday of the elective-and-majoring system, and nothing has occurred to force a change, simply because the economic situation of woman is confused by the varied possibilities of marriage.

There has been, it is true, one school of theory and practice which has brought about change: progressive education. It is noteworthy that the first progressive colleges were for women and that the chief ones are still women's colleges or else coeducational. Departure from old ways was apparently more safely tried upon women, again, I think, because of economic fact.

What did progressive education do? I have already paid tribute to its rehabilitation of teaching as a necessary art. It supplemented this with the doctrine of "needs and interests," that is, with the notion that drinking deep implies a previous thirst, and that if obstacles stand in the way of satisfying interests, these "needs" must be pointed out by the teacher to the student and taken care of by the school. This idea harks back to Rousseau's first principle: "Look at the child, and see what he is like. He is not a miniature adult, and your efforts will go to waste if you begin where you, the teacher, stand instead of at the point which the child has reached. Cut your cloth to fit the pupil and not the other way around."

This epoch-making shift of viewpoint was, however, largely misapplied and befogged by the progressive college. In its original form the precept can best be applied to the infant and the child up to adolescence. Then there should be a gradual shifting of positions. As the youth nears maturity he (or rather, I should from now on say "she") must adapt herself more and more to the ways chosen by intelligent adults for the conduct of the world's work. If at twenty-two a girl is going to marry or enter business, she must at eighteen be already able to follow *others'* needs and interests and, without stunting her own personality, learn what is "out there" to be learned.

Instead of acting accordingly, the progressive schools made the girl the fixed point and subject matter a mere flexible device. The aim was to promote "growth" — an undefined term referring vaguely to behavior at large — or to achieve "adjustment," or to develop "the personality." More than that, the student was to find her own way from point to point and by uncovering need after need, like a panorama of hills successively disclosed, to learn what she needed to know in the order of felt desires. For example, the student declares an interest in medicine (her father being a doctor). A preparatory course is laid out for her, in which she must work up some biology, which leads to the need of chemistry; this requires elementary physics and more mathematics than she has had. She probably ends by beginning with vulgar fractions. Each subject, in bits, is enclosed within another bit of another — the student standing at the center, like the core of an onion within cloudy layers of learning.

The practice of the progressive colleges is of course better than the theory: it has to be. But there is enough contradiction of an unwanted sort to make both teachers and students uncomfortable, and none of the "studies" conducted about "types," "methods," and "materials" has alleviated the pain. One student, later a good poet, expressed one phase of it in my hearing when her teacher told her at graduation that she had indeed taken a great jump forward in her last year. "Oh Miss Miller, I was growing all the time!" This is indeed the worst of launching children into the world — they keep on growing whether you are looking or not. And it may be asked whether a college is simply a greenhouse that concentrates air and sunlight while taking the credit for active cultivation.

Progressive teachers sense this and therefore redouble their efforts to watch growth taking place so as to direct it, to force it if need be, towards the proper end. But this is far too ambitious and it has led to perhaps the worst feature of the whole enterprise — the attempt to make the college a psychiatric reformatory by means of the counseling system. Where this idea prevails the weekly interview between student and adviser turns into a super-confessional unmotivated by actual trouble. Or rather, since no one's life offers a glassy smoothness to the outside eye, each student comes to believe that she has emotional perturbations worth discussing, and a hodgepodge of fancied ills, bad terminology, unconscious scandal-mongering, and pretentious soul-cures occupies the time and thought of people, young and old, who should all the while be hard at their studies.[3]

[3] One well-meaning teacher whom I know and whose heart is in the game keeps referring to the students' antecedents as their "histology."

This is reinforced by medical examinations and reports, so that the teacher beginning his week's work finds on his desk the name and diagnosis of his absentees from coryza, dysmenorrhea, or laryngitis, which is supposed to enlighten him. Then he reads his colleagues' confidential accounts of the mental troubles brewing among the same class, and he is probably reminded in the course of a tutorial on Wordsworth or the Civil War that the student before him is handicapped in research by the aftereffects of her parents' divorce.

The important point is not that these human facts reach the teacher. I showed in my last chapter how right it was that they should. The important point is that the mixing of personalities with learning is constant, conscious, and systematic. It has hardened into a new routine, which too soon and too generally has come to seem the superior way to teach. I maintained when seeing the workings at close range what I maintain now, that all help to students in personal affairs must occur only in emergencies and at the free choice of the student. The opposite course seems to me unethical in the extreme, even if it were not to be discarded on the prior grounds of interfering with instruction. Young people think sufficiently about themselves not to make them do it on schedule; and "personality" — whatever that may mean in a desirable sense — is not fashioned by increasing self-examination under false pretense of science.

I believe the tide of psychiatric interest in personality has somewhat receded in all progressive schools. The newspapers told us not long ago that the official body of progressive educators had turned away from the individual and were now devoting themselves to the community.[4] But the statement sounded much like the old slogans, expressing faith in the power of education to make this or that kind of person on demand. The "community" will now be processed according to the ancient fallacy I began this book by disputing. This does not mean that the ranking half-

[4] *New York Times*, March 4, 1944.

dozen colleges of the progressive type do not furnish an excellent standard sort of training in the normal electives plus the practice of the arts. They do, for after all not even a progressive college can secede from the union, and the world's expectations — vague as they are — end by forcing institutions that grant the A.B. degree to endow its graduates with something more than internal growth or imperceptible "adjustment."

The progressive faculties, in fact, often go too far the other way in requiring, on paper at least, that candidates for the diploma show impossible merits: "Evidence of adequate independent achievement in the following — (*a*) intensive study in some phase of college work; (*b*) more than two areas of the curriculum (range); (*c*) mastery of a definite skill (studio, field, or verbal area); evidence of a definition of interest, a clearer sense of direction; evidence of increased capacity to understand herself with respect to her present status, as well as increased capacity to assume responsibility for significant self-direction; finally, evidence of reasonable responsibility in respect to health and social life." I have noticed the same sort of phraseology in other quarters, from eagerness to prove that the liberal-arts curriculum is a dose worth the price. I think it would be wiser to moderate the tone, not to use the word "mastery," and not to pile up a list of qualities, which I for one would feel abashed to think I must put in evidence.

This brings us back to the desirable requirements for a woman graduate to possess. I have already spoken of the career woman as well provided for under present arrangements. But just as the vocational training of men must be tempered by a suitable orientation to the full contents of the modern world, so the woman technician in any field must be compelled to learn more than her breadwinning specialty. For the rest, a more co-ordinated program than they now get is clearly required. A program such as that of Columbia College, though far from universally applicable, points the way. More prescribed work, the abandonment of scholar-making, and the awareness that women are not men in skirts, are called for.

Precisely because most young women are likely to lose touch with books, ideas, and current events on the far side of the altar, they must in the four years of college obtain such a view of past and present that its outline will remain indelible once the details are gone. For this purpose, co-operative courses, compulsory for all during the first two years, should replace the History 1, Philosophy 1, English 1 — or Social Mal. These courses should stress principles rather than facts, using the latter chiefly as illustrative instances to be fully explored, rather than as working information to be remembered in afterlife.

It is true that as a general rule, girls are less interested than boys in theory, in ideas, in the logic of things and events. That is why their minds must not be cluttered up with details which they instinctively prefer — and make no use of. Girls are more conscientious and hardworking, they want to please their teachers more, and they do not want to be bothered by implications. They argue less, and the art of winning which they have been taught since the cradle has given them a respect for convention which makes them unerringly pick out the accepted hokum. At the same time they are practical enough to distrust it and the distrust ends by tainting all intellectual matters, so that one constantly meets women of fine intelligence who use their brains exclusively about concrete things such as clothes, food, and the persons whom they know. Their imagination about the distant or the abstract is completely atrophied; they are at the mercy of words, and their vehement opinions about war or strikes or politics are little short of brutish.

Though it may be hard work, the minds of women students can be forced out of their grooves of conventionality and made to cope even with abstractions. If the teacher takes pains to show repeatedly that concrete harm, good, suffering, pleasure, or profit follows from some belief or truth in question, a beginning can be made of substituting reason for memory. But that step of pointing out consequences must never be skipped until the student's imagination has been thoroughly primed. And conversely, every event or proposition must be related to human motives, lest it be automatically discounted as one of those wild things that men do or say and that count for nothing. I dare not compare twentieth-century woman to Tristram Shandy's mother, but that gentleman's observation quoted at the head of this chapter corresponds to something real.

Real or no, there is one conclusive argument for keeping women's college work close to that of men in scope and substance and yet giving them separate and different instruction.[5] This is the fact that men and women live a great part of their lives together. Most men may not be like Milton in demanding intellectual companionship from their wives, but all feel to some degree the need for other conversation than that about groceries and clothes. This is so true that I have heard many pathetic resolves taken by girls about to be married that "they would read ten books a year so as to keep up." Jim was a lawyer and loved history; they would read aloud — Lord knows what — Gibbon's *Decline and Fall*. I have advised moderate ambitions in this regard and recommended rather the selecting of friends to whom general conversation is not an unknown thing. For ordinary people, intellectual interests need a social base and an easy upkeep or they peter out. Fortunately there is such a thing as reading the newspaper and knowing how to extract from it information which too many people think only obtainable in courses. Reading the newspapers makes certain books more readable; these in turn feed conver-

[5] I have only visited coeducational colleges and cannot speak of any teaching experience there. It may or may not be significant that the term "co-ed" always designates a woman, never a man, and that institutions with women students enforce far too many minor regulations regarding conduct. In graduate and extension work, the difference of the sexes is disregarded of necessity, though its effect in learning can be seen in the questions asked or the answers given on examinations.

sation, and holding one's own in conversation is good for anyone.

With a real desire and a suitable college background (here the word is apt) a woman, however busy, can live intellectually and honorably by her wits, to her own gain and that of the children she will rear. If her husband is to continue to speak his thoughts freely to her, he must find her responsive and *au courant*. There is nothing that discourages a man's talk so much as a staring countenance and the words "I wouldn't know anything about that" — provided of course the "that" is within common knowledge — for as an old book of *Advice to Wives* recommends: "She must take care never to draw largely on the small stock of patience in a man's nature." In some women ignorantism is an affectation, in others laziness, in still others, self-distrust. Going to college should overcome all three foibles and, without making bluestockings out of a womanhood that prefers skiing, it should produce companionable, even talkative adults of the female sex, whose arrival does not immediately make the host reach for a deck of cards, but rather lends new force to the old truth that the highest form of sociability is the conversation of educated men and women. As for the workaday use of women's trained intelligence, the world of business must first clear its own mind on the subject before it can expect the colleges, or the girls, to conform with much alacrity to its dictates.

18. Adults, Workers, and Marriageable Girls

In a pompous advertisement it was announced that the directors of the Royal Academies Company had engaged the best masters in every branch of knowledge and were about to issue twenty thousand tickets at twenty shillings each. There was to be a lottery, two thousand prizes were to be drawn; and the fortunate . . . were to be taught . . . Latin, Greek, Hebrew, French, Spanish, conic sections, trigonometry, heraldry, japanning, fortification, book-keeping and the art of playing the theorbo.

— MACAULAY on the "Bubble" of 1689

SINCE THE DAYS when Macaulay reported the joke of a commercial venture to teach all subjects to all comers, it has ceased to be a joke by becoming a reality. "The schoolmaster is abroad," said the nineteenth century in its youth, and "I wish to goodness he were," added Oscar Wilde at the end of a period of unparalleled "Extension." To be sure, there were good reasons why the nineteenth century went in for it, and with fervor. Millions were being given the vote; democracy was supplying the new masters of the state and in Robert Lowe's phrase, "we must educate our masters." The task began on a universal scale when enough money was appropriated, in the seventies, to establish free public schooling in almost every country.[1]

But in taking this necessary step, the words "democracy in education" and "equal rights" (as against distinctions of class, wealth, or sex) were used so loosely that after seventy-five years we are still asking ourselves the question, "Whom shall we teach and how much?" Instead of emerging early in practice, the decision — especially in this country of vast resources — remains arbitrary and gives rise to shrill recrimination and the bitter feelings of disappointed hope. One consequence, seen during the war, was that some people felt outraged at the fact that certain young men were being taught and trained and withheld from active service while others were sent to the front. This was not "democratic." Again, in the mood of natural gratitude for the returned veterans one hears on all sides the plea that they be given a free college education, and this goes with the hope that the faculty will not be too hard on them, but give them the degree for what they have already done and suffered.

All this is in keeping with an attitude prevalent in states that maintain their own universities, where admission is open to all high school graduates. In one state, and perhaps in others, it is stipulated that the freshman class at the university must be drawn equally from all the percentiles of the high school contingents — that is, if one hundred are taken from the highest ranking 10 per cent, then one hundred must also be taken from the barely passing group, and similarly for the intermediate grades. At the end of the first term, the mortality is very high and an enormous loss through waste has been sustained. Protest against it, however, is checked at its source by the belief that the truth about inequality of brains is unpalatable, nay undemocratic; so that if it were mentioned and

---

[1] Until that time, the only countries where everybody could read and write were Prussia and adjacent German and Scandinavian states. Since 1900, the most "literate" country has been Japan.

acted upon we should be in contradiction with our cherished form of government.

This is a false belief, which goes back to a double confusion involving the nature of education and the meaning of equality. Rightly understood, there is nothing unpalatable about the facts of intellectual aptitude and nothing undemocratic or iniquitous about selecting the best for the highest training. Every citizen of this country understands the true principle perfectly well when it applies to Big League Baseball, the Army, science, or business organization. How should I be greeted if I demanded a place on next year's All-American football team because I am a citizen and therefore the equal of any candidate for a place? Does the enlisted man get his turn at playing commander of the forces in the field? And would anyone claim as a right the direction of the hospital in which he is a patient? The examples suggest absurdity because they relate to concrete activities where disaster would follow a confusion of ranks and duties.

But how does subordination of functions impair equality of persons? In no way. And the ladder of learning is no different from the ladder of promotion and power in an army, a hospital, or an athletic organization. In all these activities, it is possible to make wrong choices and to put forward incompetent men, but the mistakes do not alter the fact that a fair ratio must obtain between ability and responsibility, otherwise the system breaks down.

Let me grant that in education a greater freedom of opportunity than elsewhere is desirable, both because it affects young, unformed people and because the risk of error costs less for a possibly greater gain. In short, let us give every intending student the benefit of the doubt. Still, the principle of choice must not be damaged or destroyed by this generosity and the right to education must remain on an equal footing with every other right, namely, the footing of being available insofar as the claimant shows the power to deserve it.

What creates bitter feelings about the sifting out of those worth a college training is that people both admire and despise the degree. They despise it unconsciously by believing that any good-natured youth who sits through four years of class work has done enough for a diploma, and they admire the A.B. by very consciously wanting it for themselves, their children, and their employees. Now it may be indiscreet to tell people that they squint, but if they distort the situation, they must be told the truth. The truth is that the existence of superior brains does not touch in the slightest the theoretical bases of democratic government. Democracy in education is something very precise to uphold and work for. It does not mean "Everybody in college" or "One man – one A.B." It means, every man or woman freely endowed with the right to a college education if he or she is previously endowed with the ability to profit by it.

In Jefferson's plan for education in Virginia, he makes the provision that "the twenty best geniuses be raked from the rubbish annually" and sent to the University. No one can accuse Jefferson of harboring undemocratic or snobbish feelings, although here I am ready to stand with the mob and object to the hasty expression of "rubbish." The rejected applicants are "rubbish" only with reference to collegiate work, just as Jefferson was rubbish for the boxing ring. We are all rubbish in relation to some demand or other, and if my view of intelligence as an adaptable power is right, there is no disgrace in being a duffer at book larnin', or in being pure rubbish in any of the many arts which human intelligence has created. The true notion of equality is not identity, but equivalence of treatment. That is why handicaps are given to horses in racing and to men in playing golf. Walt Whitman – another unquestioned democrat – has a line which defines equality once for all with great accuracy: –

By God! I will accept nothing which all cannot have their counterpart of on the same terms.

Applied to college training, this means: I cannot expect to get free of charge and without good work or real interest on my part what others are getting by the expenditure of both.

Ideally, I suppose, it would be possible to bring the great majority of boys and girls to the point where college would profit them. This would mean untwisting every kink put into them before eighteen by unhappy circumstances reaching back to the cradle. Since teachers, time, space, and money are limited, competition ensues and selection is inevitable.

Now to ensure genuine equality of treatment in selecting, the needful thing is to keep an eye on educability and disregard irrelevant considerations. In practice this comes down to appropriating enough public money so that the college population shall represent the best young brains of the country and not a haphazard mixture of brains and bank accounts. It has been estimated that for every youth attending college there is one equally capable who cannot afford it. This fact defines with blinding clearness and simplicity what a democratic nation must do to provide a democratic education: pay the way of its most valuable natural resource — the intelligence of its youth.

If every college were in a position to replace the lower half of its student body with a group equal in caliber to its present upper half, one of the great dilemmas of college teaching would vanish. For among teachers, there is a professional meaning to the question, "Whom shall we teach?" That meaning is, Shall I work upon the top students in the group before me or spend most of my time whipping up the laggards? The layman may think at first that this is an artificial division. I beg him to believe that it is a tangible fact — like the waterline of a floating ship. In a normal class, the break comes somewhat below the median. A student of "C" grade is either a good man not working or a really poor bet. This is sufficiently recognized whenever a "screening" for putting students on probation takes place; and in pedagogical literature, the "average" student forms the subject of innumerable attempts to raise or rouse him. This is the man I should prefer to call "subaverage," in the belief that if we really tapped the best talents in the country, the average would be of astonishingly good quality. But so far the only schemes proposed for coping with him consist either in segregation by means of placement tests, or in designing special courses, slower paced or somehow diluted. I have even heard it said that the new Area Studies were the ideal thing for the stupid boy. Unless I miss a hidden joke, this strikes me as the parody of college training and the self-stultification of the teacher.

Every conscientious instructor tries to keep a class together. Some students have to march in the rear ranks and must be cheered along; others want to run ahead and have to be gently kept from running out of sight. But the group is a unit, and it is excellent for both its extremes to see how the other half thinks: the more gifted learn to appreciate other men's difficulties; the less, to gauge other men's powers. Both can hence deduce a scale of merit between genius and normal parts. Moreover by good instruction, qualities cutting across the main line can be pointed out: quickness and depth and accuracy and elegance of thought do not necessarily go together, nor is the coupling of any of them fixed by rule.

But beyond the line that separates the educable from the rest lies a wasteland that would require vast irrigation and incubator nursing of each weakly plant to turn into a flowering plain. The sluggish minds are stunted, timid, rooted in resentments, and paralyzed by a laziness which is not of the body merely, but of the emotions. They are not so much hopeless for teaching as themselves without hope of learning, and if no fairness of form or skill of hand redeems them in their own eyes, they are indeed the disinherited.

To sum up, there should be in college only one sort of student — quite obviously, the college student. For learning, however diverse in detail and appeal, is one. If we compare its demands upon intellect with those of, let us say, survival in the jungle, we can see that study is something separate and homogeneous. Hence there should be no tampering with either its ingredients or its standards of quality. We must teach those who can learn, having first found them wherever they may be and cleared the path that leads to the campus.

II

But having just said this, I want to modify it in favor of a large section of our population who love learning for its bright glow without being willing or able to stand its heat. This vast group is chiefly composed of adults, whose claims upon the attention of many teachers ranges from Woman's Club lectures to so-called educational radio programs. Adult education, strictly defined, is outside my present classification. It consists, as everyone knows, of classes in elementary or technical subjects given outside business hours to mature men and women who are striving to better their lot. These people are real students taught in the standard way and their efforts are both touching and magnificent.

The other adults I speak of are not students in any real sense and should not be treated as such. But neither should they be disregarded or despised. For them, I should even willingly loosen the bands of learning, with an occasional reminder that the genuine garment is a tighter fit than they can stand.

The great instrument of, shall I call it, "popular teaching," is of course the public lecture. Before the movies and the radio it rivaled the theater and the church as sources of entertainment. The Lyceum flourished here and its counterparts abroad. All the great men of the period lectured. "What do you do it for?" someone asked, I believe, of Wendell Phillips: "Fifty dollars and expenses." The answer expresses fatigue and discouragement rather than cynicism. For if you read the accounts left by Emerson or Oliver Wendell Holmes, Tyndall or Huxley, William

James or Mark Twain, you find that popular lecturing was always the unsatisfactory thing it is now. The prince of lecturers, Michael Faraday, put his finger on the trouble when he was asked what he could assume that the audience knew: "Nothing."

This is what keeps the devotees of lectures from being students — and from learning anything. They know nothing, not individually but as a group, and when I said earlier that a Woman's Club is not the ideal place to resume intellectual interests dropped in youth, I meant just this. The lecturer cannot take anything for granted; he wears himself out building on sand. In doing it, he bores some and bewilders others. The lecture clubs, feeling no progression, flit from topic to topic and from speaker to speaker. If led by a sensible program chairman, they finally agree that they have the best time with a lecturer who exudes charm unadulterated by knowledge, or with a man who brings slides or films. I should add the autobiographical lecturer — "Storm over Ploesti" or "I Was a So-and-So."

All this is entertaining and even informative, but it does not instruct — much less educate — for it has no links with anything else, and the resulting confusion and vagueness are accurately rendered in the captions to Miss Helen Hokinson's drawings.

Least satisfactory of all, I think, are the lectures by authors about their own books; not of course the books of adventure, but the serious novel or prose discussion. There stands the poor fellow who has labored hard to make his point clear in three hundred pages. He thinks he has done his work and yet it is still to do before an audience which plainly says to him: "We don't want to read your book. Tell us about it in fifty minutes — and don't make it difficult." I remember appearing on some such forum platform with Mr. Thomas Mann, who began by explaining what he had said in a little book about Democracy. I followed on "Freedom," then we answered questions, and finally we looked at each other, in what I trust was mutual commiseration. Do not imagine that we had the feeling of having miscast pearls. The audience was a perfectly good audience, individually intelligent and receptive, collectively impervious and unhappy. It was our little talks that were at fault — at least mine was, because I took literally the assignment of summarizing the thesis of a book. I have since learned that such an audience can only take in one point in one lecture. It must be a simple point, preferably one they are familiar with, and it must be driven in by hammering repetition — until the lecturer himself begins to doubt it.[2]

When you go from the platform to the microphone, the difficulty multiplies, with only one compensating advantage. Millions are listening and therefore no common denominator of interest or knowledge can be guessed at. But at least one is speaking conversationally to single listeners or at most to a small group in a living room. The audience, moreover, is one of free men and women who can turn off the speaker instantly without qualms. This is a boon to both parties. The speaker, relieved of the necessity of lecturing, and sure that he will not constrain those whom he fails to please, can be himself and talk in easy friendly fashion to what resembles a wide circle of unmet acquaintances.

What is unfortunate is that no efforts have been made by the radio industry to capitalize on the public's habit of regular listening. I am thinking of course about "educational" programs and particularly of the relatively successful "Invitation to Learning." [3] By treating such programs exclusively as "shows" which must appeal chiefly to the new listener, the value of cumulative effect is lost and the old listeners are cheated of legitimate pleasure and profit. It is possible, I am convinced, to make such a program truly educational by establishing a real progression from topic to

[2] My friend Theodore Spencer of Harvard once wrote a fable in the style of Joyce, which bears on this situation. It begins: "Once there was a poorflosser of Angleish Littlesure who was axed to deliver a spleach. . . . All he was used to undoing was to dequiver a lacksure. And his hawdiunce was exhumausted from laxatures. . . ." (*Atlantic Monthly*, September 1939.)

[3] The estimated number of listeners to this program ranges from two to three millions every Sunday.

topic — not so tight-knit as in a regular course, but comparable to, let us say, the effect of a book of essays from the same hand.

Of course any radio broadcast must in part remain a "show"; it must be as dramatic and lively as a good lecture or discussion; but it needn't always start at the same point, assume the incurable ignorance of the public, and entice chiefly by the false glitter of big names or easy culture. Why not frankly face the fact of a limited appeal comprising three million highbrows and satisfy *them* instead of trying to cater for all and disappointing the fraction of actual devotees? Not even they will be contented throughout, though they would gladly put their trust in an average performance if they could be sure of being spared vaudeville effects. One radio executive of my acquaintance who feels as I do expresses on this point a resigned cynicism. On one occasion, when I was scheduled to broadcast, he asked me what the discussion was to be about. "Ruskin's *Stones of Venice*." "Who is on the program with you?" "John Morse, editor of the *Magazine of Art*, is the chairman; I don't know who the third man is." "Well, I think I know. You see, you're on for Ruskin — he's in your field; this art editor is on for the Stones, and for Venice, they'll find you a gondolier."

Actually, the desire to make learning attractive is perfectly sound. What is unfair to the public is to suggest that attraction and ease of learning are synonymous and that what seems strange or new will remain incurably so unless the expositor jazzes it up. This point of view is fatal, for what seems outwardly exciting is often less palatable than a more modest article close by. I once tried to suggest to a director managing a series of talks on the great philosophers that it was a mistake to put down Hume's *Treatise of Human Nature*. He argued that everybody was interested in human nature. True, but it so happens that the book of that name was Hume's first and worst. Its flat failure on publication led him to rewrite it in shorter form under a new title, and it is almost certain that an unprepared reader looking into the first version would feel exactly as did the original audience. But these facts made no impression against the pulling power of the phrase "Human Nature."

This vain endeavor of mine recalls the difficulty I mentioned before as affecting some colleges: the directors of semi-instruction for adults are professional managers who know little of what they handle. They are pure empirics who follow either the box-office returns or, in public institutes, the last person's casual gossip. A real consensus would matter and its expression in cash would mean something, but both need interpretation as well as carefully compiled data. In short, to build up a program or a public for popular teaching, it is necessary to have a sound idea, a sensible way of testing its intrinsic success, and the faith to carry it out until it gathers as many followers as properly belong to it.

III

In between the nondescript lecture public and the true adult student in continuation schools, there is a third category of grownups, who follow the so-called extension courses offered by our great universities. In the boom days before the depression the most ancient and respectable of our seats of learning did on a vast scale what Oxford and Cambridge had done for thirty years — send out teachers to near or far cities to conduct classes in a wide range of subjects. In addition, our institutions offered evening classes on their own campuses and some also undertook to guide home study by mail. Though changed economic conditions have reduced the output, the principle of extension work is now firmly fixed, and the only questions about it are, Whom is it intended for and what should it mean in academic terms? This is an especially important inquiry at the moment because of the returning veterans, not all of whom will wish to undertake regular college work, but will rather hope to supplement their knowledge by following higher studies, as it were, à la carte.

Extension courses have been held up to ridicule, notably in Mr. Flexner's book on *Universities*,[4] because the list of courses offered by Chicago or Harvard or Columbia reads very much like that of the *Royal Academies Company:* by paying your fee you can obtain tuition in any regular academic subject. Occasionally, courses are offered in more recreational arts, such as harpsichord playing or fly fishing. The public assumes that "extension is easier" and over the whole enterprise hovers the vision of a degree. It seems as if the universities had sold out to vulgar demand; yet this not unnatural impression is in fact erroneous. No reputable institution has ever counted fly fishing or its subacademic counterparts towards a degree, though it is true that a program of connected extension studies in an academic field entitles the student to a certificate showing that he has completed them. If that student then says he has a "diploma from Chicago" and it is known that he studied animal husbandry, the institution is simply misrepresented.

In the state universities and some self-supporting city establishments, the confusion which already exists about Columbia or Chicago is made worse by the fact already mentioned of custom-tailoring collegiate courses to future vocations. Thus on one campus I was introduced to a young man and his girl companion: he was, so he said, a pre-Mortician and she a pre-Air-Stewardess. I had no chance to inquire what these preliminaries comprised, but I found myself irrationally resenting the association of the ultimate subject matters with the university I was visiting. So far has the careless wording gone that in certain places the students of the liberal arts aiming at a Bachelor's degree are classified by a negative: they are known as *non*-pre-professional students.

But all this is a matter of usage which one hopes the present "crisis" in education will clear up in one way or another. The work, academic or practical, which is offered in extension courses

[4] Abraham Flexner, *Universities — American, English, German.* New York, 1930.

is fully justified by its aim and its results. Roughly speaking, it is or should be designed for the three categories that form the title of this chapter — unclassified adults, ambitious manual workers, and marriageable girls. I intend no irony when I say that if a woman in search of a husband seeks him among the fellow students of an extension course taken by her with that object in mind, she is acting perfectly legally, sensibly, and even praiseworthily. There is no reason why it should be proper for well-to-do boys and girls to attend colleges affording pleasant chances of finding mates, and somehow shameful or ridiculous to take up radio-script writing with an eye to captivating an eligible man whose profession that will be. If the girl's work is unsatisfactory she fails the course; for matchmaking — despite appearances — is not equivalent to good radio scripts. But the teacher need have no qualms, for extension work presupposes that the students are old enough to know their own interests, and expect no shepherding.

Naturally, an inveterate teacher will always try to save every sheep he can. As one energetic man who has by choice done only extension work said to me, "I don't *ex*pound the stuff, I pound it *in*." But it is unfair to the extension student to require of him or her the same zest and attention that is expected of regularly enrolled college or graduate students. For one thing, extension students bring tired minds to the classroom. Most of them work for a living, hence classes are held at night — a bad time at best. Many are past middle age, and hampered by poor preparation, bad habits of mind or pen, heavy personal responsibilities. They are in fact showing great fortitude and admirable feeling in desiring further instruction. They are aware of their handicaps. Some have told me that all they wished in a given course was to find out how their native land had fared in centuries past: they have no wish to be historians, or students of history. They simply want to hear; they enjoy the contact with learning. I see no harm in the fulfillment of their desire. Their superiority to the lecture audience is mainly moral: they come regularly, they work as much as they can, and they do not expect a snake-charming act in place of the proper contents of the course. Above all, they are unpretentious. A colleague once told me of an old man who after a year in philosophy class said to him, "I'm sorry, I have already forgotten most of what you said, but I've always wanted to know what philosophy was like and I think I know now: it isn't at all like newspaper advice to the perplexed."

These cases, though exceptional, are indicative. The results of even such casual flirting with great subjects are far from negligible, for real culture does not thrive solely in upper air. It needs roots and gradations of soil. The rare plants at the top require for survival a whole hierarchy of consenting minds below, and it is a social good to have an ordinary man who knows nothing about philosophy still know enough to respect its existence and that of the men who create it. The fact that among extension students, some come to believe they know more than they do is another matter altogether, which I shall say a word about later.

Meantime it is hardly necessary to stress how much pleasure and profit university classes in manual arts or in hobbies or in commercial techniques afford to our population, especially in centers like Chicago, Boston, and New York. If the university, though indebted to the public as a tax-free institution, cannot render this service — a service which its standards of scholarly competence guarantees from quackery — what other establishment should give it and how can the claim of these same institutions on the public purse be justified?

No doubt exists in my mind as to the answer. I am utterly insensitive to the obvious charge of desecrating the playground of the Muses. Let the colleges that have never accommodated learning to football or to alumni bequests cast the first stone. And let the universities simply forestall misconceptions by making clearer than ever before, in their catalogues and releases to the press, the difference between, say, organized studies for the A.B. in Columbia College and the galaxy of evening classes in Columbia University. Men returning from armed service should be particularly informed of the kind of instruction they may expect in one division or another. We Americans too readily believe that a course is a course — restaurants bank on this in printing their menus. But in a university the buyer should not have to beware. Accelerated work, refresher classes, and other inducements will be used to draw the veterans here or there. But in reputable institutions, Harvard and Princeton's examples [5] will be followed, of repudiating academic inflation and shinplaster degrees by sticking to the requirement of real academic work for full academic credit.

For my part, I should wish to see a major addition to this extension offering. I should like to see the large universities take thought and set up courses especially meant for workers. Of late years, a growing interest has been shown by industrial labor in the values of higher instruction. Several colleges have held summer conferences, but seemingly always about labor problems. At the same time, groups of workers and employers have tried to secure the services of college teachers for instruction, notably in English and economics. There seems to be a shyness about taking on a wider curriculum and braving it in an academic setting. Or perhaps what I called shyness is snobbishness. Whichever it is, the proper place for manual workers to learn what they want to know is the campus. They should have separate classes only if they wish them. If they come singly or in groups they will find many teachers of all grades and ranks throughout the university ready to teach them to the best of their ability. The atmosphere of the place will in itself be an educational influence, and one which, from the nature of education itself, cannot be duplicated at will. The story of Mark Hopkins at one end of a log and a student at the other contains a truth, but it is a half-truth. The concourse of teachers treading their own ground, of books in

[5] *New York Times*, August 7, 1943.

rows upon rows, of halls lighted at dusk and filled with fellow students — these are things that no one can experience untouched. It was what drew Jude the Obscure to Christminster, but his rebuff by that citadel is no model for a democratic university, nor is it likely to be taken as one by any higher institution, public or private, against the workers of America knocking at the gate.

19. *Our Nation of Highbrows*

> All generous minds have a horror of what are commonly called "facts." They are the brute beasts of the intellectual domain. . . . I allow no "facts" at this table.
> — *The Autocrat of the Breakfast Table*

PRESUMABLY all this vast machine, this teaching and course taking, this examining and graduating in all kinds, works towards some great end. Above the social need to read and write, above the skillful doing of technical tasks, above even self-fulfillment, there must be a result — conscious or unconscious — affecting the country as a whole. I can only think that this ceaseless activity answers the need of every nation to have a head, that is to say, a portion of itself devoting all its energy to leadership in intellectual matters — science and art and government and literature and education.

Do I mean a group set apart and known as intellectuals? No, that is a loaded word, at once too contemptuous and not inclusive enough. A top layer of highbrows? Well, that is the common term, but in my opinion a bad one, because it suggests that the body of the nation is composed of lowbrows, whereas the truth is that highbrow and lowbrow are by nature one person, and that person is every American, more or less. The two words "high" and "low" simply denote two phases, like the alternating light and dark of a blinker; and I very much fear that some of our teaching and learning encourages not only this lack of steady glow, but the bad emotions that go with it. Always beware of a man who begins: "I'm only a lowbrow, of course, but I want to tell you that — " Nine times out of ten, what he will tell you is fact, or prejudice passing for fact, of which he is intensely proud and for which he claims your admiration. That is, he is a highbrow, or in older parlance, a pedant. Only, being a partial and not a thorough pedant, he also exhibits the other character of lowbrow and belongs to the huge class I should like to call the "high-lows."

There is no snob under heaven to equal this type, and its characteristics are by no means new. "Who does not know fellows," asks Holmes the Autocrat, "that always have an ill-conditioned fact or two which they lead after them into decent company like so many bulldogs . . . ? The men of facts wait their turn in grim silence, with that slight tension about the nostrils which the consciousness of carrying a 'settler' in the form of a fact or a revolver gives the individual thus armed. . . . What! Because bread is good and wholesome and nourishing, shall you thrust a crumb into my windpipe while I am talking?"

This is uncompromising enough, but for a teacher and a scientist to disallow facts and condemn "men of facts" calls for explanation, particularly if, as I hinted, some national issue hangs upon it. To many good people, our American zeal for acquiring and storing facts is praiseworthy, and I am ready to concede that once in a while the presence of factual minds in our midst is an asset. In a vast housekeeping operation such as war, the men of facts can be mustered out and pumped dry for the good of the state, their scattered drops of particular knowledge being caused to flow together into a great reservoir. But even in war this is useful only if the scarcer and more valuable type of man is available, the man of ideas, with a mind accustomed not merely to holding facts in solution but to crystallizing them for use. And the making of such men in sufficient numbers and varieties ought to be the great end of all our teaching.

The highbrow or man of facts is a mere container. His mind is a sponge, which takes up so much and gives it out again on a little squeezing. You will recognize him in the character of Howard Littlefield in Sinclair Lewis's *Babbitt*. His conversation, you remember, is made up of facts about the various derivatives of coal tar and the gross income of some corporation or other in Zenith. The trouble with him is not that he knows these things, or even that he repeats them, but that they are idle possessions of which he is proud and for which he is alternately hated and admired by his friends.

Now I contend that he and his kind are a drag on the nation's intelligence, that his view of things and men is part of a false ideal mistaken for practical wisdom, and that its corrupting influence in our culture argues a recurrent fault in our scheme of instruction, from the primary grades to the highest reaches of scholarship.

Perhaps the proposition I must chiefly document is that we are a nation of highbrows, for we affect to scorn the species and boast of our unspoiled simplicity of mind. Yet we can see the young highbrow, like the silkworm on its mulberry leaf, develop from earliest reading days upon the sports page of the newspaper. It is there that every boy begins to lay in his stock of facts — batting averages, names and records — which he prides himself on knowing and for which "the fellows" admire him. At school, as we know, the teaching of history, literature, or general science encourages the same habit, even when the boy disdains the school's less exciting collection of facts. The good pupil, the grind, is simply the boy who sops up the facts of American history instead of baseball history.[1]

Grown to man's estate, the American boy goes on acquiring facts — tons of them in his professional school, cartloads more in the course of his career — not working facts used in business, but honorific facts hoarded from pride and to fill a vacancy. The

[1] Proved by the kind of tests in American history used to show up our ignorance of the subject. See *New York Times*, April 1943, *passim.*

lawyer learns market quotations, and the Railroad Traffic Manager the serial number of freight cars. Most of the printed matter
which our representative man buys or receives deals with facts.
His favorite magazines boil them down so that he can take in
more. On his suburban train, he reads advertisements which, when
they are not simply erotic, give out facts — the pedigree of the
sheep at the basis of somebody's blankets, or the mileage of steel
cable used in the latest suspension bridge.

The fiction our citizen enjoys must have a solid ballast of correct information; else he writes to the editor about the discrepancies, and the editor thanks him in the same mail as he repri-
mands the storyteller. As for his hobby, it reveals another facet of
his cubic intellect. He probably "loves the woods" and thinks of
himself as an amateur botanist or ornithologist, but he is really a
mere collector of facts about leaves, bark, birds, and ferns. He
does not know how often he lectures, and it is you — the author,
the teacher, the scientist — whom he vaguely disapproves of for
doing it professionally. You, being in the minority with respect
to his kind, exist on sufferance and should be correspondingly
shamefaced. See how the newspaper betrays this expectation: —

Months before the invasion [of Normandy] parties of civilian
scientists landed . . . and obtained samples of sandsoil so when
the tanks and trucks bustled ashore the drivers would be prepared. . . .
The dramatic story . . . which began in musty libraries,
shifted to laboratories, and ended on shell-swept beaches, was told
today by a mild-mannered professor in baggy clothes.[2]

The tone of this report is friendly but the condescension is
plain. The "musty" libraries — unlike the airy tanks — and the
mild-mannered professor — unlike the fierce truck drivers — establish the superiority of the lowbrow over the man of knowledge.

[2] *New York Times*, June 10, 1944. See also the attack on Freudian psycho-
analysis for its reliance on "words" and "ideas" to cure mental ills as against
the "factual" use of insulin. *World-Telegram*, January 4, 1943.

Yet at the same time, it is the remarkable feat of knowingness that we are asked almost pruriently to admire.

This double standard is reflected in our best sellers (fiction apart), most of which are bulky recitals of fact — sometimes little more than compilations of newspaper clippings seasoned with backstairs gossip — yet professing to supply an understanding. Books of reference, anthologies of the best this and that, works of the "Quick, Watson, some culture" type, and fashionable popularizations — all feed the same insatiable appetite without perceptibly lessening ignorance, prejudice, or dullness. Impressive by their mass and reassuring by their factuality, these books escape the odium of being highbrow because they do not call for reflection but only for absorption. Built on the "and" principle — "this is true *and* this is true, *and* also this, *and* yet again this other thing" — they follow naturally in the worst textbook tradition, blandly ignoring how one fact is subordinated to another, or the whole set of facts to things outside the covers of the book. Summaries there may be, but no principles. For publishing experience does show that faced with an idea, no matter how simply expressed or illustrated, the layman is shocked into resistance. Automatically, his brow wrinkles in self-defense and shortens its span from natural high to affected low.

This seesawing between high and low is unquestionably a national tradition. Whereas the brain trust was a joke before anyone knew the men who belonged to it, the country has again and again given itself over to factual pedantry with great enthusiasm and no sense of ridicule. As Mr. Henry Morton Robinson has pointed out, "while naval petroleum reserves were being looted [in the 20's] American citizens were furrowing their brows over 'a drupaceous fruit beginning with "g." ' " [3] Then followed the "Ask me Another" craze — encouraged by the All-American sage, Thomas A. Edison — which in turn was followed by its modern embodiment, the "Information, Please" radio program and related

[3] *Fantastic Interim*, p. 71.

quizzlings. Not once but many times, I have heard the chief fact-givers in these shows credited with supreme intellect and culture — which they may indeed possess, but which they surely have no opportunity of displaying under the rules of the game.

Perhaps this misjudgment by people who should know better is the best illustration of my belief, that facts drive out true culture in the same way that cheap money drives out gold. When everyone is talking fact, who has ears for opinion? Who observes the distinction? The pleasure that should normally be aroused by a question, a hypothesis, a difficulty, a paradox, an unexpected point of view, becomes attached to a statement of fact; and conversely, the boredom that properly belongs to the recital of bare fact comes to be associated with the discussion of principles. Hence the dreary exchange of affidavits which passes for conversation. Nothing follows upon anything else. The doctor tells medical anecdotes which do not mesh in with the stories of bank loans and legal misadventure, while the emptiest mind present interposes locker-room stories with a "that reminds me" — which becomes the falsest phrase in the language.

Why am I so bent on conversation? For pleasure first, pure selfishness, but also because conversation is a school for thinkers and should be a school for democrats. When one finds supposedly educated people arguing heatedly over matters of fact and shying away from matters of opinion; when one sees one's hosts getting nervous at a difference of views regarding politics or the latest play; when one is formally entertained with information games or queries cut out of the paper about the number of geese in a gaggle; when the dictionary and the encyclopedia are regarded as final arbiters of judgment and not as fallible repositories of fact; when intelligent youth is advised not to go against the accepted belief in any circle because it will startle, shock, and offend — it is time to recognize, first, that the temper of democratic culture is tested at every dinner table and in every living room — just as much as at school, in the pulpit, or on the platform; and second, that by this test and despite our boasted freedom of opinion, we lack men and women whose minds have learned to move easily and fearlessly in the perilous jungle of ideas.[4]

The evil arises from a radically false relation to knowledge, which is only a step away from a radically false relation to life. Undoubtedly, no man can think without facts, and that is why teaching is of facts and about them. But if they are stored up by thoughtless habit as a squirrel stores up nuts, kept as exhibits and never stirred about to see how they mix and react, their only use is the sterile one of filling the void from which they first came. The men of fact wait in grim silence, as Holmes said, to make a throw and claim a point.

To be sure, some predicaments seem to call for pure information, as when one of my students, now a war correspondent, had to navigate a fishing boat to escape by night from the enemy. "I knew," he said, "that the stars moved, but not in what direction." Yet he "thought" his way out in the end. No one can know all the facts he might possibly need, though many students confess to having this Gargantuan appetite and try to feed it. But the scheme is unpractical: life is too short, memory balks, and worst of all, while the scholar turns himself into a human silo for grains of knowledge, thought starves in the midst of plenty.

It would only be a slight exaggeration to say that facts grow out of knowledge, and not knowledge out of facts. In any case both should remain means to the good life and never usurp the place of ends. Why does it never occur to the hardened highbrow either that you already know his facts and do not wish to have them rehearsed, or that although they are new to you, you are not seated at his festive board in order to cram, either physically or mentally? The only answer to this is that he has no notion of what life is for. He is indeed aware that although one eats food

---

[4] See my article on "The Literature of Ideas" in the Anniversary Number of the *Saturday Review*, August 5, 1944.

to keep alive, a certain artistic form and pleasure can be given to dining. But he fails utterly to make the parallel applicable to his raw facts, and never suspects that they may all be variations of one dull dish, savorless and indigestible.

In a great passage of his *Psychology*, James gives a suggestive account of this blindness from the point of view of his science. And the real meaning of the light touch and the allusive manner is so often overlooked or denied in our day that his conclusions are worth quoting at length, with the warning that in contrasting "gentleman" and "plebeian," James is not thinking of fixed social classes but of mental types; he might as easily have said "acrobat" and "clodhopper": —

When two minds of a high order, interested in kindred subjects, come together, their conversation is chiefly remarkable for the summariness of its allusions and the rapidity of its transitions. Before one of them is half through a sentence, the other knows his meaning and replies. Such genial play with such massive materials, such an easy flashing of light over far perspectives, such careless indifference to the dust and apparatus that ordinarily surround the subject and seem to pertain to its essence, make these conversations seem true feasts for gods to a listener who is educated enough to follow them at all. His mental lungs breathe more deeply, in an atmosphere more broad and vast than is their wont. On the other hand, the excessive explicitness and short-windedness of an ordinary man are as wonderful as they are tedious to the man of genius. But we need not go so far as the ways of genius. Ordinary social intercourse will do. There the charm of conversation is in direct proportion to the possibility of abridgment and elision, and in inverse ratio to the need of explicit statement. With old friends a word stands for a whole story or set of opinions. With newcomers everything must be gone over in detail. Some persons have a real mania for completeness, they must express every step. They are the most intolerable of companions, and although their mental energy may in its way be great, they always strike us as weak and second-rate. In short, the essence of plebeianism, that which separates vulgarity from aristocracy, is perhaps less a defect than an excess, the constant need to animadvert upon matters which for the aristocratic temperament do not exist. To ignore, to disdain to consider, to overlook, are the essence of the "gentleman." . . . All this suppression of the secondary leaves the field *clear* — for higher flights, should they choose to come. But even if they never came, what thoughts there were would still manifest the aristocratic type and wear the well-bred form. . . .

I may appear to have strayed from psychological analysis into aesthetic criticism. But the principle of selection is so important that no illustrations seem redundant which may help show how great is its scope.

The analogy with art is suggestive, and neutralizes any irrelevant overtone that might come from the word "aristocratic." For it has often been remarked that many simple people who make no pretense to culture, and even less to high birth, have the ability to endow whatever they say with charm and meaning. Often this power seems to go with the practice of a handicraft or of a trade that enters into conflict with the elements. From which we might argue that a habit of shaping matter by hand, or the need to cope with nature, liberates the mind from facts by spurring the creative will to act upon them. Is not this in truth the main point of Thoreau's *Walden*, which we Americans keep reading and reprinting without taking to heart its emphatic lesson?

II

If this addiction to fact — from which none of us is wholly exempt — is indeed nationwide, it can cause no surprise to hear that even in the open city of the intellect one finds mantraps and impediments of the same sort. The observer finds that even where brows are all of a good size, some are higher than others; some kinds of facts are admired, others despised. I have already spoken of the rival faculty clans for or against science, for or against the study of history or of a foreign language. These are the most obvious rifts. Behind the monumental gates, the garment of learning is the object of a tug of war that leaves it looking like a collection of rags. A number of times I have attended informal discussion groups made up of university men; always I have found manners apologetic, susceptibilities raw, and discussion scurrying to take refuge in the shelter of a specialty. In fact, such groups do not long hold together, for there is no common ground and too much common restraint. Discrepancies of age and rank add further obstacles, and one wonders whether there ever was literal meaning in the phrase "a *company* of scholars."

The lines of snobbery do not coincide only with subject matters. A vast distance separates the college professor socially from the high school teacher, and both from the instructors in preparatory schools. Prejudice thrives in the no man's land, to the infinite harm of all concerned; for no routine scorn on the part of colleges and no complacency about doing the harder job on the part of secondary schools is going to unify the course of studies through which every able American boy must pass. It will therefore continue to be an ill-joined affair precisely at the point where students find it so difficult to keep in stride. Better understanding may come from the scheme already tried out of sending to college selected high school seniors, but surely intellectual contact between a teacher of science in the twelfth grade and his successor in the college freshman course should not wait upon innovations affecting only a few among the school population. How can there be a regular gradation of trained minds throughout our society if hairlines of difference act like the Great Wall of China?

Again, why must there be arbitrary barriers, not only among the several disciplines on a single campus — that is known to be bad and a change is in sight — but also between journalism and literature or journalism and scholarship? One would suppose the substance of these three was three different things instead of one presented in as many ways. But the prevalent attitude splits the field and generates undisguised hostility. A reporter from a large news agency — an entire stranger — once rang me up for the favor of a brief consultation. He came, bringing with him a large roll of pictures to be syndicated throughout the country. They showed important events and figures in European history, for which he had written the captions. Were they correct? Of the fifteen or twenty sizable blocks of print, perhaps three or four were right enough to pass. The others all contained one or more serious errors, not of incidental fact, but of major significance. I suggested changes, but as I half expected, my visitor argued. Was it so very wrong, he wondered, to represent Bismarck as always seeking war? The important thing, he felt, was to have the dates right. I pointed out the relative values of fact and truth and reminded him that he was the one who came to ask my opinion. Where-upon he shifted his ground and maintained that what he had written came from a good encyclopedia. Why was I questioning it? I could not tell him that he had misread and misinterpreted, and he went away, as disgruntled, no doubt, as I was discouraged.

In such an instance we come close to the root of the whole cultural problem, the inherent weakness of all modern literacy: it is half-baked and arrogant. It trifles solemnly with the externals of things, neglecting even the surfaces or the handles by which a truth may be seized: it goes like a child for the false glint or striking triviality of detail.[5]

This vice is not limited to journalists as a group but to all "in-tellectuals" who trust the journalistic way of bottling and labeling information. Why does every war against Germany bring up the same old platitudes about Fichte and Hegel and Nietzsche, which later on are forgotten or disavowed by their authors? Simply because the college-educated mind is a collection of such ideas, barely scalp-deep, and all the more treacherous that they have the rounded self-sufficient appearance of "facts." If you say "Nietzsche" I think "Blond Beast of Prey"; if you say "Rous-seau," I think "Noble Savage"; if you say "Emerson," I think

---

[5] We were told by radio during the siege of Cherbourg that the fortifica-tions of the town had been built by Vauban for Napoleon. Why? Probably because Vauban's name occurs in some article on Cherbourg and Napoleon serves as a generic name for all French rulers and conquerors.

"Self-reliance"; if you say "Darwin," I think "evolution"; if you say "Farewell Address," I think "no entangling alliances." I think no further because "I know it for a fact." Yet there would still be not one grain of accurate sense in any of these associations, though every jury in the country should acquit me of misrepresentation. Wouldn't it be far better, as Josh Billings remarked, "not to know so much as to know so many things that ain't so"?

Far better, because there is something incurable about the organ that wraps itself around such "facts." Nothing new will penetrate it or mingle with them, and since all true learning depends on fitting and refitting the new to the old in the mind, self-education stops on the near side of any catch phrase. When a student comes to college stuffed with ready-made notions, it is still possible to say to him: "You know nothing if you only know these things; forget them; pull them out one by one and go bury them." But no one can serve corresponding notice on an adult who thinks he has *finished* his education. Even when the ignorant or half-educated are humble enough to consult a genuine authority, he turns out not to be wanted — he disappoints — unless he brings a special jargon that can be laid on and shown off without compelling the inquirer to learn or change his mind.[6]

Surely this deserves to be called mental cowardice — a vice that differs from laziness and often masquerades as modesty. The man who calls himself a lowbrow is of course boasting and lying but also shirking. The educated woman's "I wouldn't know anything about that" is not modest, but defensive. "How do you know you wouldn't? Your very ignorance refutes itself. Wait and see: read to the end of the page; listen to the end of the sentence; DON'T

[6] A colleague of mine in the classics was rung up by a firm that wanted to know the Latin term for "advertising man." When he said there was no such term, he was asked to make up one, which he did, but this did not suit, because they had one of their own, which they wanted approved, namely, *Homo publicitas.* The copywriter who struck off this gem must be the same who was impelled a little later to call television "the video art." Pedantry in low places!

RUN AWAY! For even if the new idea fails to enlighten, it will not hurt you. Remember that what one fool can do, another can; and by good luck and the use of a little mental courage, you *might* after a while be able to recognize a syllogism or to tell 'God Save the Weasel' from 'Pop Goes the Queen'!"

The nearer one gets to popular tastes and unstudied actions, the more widespread the signs of mental cowardice. Observe how timid and sensitive and frightened are the readers of cheap fiction: the slightest novelty, the least deviation from formula, scatters their mind in a panic; so that the art of catering for them as magazine editors consists in being in a perpetual sweat of anxiety about particular ideas, feelings, and words. Compared to them the so-called esthete is a tough character ever ready for a word and a blow, even if the blow is aimed at his solar plexus and the word is one made up of six others, scrambled together by the art of James Joyce. Not that "intellectuals" do not also huddle in cliques with a very narrow range of physical tolerance for the unfamiliar, but at least their pride is on the side of intellectual adventure.

I suppose that the frantic clutch for a mental security card has something to do with the dread of all realities and the increasing difficulty of getting at them. For most people the objection to intellect is the same as the objection to art: both are too strong, too direct, too close. So it is better to pretend that intellect is out of reach in the clouds. But the clouds are not what they are thought to be. They exist, but they are not natural to intellect. Rather they are smoke screens, which we owe to commentators, to journalism, to "literacy." The clouds come from the objectors themselves. The result is that for a man to find his way through to the real Nietzsche or Darwin is a laborious task. He must forget what he "knows" and read Nietzsche himself, not one book merely but perhaps as many as three, lending his mind to each, while comparing and assimilating. He must consult biographers and critics and sort out the chaff; and when he has done, though he has satisfied his curiosity and come to grips with the real substance behind the word "Nietzsche," he finds that he has only cut himself off from newspaper-educated opinion.

No wonder most people prefer to invest their mental energies in tasks requiring less gumption, and that these tasks acquire an unmerited worthiness. If you notice, we are all scholars now, we do research — the man of business like all the rest. But the research is of the assembling-and-packaging kind. There is a tremendous demand to "know" — to know what? To know the ratings of soap operas or the length of time it takes to read the Constitution; to know the average life of a front tire on a four-door sedan, or the five hundred best books of the decade, classified in groups and rated in order of merit by leading librarians.

Hundreds of study groups and fact-finding commissions, public or private, give their members in this way the pleasant illusion of being practical scholars and social "scientists." The facts usually lie in surface soil — supposing they are facts at all and not verbalisms — and they can be had for a little scratching. The results are then published and we have another layer of paper wadding between us and the horrors of life. Just as there is a business concern that will remind you by telephone that it is your wife's birthday, making you a model husband, so "research" has now progressed to the point where our culture has been broken down into published "facts," making you a realist. You can find a hundred specimen cases, fully charted, of almost anything you are interested in; which should give you the double satisfaction of quenching your own thirst for facts, and of knowing that the preparation of the study fulfilled a similar need in the researcher. He is proud and you admire him, looking down — both of you — on other highbrows.

After your labors, no one need ever again open a real book — let alone the mind's eye. All one need do is consult the Progress Report, the Summary of Findings to Date, or the Study of Fifty One-Armed Paperhangers. In the end, the nation may not have a very clear head, but it has a Gallup poll.

20. *The Little Money*

> What the average citizen desires
> to have done in education gets
> itself accomplished, though the
> process should involve the ex-
> tinction of the race of educated
> gentlemen.
> — JOHN JAY CHAPMAN

THE HIGHBROW TRADITION evidently does not exist in a vacuum;
it is not self-supporting. It is sustained, in part, by the flow of
money through accustomed channels. We get what we pay for,
and we pay for what we want — or think we want. If instead of
Howard Littlefields we wish to make something else out of the
wonderful vitality and intelligence of our youth, we must show
in substantial ways that we value that something else, and why we
value it. We must put a premium upon intellect, and a premium
is always money. Despite the convention that love of learning
lessens the need for material things, brains are attached to organs
that require sustenance. No person of intellectual ambition or
attainments should feel ashamed to own that he needs three meals
a day, a roof over his head and, in addition, a quantity of expensive things like books and music and leisure, which the ordinary
man would consider luxuries or superfluities.

Although it is true that a good deal of money is spent in and
around education in this country, the prevailing style among those
engaged in learning and teaching is the shabby-genteel. Money
and good will have not been wanting, but the distribution has
been haphazard, often wasteful, and almost always thoughtless.
Wherein does it go wrong?

To take one important heading of appropriation, there is by
and large no respectable collegiate policy with regard to student

scholarships. The present Congressional law guaranteeing liberal maintenance and full tuition to qualified veterans is the only one based on a correct principle, and it is perhaps best not to go into the motives of its drafting. Normally, a scholarship holder on an American campus belongs to one of four categories. He may be an athlete supported by a local alumni club — his chief contribution to scholarship in the other sense occurring eight Saturdays during the year on a muddy field. Or he may be a poor boy of middling quality who has applied for financial help and received it, to continue during good behavior at the same level of academic work. Or the scholarship holder may have been given aid as fulfilling certain specifications of age, training, nationality, race, or vocational purpose. A particular deed of gift called for certain characteristics and he alone possessed them. Or finally, the incumbent may have won his award in competition against others in the state or in the college, by means of marks or examinations. This is the only scholarship that represents scholarship and deserves the name.

Most likely none of these awards keeps its man. True, there are also available to the needy grants-in-aid and loans for payment of tuition. These are fairly liberally administered but they are probably withheld from scholarship holders, so that every campus counts students who are forced to combine study with an excessive amount of remunerative work. I have mentioned in an earlier chapter actual cases of paralyzing need and heart-rending effort. If the victims are men of the highest caliber, this is an egregious waste of their gifts and of the institution's opportunities. The incidental training of "character" is either negligible or priced too high to be worth a thought. Far from dwelling on it complacently, any establishment that calls itself a seat of learning should put its pride in freeing all its distinguished minds from drudgery, even that of washing dishes or airing dogs for pay.[1]

[1] It follows that I view with a lackluster eye the housework program which is part of the Black Mountain curriculum.

This means that the committee on scholarships should stop acting the fairy godmother and adopt instead the single-minded policy of subsidizing merit. The criterion for awarding funds should be, not the need of the student for a college education, but the need of the college and the country for top-notch students. There should be an end to the required confession of poverty, which is irrelevant, degrading, and sometimes mendacious. All questions of health and character — except in cases so extreme that they probably would not arise — should be omitted, and the only proper inquiry should be satisfied by evidence of talent, achievement, and promise. The committee should be composed of a majority of teachers, men committed to intellect and indifferent (as administrators notoriously are not) to smooth manners and apple-cheeked innocence. "Nice boys" have their place but it is not *ipso facto* at the top.

The waiver of the health qualification may shock some readers. It is indeed a revolutionary proposal. Just recently a great foundation denied a grant to a man of acknowledged ability, whom they themselves had gladly accepted until they found that he was not in absolute physical trim. Whereupon they gave him the stipend but withheld the title of the fellowship — in short, stultified their own rule. Dr. Johnson's is far sounder, being based on a much longer series of cases. He says, in the memorandum jotted down for his *Life of Pope* — "Motives to study: want of health, want of money." One need only reflect upon any imagined hall of fame to agree that it would be folly to turn down Beethoven for deafness, Keats for tuberculosis, C. P. Steinmetz for a hunched back, or Lafcadio Hearn for near-blindness.

All but a few of the scholarships awarded should be large enough to provide full tuition and living expenses. It is useless to offer a hundred dollars a year to a penniless boy; indeed this is to tantalize him in an almost immoral fashion which can only lead to worry, overwork, and academic failure. If a country as poor as Scotland can see to it that every able man, were he the son of a washerwoman, reaches the university — a policy now almost a century old — we ought with our greater resources to do as well or better. Oxford and Cambridge are still considered discriminatory on economic grounds. Yet *more than half the students* who attend them receive scholarships ranging from $160 to $1000 a year. In this country, full scholarships will require three to four times the amount of funds now available; colleges and universities should therefore open the campaign by educating their friends and alumni. This should be part of a wider undertaking to present their general financial case more forcefully to the public, and I should like to see the leading institutions forming on this subject a united front: it is a national concern, and only a concerted drive will succeed.

If the alumni must have invincible teams, let them continue to send promising athletes to their alma mater, but since this often requires steady "co-operation" on the part of the admitting authorities as well as the teaching staff, let the alumni clubs be told that every second recipient of their support must be a genuine student. Let the college authorities at any rate drop the too frequent pretense of apologizing to the old grads for keeping up an illicit connection with learning. No person or institution can hope for more respect than it pays to itself, and hitherto academic behavior in front of the business world has been excessively worm-inspired. There have been deception, self-deception, and reciprocal injury. Under the pretext that gift horses should not be orally examined, colleges have let themselves be burdened with buildings they could not afford, research departments they could not staff, and grants for "studies" they could not carry out. At the same time they have lacked funds for an adequate teaching staff, for working equipment, and for student scholarships. They were not land poor, but plant poor and grant poor.

In spite of this, ever since Andrew Carnegie supplied the country with libraries, the public has thought of millionaire munificence as endowing learning. This has hardly been true for twenty years. There have been vast outlays for brick and mortar — for memorial halls which could be named after the donor — but these were already anachronisms. The universities had physically expanded up to and beyond their legitimate size; what they now needed was the means to support living talent. They still need it; but unfortunately for higher learning, the typical bequest is one of thirty thousand dollars for cancer research. I have no love of cancer and no jealousy of medical research, but it is plain that this sort of gift does nothing for higher learning. It springs from a sympathy grounded in animal fear, leaving untouched the duty to train young minds while they are still free from the deadly scorpion. Taking at random a recent announcement of gifts to one institution and analyzing it, I find that of $69,900 the bulk was earmarked for medicine, chemistry, engineering, and allied sciences; a small fraction went to history, public law, business, and occupational therapy; and an anonymous donor assigned ten thousand dollars to research in syphilis. If we count the subjects, the ratio is two to one in favor of serving animal needs — and the distribution of cash makes it more like one hundred and fifty to one.

We meet again our national faith in facts and our distrust of mind. This might be a permissible choice if it did not also amount to a mistrust of men. We think the American way respects ability and trusts in individual initiative — it may be so, but not in education. A glance at the policies of the great educational foundations will make my meaning clear. All of them naturally feel a serious responsibility in administering their vast resources. They want to avoid mistakes and they would like to see results. Nothing could be more proper, were it not that the word "see" is ambiguous, and that since the money must be given out ahead of performance, a safeguard is found in carefully planned "projects" which look as if pregnant with results. The seeing eye naturally jumps to the concrete, the familiar, and the upshot is an unfortunate subsidizing of measures instead of men, coupled with a strict accounting of "progress," of work published, in short, of "results."

I say unfortunate because I am persuaded that this is not the way to lay out money and get the most out of it. If we are agreed that the funds are meant for education, scholarship, science, art, wisdom, and good teaching — one foundation is for the advancement of teaching — then the only safe and profitable thing to do is to cast the bread upon the waters, to invest the money in men — men and women — not in things, not in projects, and not under control.[2] What do I mean by "things"? I mean the secretarial apparatus, the mimeographed paper, the steel filing cabinets — of which the granting authorities are usually lavish, while they are exceedingly "careful" about awards to human beings. When I am despondent I see in my mind's eye an endless row of steel files, reaching, dark green, to the moon: they are filled to bursting with records and tests and graphs, and upon each cabinet sits the pale ghost who filled it in return for his stipend. "For the same money" — to use the vulgarest standard — he might have been a scholar, a critic, a poet; or simply an educated man, a thoughtful citizen and capable parent, with no other "purpose" in view than his own and his country's good. Which, I wonder, is the truer execution of the testator's billion-dollar bequest?

I might add that when I am despondent I do not necessarily exaggerate; perhaps I only see more vividly and comprehensively: I happen to know that it costs one foundation twelve hundred dollars a year to maintain a young man who is working with great knowledge and fervor at musical composition based on new scales and instruments. Well, at the institution where he works are whole attics filled with discarded tests, once part of a great piece of educational research. Counting all the wasted typing and man-hours of drudgery, one attic's worth would keep the musician in funds for ten years. Double his grant and he might achieve

[2] The American Council of Learned Societies and the Guggenheim Foundation should be excluded from this generality. They work on the principle I advocate and their experience justifies it.

his results in less time, certainly with less wear and tear. The great obstacle to this obvious improvement is that the educational tests were tangible, undeniable "facts," though useless; whereas a piece of strange music or even an instrument bristling with stops and keys seems dubious, unsubstantial, hardly fit for impressive listing in an Annual Report.

And so the rich subsidies of education are frittered away in schemes. I have before me an Evaluation Study of a whole college — ten thousand dollars; a report on freshman exploratory work — thirty thousand dollars a year for five years; a test on "forms of thinking" conducted at a school of education — twenty-seven thousand; a project on "approaches" to history — five thousand dollars renewed for three years; a comparative examination of methods of conducting field work — x hundred dollars. The printed mass takes up the room of a good set of Poe's works or *The Three Musketeers* with all its sequels. It cost eyesight, adrenalin, and the social investment of several dozen college educations before the first of these thousands of useless pages could even be penned. And do not think that it is one man's biased view that puts their value so low. Go to the very institutions where each "project" was undertaken and look for its "results." They are nonexistent. The very memory of the deed has been forgotten, and of all those who received the handsome report fresh from the press I am perhaps the only one who has kept it. Its use, if any, begins now, on this printed page of mine, as an example of How Not to Do It.

II

The same considerations apply to Faculty salaries: the money should go to men, and by preference to men who teach. It is too often taken for granted that one administrator or one research man is worth three teachers, and it is only when the latter — or rather a few among them — reach their last years of service, perhaps in an endowed chair, that they begin to receive a salary — I will not say adequate to their merit, for that would be an incommensurable expression — but adequate to the standard of living which it would be *desirable for the country* to have them maintain. I do not know what the Romans paid their college of augurs, but if they wanted the people to have faith in their auguries, they must have taken care to support those gifted persons as befitted their importance and their devotion to the state.

With professorial salaries in American universities reaching the not very dizzy height of nine or ten thousand dollars a year,[3] the only way a teacher can reconcile his self-respect and his money sense is by considering that he earns only a retaining fee. He may work himself to death in an effort to teach during every moment of presence in class, but he reflects that since the spirit bloweth where it listeth, he is paid only to put in an appearance at the scheduled hours. Therefore his pay is ample, particularly if he keeps a portion of his genius for other uses. This beautifully takes care of the dilemma, as old as the Greek Sophists, whether a man has a moral right to sell knowledge instead of giving it away. The American teacher unquestionably gives it away, while managing somehow to live on the bonus which a grateful society offers him for giving it away in one place rather than another.[4]

It is the "managing to live" which is the bad feature. Society expects that teachers shall dress well, live in a suitable district, and frequent good company — all on the salary of a policeman. Some colleges have recognized this quasi impossibility by refusing to appoint young men as instructors unless they have at least a

[3] From the start, the Institute of Advanced Study has bettered the highest professorial salary by about half.

[4] The lower depths of the profession's earning power are painful to think of and undercut any irony; e.g. in 1940 there were 433 junior colleges, whose salary scale ranged, on an average, from $1572 to $2130 a year; and 177 teachers' colleges, for which the figures are $2433 and $3600. Needless to add, 98 per cent of each group want nothing but Ph.D.'s on their staff, though they do not always get them.

small independent income. Another way would be to have promising young men in the profession advertise for wives with dowries; or perhaps one of the foundations could subsidize campus eugenics: the academic couple would submit the baby as evidence of good faith, and meanwhile a member of the profession would have benefited from the one freedom it most needs — the freedom from care. Not long since, I was shocked to read the announcement of an article by the wife of a college professor, entitled "Ouch! How that white collar pinches!" How entertaining for the readers of America's oldest popular magazine to learn the sordid details of high thinking and plain living on two thousand dollars a year! And how becoming for the richest civilization on record to number its men of learning among the lowest grade of routine office workers — once cleric, now clerical.

If it is true that the student whose mind is being formed needs books, pictures, travel, and leisure, all the more does the man who is to exert the formative influence. A soul, as Bernard Shaw has pointed out, is an expensive thing to maintain and it perishes if starved. It may safely neglect both the coarse pleasures and the monumental vices, but it must feed steadily and without stint on articles of diet which are at once costly and rare. Some of them indeed are only to be found by good fortune — pleasant surroundings, agreeable companionship, quiet of mind and body. This and other desires may seem self-indulgent, but they are, whether acknowledged to be so or not, indispensable professional expenses. In a remarkable passage of his autobiography, John Stuart Mill, who was surely austere enough to be a fair witness, has recounted the educational effect upon him in early youth of visits to Bentham at Ford Abbey. "Nothing," he says, "contributes more to nourish elevation of sentiments in a people, than the large and free character of their habitations. The middle-age architecture, the baronial hall, and the spacious and lofty rooms of this fine old place, so unlike the mean and cramped externals of English middle class life, gave the sentiment of a larger and freer existence, and were to me a sort of poetic cultivation." [5]

"Larger and freer existence" are the operative words here and they need not be taken as exclusively pointing to Gothic architecture. We might bear this in mind when we condemn American collegiate styles wholesale: they are at least symbols of space and liberality of design. We can even regret that in so many institutions the faculty cannot live in collegiate dwellings, near their work, though sheltered from students; but must return after the day's work to the "mean and cramped externals" that Mill justly deplores. As for the greatest and freest American style of building, the style of our century, we must hang our head in shame to think it has made as yet no mark on our centers of learning. We have the most beautiful campuses, with lakes and hills and greensward, but our newer buildings seem to be ever more cramped and uninspiring — those devoted to faculty apartments worst of all, built as if on purpose to depress, each suite, in Trollope's phrase, "a suicidal set of chambers." What do our teachers do? Paradoxically, they must resort to Europe every other year or so, to restore their souls with sensations of largeness and freedom.

The evil we must even now stave off is that with the interruption caused by the war, with heedless cries for accelerated courses, with economic uncertainty and roller-coasting prices, poverty will tighten its grip still harder on those who should by profession be able to afford disinterested lives. We know too well the endless round in which more than one victim, great or humble, has succumbed: to lead the good life takes money — enough money not to be always thinking of it; money takes laborious time to earn; and this leaves none for leading the good life. How many, like William James — who still enjoyed what would be called "advantages" — have overdone and exploited certain talents in order to keep their best self fairly nourished? It was always the Summer

[5] Ed. New York 1924, p. 39.

School, the paid lectures during the Christmas recess, the article for the popular magazine. With modern acceleration, it will be the "chance" to teach all three terms every year for extra compensation, or else the filling in of the vacation with similar work at another place.

Already before the war summer schools had attained an insane popularity. The lovers of art, literature, science, and politics apparently could not keep away from one another more than a week. No sooner had academic hostilities ceased in one spot than they rushed into country meant for summering and set up the tents of war for further battle. One saw straggling back to the campus in mid-September haggard, sleepless students and instructors, the former full of glory and "credits," the latter richer by a few hundred dollars, and poorer by incalculable sums. Truly, as Sidney Lanier said, "we have lengthened life by shortening leisure."

From these and other facts some have argued that teachers should organize themselves into unions and demand the standard of living they think they are entitled to. This might be a practicable way if it could ever be determined what leverage teachers can employ and who their employers are. I feel a strong corporate sense binding me to my colleagues, and once upon a time I joined a so-called union to see what it could do. It could obviously help teachers in public schools and other tax-supported institutions by lobbying at the legislature in the approved way. But the members of an endowed college or university are in a peculiar position: they do not work for themselves, nor truly for their clients, the students; nor for the administrative heads, who are mere agents; nor for the trustees, who do not run a profit-making concern. The university teacher clearly works for the public. But he cannot strike, expostulate, bargain, or picket. The fact that colleges are of so many different kinds, run on so many different financial plans, may obscure this common role and their common needs, but the profession being by and large under the control of public opinion, it is before the public that teachers must present their claims.

The proper body to accomplish this is then not a union in the ordinary sense, but a guild — of which one or two approximations already exist — whose chief object should be to establish and maintain intelligent and dignified public relations. It should endeavor to tell the people what teachers are for, what they do and what they want, and why it seems best to support them more liberally than hitherto. This would have a double advantage: the first, a raising of the dignity of the profession; the second, an indirect training of the population in matters upon which they pass judgment whether they know it or not.

When one considers that almost every adult necessarily comes in contact with education by being a parent, a taxpayer, a member of a school board, a reader of books and periodicals, a library and museum visitor, or a radio listener, one can see the political need for closing the rift between the laity and the teaching profession. Parent-teacher associations cannot do it, or at least have not done it, for reasons too numerous to go into. But an association of teachers of all ranks and specialties, and serving the interests of teachers before the public — a real and inclusive professional body — might in time improve a multitude of conditions, of which not the least is the reallocation of funds for the sake of a freer, richer, and more irresistible instruction.

A suggestion more ambitious still, but one which I find attractive and just in principle, would be to organize every college or university into a genuine company of scholars, the proceeds of whose work should be shared among themselves on some equitable basis. Individual initiative could be encouraged by reserving a suitable portion of earnings and royalties to the author, while the rest would be credited to a fund for annual distribution among the group.[6] In most cases, the university press could be the main

[6] President Hutchins's proposal, akin to this, has much to recommend it. He would raise all salaries, abolish intermediate ranks, appropriate all

agency for marketing the products of scholarship, both local and general. A healthy regional competition could arise and a somewhat stouter direction be thereby given to research.

Whatever may seem utopian about this proposal — which has been made at various times and places — is really not so, for absolute individualism in scholarship is an illusion. Scholars already engage in many co-operative ventures whose profits go into the General Fund; publishing a set of source and textbooks is a case in point. The knowledge of twenty people goes into the work and returns seldom accrue to the doers. Conversely, the "authors" draw upon the brains and experience of their colleagues as well as upon the facilities, the books, and the time that belong strictly speaking to the community. A redistribution of joint annual earnings would be simply a clearer business arrangement.

I am so far from desiring a slovenly pooling of thine and mine in academic life that I should like to see at work within it a sharper sense of business values. Too many persons, inside and outside the profession, act as if a teacher's time or thought were a free commodity. It is flattering to be considered on the same plane as sunlight, but any guild of scholars should set its face against this belief and train its membership to put a proper price on their services. I do not urge this to inaugurate monopoly gouging, but to safeguard quality and conditions of work, including self-respect.

As things now stand abuses are rife. Within the profession, nothing is more common than the request for free lectures, free concerts, even the free gift of books which one has written. Except when this type of charity has a clear excuse, all such requests should be steadfastly refused, with a precise explanation of the reason why. One college I know used to cry poor according

---

royalties, and grant two months' extra leave for "producing." My sole objection is to the reduction of the normal vacation to a single month, and to its extension only for the sake of turning out work. I am certain that teaching would again suffer. Three to four months free, without imposed obligations, is a strict *minimum* for all teachers.

to a set form, so as to obtain cheap the most interesting outside lecturers; yet it always had enough funds for the elaborate entertainment of Trustees, parents, and graduating classes, as well as for expensive printing on all occasions. This amounts to the cynical and unethical practice of paying for luxuries by bilking the butcher. Choosing may be hard, but a college has a duty to find out whether it loves wisdom better than teacakes, for as one student absent-mindedly wrote in a paper, "You cannot serve God and Gammon at the same time."

Outside the profession, all sorts of persons, clubs, and commercial firms have learned the same begging habit for obtaining professional services gratis or at a nominal fee. One wealthy and powerful publisher wishing an expert opinion on a manuscript intimated that since the firm examined so many books, it could only pay a few dollars to have each one judged. Does the head of the house speak to his doctor or lawyer in that graceful cadging way? The reverse of this attempted graft is of course the distribution of free books, and teachers should have enough moral fiber to decline such gifts (which they ultimately pay for in the price of other books) so as to have a clear conscience when putting a price on their opinion as experts. Another well-dressed mendicant said to me: "This is a book you'd read anyhow. Read it for us in manuscript and we'll give you a copy — if we publish it." The mixed appeal to the gambling instinct, the love of bribery, and the urge to self-depreciation reaches here its perfection.

If the corporate business spirit has a proper role in our society — and it seems to be built into our very laws — the man of knowledge has a clear duty to insist on due remuneration. It is not because it only takes him a few minutes to give out information that therefore the information has cost him nothing. It is not because someone else's purpose is "educational" that therefore he must fulfill it free. As a distinguished violinist said, "I will gladly play without fee to your students — if you refund to them the afternoon's tuition." And an author who was being "reasoned with" on the ground that his giving a judgment on an anthology would really mean a pleasant evening's reading, cut the begging short with — "Sorry, my education's been too expensive."

The teacher and thinker must constantly bear in mind the special conditions that define his craft. He cannot count as aids to his advancement the pain and fear that favor the doctor, nor the apprehensions of loss and disgrace that favor the lawyer. He has on his side only mankind's desire for light — the light that gives all other things their shape; and this, though a strong motive, is easily obscured by more immediate demands. The teacher must consequently sustain it most steadfastly in the very persons who neglect or forget it easily. He must do this not for their good merely, though that is a real reason, but for his good whenever it is identifiable with the good of his calling. Like any other man, a teacher may be selfish and mistake private ends for public, but this possibility must not keep him from upholding the public ends he represents, even though those ends are expressed — as they are bound to be — in money. Without money, intellect is crippled, art starves, and science stagnates. If the Field Marshal is not ashamed to admit that money is the sinews of war, the teacher should feel no qualms in proclaiming that *alma mater* means first of all the nourishing mother.

21. To a Young Man Who—

> Let no man say, "Come,
> I will write a duodecimo."
> — STERNE

THERE IS on my shelves a book of late Victorian aspect which I once picked up at a secondhand shop for a very small sum, and which I occasionally dip into for pleasure and wisdom. It is called *The Intellectual Life,* and was written by Philip Gilbert Hamerton, around 1875.[1] I bought it because my eye happened to catch one of its best chapter headings: —

TO A YOUNG MAN OF INTELLECTUAL TASTES, WHO, WITHOUT HAVING AS YET ANY PARTICULAR LADY IN VIEW, HAD EXPRESSED, IN A GENERAL WAY, HIS DETERMINATION TO GET MARRIED

This is followed by marginal summaries equally alluring: "Only two courses open for the intellectual . . . Danger of unequal marriages . . . Peasant girls . . . Opinion of a distinguished artist . . ."

The combination of ludicrous primness and outspoken good sense in Hamerton's pages makes the work an ideal bedside book, but it is for the deliberate treatment of his subject as a whole that I respect and value him. There are no books, or very few, about the intellectual life, with the result that after ten millennia of culture this particular vocation of man remains a vague mystery. We know about the fisherman's life from Izaak Walton and about

---

[1] Hamerton was a remarkably prolific writer, of English birth, widely traveled, and especially competent in treating of the fine arts. His *Life of J. M. W. Turner* is full of excellent ideas and his books about France and the French are truer and wiser than many works by later writers.

the naturalist's from Gilbert White, Darwin, and a host of others, but apart from hints here and there in the letters and diaries of thinkers and artists, we rely chiefly on crude superstitions about the conditions, pleasures, and pains of the life of mind. One of the merits of *The Autocrat of the Breakfast-Table*, by the way, is that it contains many sound observations on the man of thought. But crumbs are not enough; the intellectual life is a real subject for description, because it is the goal at which the highest instruction aims, and because it is synonymous with education, scholarship, and culture truly defined.

This being so, Hamerton's concern in the chapter about marriage — one of nine on the subject of women — is certainly of prime importance. But it rests on a simpler truth, which is that the world is not organized for the life of mind. The world is organized for business and domesticity. Feeding and clothing its members and reproducing its kind are humanity's primary tasks, necessarily so; and no civilization that we know of has ever put these activities in the second place. First live, said the ancients, then philosophize. Americans therefore are in the great tradition, and may safely disregard the common charge of being excessively materialistic for simply doing on a larger scale what other peoples have done before them. Because we have cleared and settled the land, built upon it, multiplied comforts and refined machinery, we are not automatically damned. The damnation only comes from going on, after these achievements, to deny space, time, and money to the servants of intellect. This denial, so far as we have been guilty of it, has come less from deliberate intent than from ignorance and heedlessness. I described how and why in the two previous chapters on the highbrow tradition and the habit of looking for quick and obvious results.

But if we consider our history as a whole, we are struck by the persistence of an opposite tradition, a minority tradition, perhaps, but of remarkable strength and distinction. Our great figures — the most popular as well as the most withdrawn — have stood for intellect: not Hawthorne only or Melville or Jonathan Edwards, but Franklin and Lincoln and Artemus Ward and Theodore Roosevelt. Jefferson was not, as is commonly supposed, a sentimental lover of the small man with a small brain, but an encyclopedic learner with a passion for thought and knowledge. New England was made great by force of mind. Whitman's *Democratic Vistas* is not exclusively a hymn of praise for common virtues but also a denunciation of common superficiality of thought. A representative Westerner such as Mark Twain, a delineator of the commonest man such as Ring Lardner, even a cowboy wit like Will Rogers — all express the same faith in the superiority of man thinking.

Perhaps it took the depression of 1929 to make us recognize how insecure our other resources could become if we lacked the brains to hold them and keep them serviceable. And the same catastrophe helped us to take stock, through Federal projects employing writers, actors, scholars, painters, and musicians, of how much talent we really had available. We now know that the good life does not come into being automatically and that a proud culture calls for the support of culture makers. What we do not yet know sufficiently for our good and for theirs is what the intellectual life requires.

The first truth about it is that it is different from other kinds of life. We expect the miner to work underground and the aviator in the clouds. We must expect the thinker to have his special haunts and ways, which we must accept with due humility. One of the great obstacles to a decent organization of the intellectual life is that it is at the mercy of the majority's snap judgment, which means that it is forced to square itself with the ideas of the man of business. Now although the products of mind turn ultimately into business products — books, pictures, scientific appliances — their creation follows rules diametrically opposed to business rules.

From the outset, the two modes of production contradict each other. A business occupies space, it has tangible assets and it makes a noise — the hum and bustle which prove that work is going on. In the artistic or intellectual life, the engine that does the work is silent, locked up like the motor of a Rolls Royce in a box that you only open at your peril. Not only can you not see the wheels go round, you cannot, most often, see the fruit of the day's work. It is invisible, and remains so, maybe, for twenty years. Or if visible, it fails to make any deep impression — it can be as slight of bulk as a sonnet or a formula. That is what is so embarrassing. To the man who can dig a ditch, to the athlete who can pole-vault twenty feet in the air, to the physician who delivers a baby after hours of back-breaking struggle, the world says "Well done" and hands him his fee. But to the man who says or writes or paints a true thing tolerably well, it hardly knows how to give praise or reward. It disputes his merit, his industry, his "seriousness." He is at best "a clever fellow."

This fact is central, and any young man who intends to teach or be a scholar had better give up his ambitions at once if he hopes to receive in any satisfactory degree what is called "recognition." As a realtor, he could advertise his volume of business; as an engineer he could point to bridges and tunnels, but as a thinker and instructor of youth he will find most persons suspecting that he properly belongs among the unemployed. Let him, if he can, compromise on being an artist in marble or at the piano. The heavier and the more public the effort, the better. Let the crowd see that you are in a sweat from pounding the keys or heaving the block. Yet even then, the moments when you are ostensibly "doing nothing" will be held against you, however much they be the instants of decisive, arduous inner toil. To be sure, if you are a scientist, your working life will be respected, for advertisements have made it widely known that the inspired fiddling of the laboratory may result in a cure for colds or a plastic substitute for bread. But you must wear a white coat and that puzzled frown which shows that you are undergoing the rigors of thought.

I may seem to be speaking as if the main end of the intellectual life were to earn a pat on the back for sheer effort. That is not the point, although it is true that any worker likes to have his performance known for what it is and that all intellectual work is in fact physically exhausting. There may be no such thing as brain fag but thinking is done with the whole body, and sixteen hours at a desk composing in words or notes is an ordeal that few strong men not trained to it could withstand. As Shaw has pointed out, his kind of life would cause an instant strike among the navvies.[2] The more important point is that the brain worker is like everyone else dependent on his neighbor's tolerance. In order to carry on his work, he must "justify" himself, not in so many words, but through the emotional give-and-take between him and his environment. It is doubtless for this reason that artists and thinkers tend to flock together and to lead in chosen spots what the public calls a bohemian existence. The "artistic temperament" is held to be a thing apart, erratic and more than a little reprehensible. Yet the withdrawal from the respectable business and residential sections is well-advised. Leaving aside financial reasons, or any given artist's love of personal disorder, bohemianism simply expresses the desire to maintain the conditions suitable to thought.

One of these is the absence of noise — hence intellectual work is best done at night and sleep during the day. Another is continuity of work when the fit is on. Hence regular meals are a nuisance. A third is the need of space, closely allied to keeping the workbench *in statu quo* while work is in progress — hence the housekeeper's poking and tidying is a cause of war. Again, the need for long incubation is an inescapable fact — hence the princely use of leisure and the disinclination for "regular work" have a meaning. Whitman has told us of the long period of "loafing" that preceded the writing of *Leaves of Grass*. This necessity knows no law except that in producers, loafing is productive; and no creator, of whatever magnitude, has ever been

[2] See his discursive but revealing essay "On Going to Church."

able to skip that stage, any more than a mother can skip gestation.

Some of these facts are presumably well known. Yet it is apparently one thing to nod assent and another to act upon them. People who are not systematically broken in to living with a professional thinker cannot overcome their ingrained disbelief in the reasonableness of so irregular an existence. They interrupt and say, "Oh, I thought you were only reading." They make an infernal racket without giving notice. They comment, "You haven't done anything this morning — not feeling well?" They crow gently: "Well, while you've been playing with your little papers, I've weeded the garden." They mesh into your machinery with a thoughtless demand for information on your subject and do not see that it is as if they consulted the doctor while he was swimming for his life.[3] Worst of all, they cannot see why domestic or business routine, just because it is a routine, should not take precedence over the will-o'-the-wisp of mental effort. Yet all the old phrases — wooing the Muse, waiting for the spirit, catching the breath of inspiration — are strictly accurate metaphors. They are not an affectation but a record of neglected fact. Too few brain workers, alas, know how to protect their vigils, and too often at the ringing of a bell — door, dinner, or telephone — priority goes to the thing that might be postponed as against the thing which if postponed may be lost forever, namely a thought.

This is not all; there is the dreadful aftermath of creation. The war has made us familiar with the term "combat depression," which could fittingly be applied to the thinker's case. Soldiers are given leave or excused for the misdemeanors committed under its influence, but what is it? It is the breakdown of the centers of control after a struggle in which all a man's energies have been bent toward a single end. It is a sort of inner disconnection of all the lines of force once the great task is accomplished. The thinker or artist or scholar does not run the risk of sudden death, but he is in the same kind of death grip with unyielding

[3] Overheard in a museum: "Oh, Professor, tell me all about paleontology."

obstacles. It is not fear of death that strains the soldier but anxious doing, as was shown by the suicide of a staff officer behind the lines. The man of thought feels the same anxiety, the same danger of effort coming to naught, and when this is happily over, he collapses, grows moody, listless, disgusted with work and life.

This is perhaps the hardest phase for the onlookers, who are still cheerful and of good appetite. Accordingly, one of the morals that Hamerton preaches has to do with suitable marriages for "young men who — " How many careers have been broken near their beginning by the demands of some insensitive and possibly jealous young wife of good family who "could not see why John must work at those musty old papers every night." Those who cannot see why will seldom accept an explanation, unless they are like Blake's wife, humble souls of different station from their lord and master. But this is becoming increasingly improbable and Hamerton's recommendation of peasant girls for artists is only the afterglow of a golden age: there are no peasant girls. The man of thought must face the educated woman of the twentieth century — if he can find one to his taste — and work out his intellectual salvation with or against her.

In this regard also, the men of science have a great advantage over their fellows: they work away from home in special buildings filled with material objects. The crudest boor would not jog the elbow of a man pouring water into a beaker, and yet the operation is probably far less important than the search for the right word done by a motionless man with a vacant stare on his face. The man who is reading or writing or imagining is so much more vulnerable that he who has not had a thread of thought broken does not know the full meaning of frustration nor the strongest temptation to murder. I believe Samson brought down the temple on the Philistines because they — and particularly Delilah — were what their name now implies, and he had found no sanctuary before the crash.

II

Teachers, who *must* be thinking in order to be effective, are, to be sure, well enough protected in class and they presumably have an office to retire to for meditation. But the conditions are really less satisfactory than they seem. Many classes are held in close proximity to musical practising, outdoor games, or city traffic. With the lapse of mannerly discipline, corridors are often noisy — even in the most peaceable of rural settings, perhaps as a contrast to the stillness of Nature trying to favor mind. As for the instructors' office, it seldom warrants hanging out the sign "Hush! Realm of Pure Thought." Usually, the younger men huddle three or more in a largish room. It has a telephone, and custom allows anyone to come in at any time on any pretext. In all my experience, I have met only one man who could do real work in his office, and he is of that very rare self-insulated type which needs no privacy or preparatory mood. He can add a sentence to his manuscript during the five minutes between two classes; so easily that once in a subway rush hour as we swung from straps in a cluster, a colleague exclaimed, "Harold, why don't you get out your typewriter?"

In talking of Ph.D. dissertations, I said how difficult it was for most young instructors to teach and write their first book concurrently. The matters I have just mentioned supply a few of the reasons. The author lacks sufficient stretches of time to himself. Unless he can afford a room of his own at home, he must write in the library and here new obstacles offer. Composing in the general reading room is difficult if not impossible. Cubicles available in some libraries are private but lack all atmosphere — the Prisoner of Chillon had a better start; besides, of necessity, the library expects you to take only the few books that you need to use at the moment. Reference works are miles away: you cannot consult, roam, or grope your way to the heart of your subject.

Do not hastily conclude that I am coddling the youthful writer and do not say, in rebuttal, that he "ought to be able to stand" the annoyances I detail. Of course he can stand them, but doing so changes the character and the quality of the work in hand — or rather "in head." [4] The less we know about the future powers of the promising youth, the more we should make his conditions of work propitious, short of extravagance. It is not solely the whims of the great artist aged eighty that we should consider, but the needs of the fledglings. We know that to compose, Wagner had to wear a silk dressing gown, that Sacchini wanted cats in the room, and Schiller a drawer full of overripe apples. Mark Twain very sensibly preferred to write in bed, and I am happy to know that William James, writing in a public hotel room a hundred and twenty feet long, calls it "just about the right size for one man."

We smile, but the principle behind all these wants is the same: the desire for a fixed setting. Moreover, intellectual work, occupying as it were a dimension athwart the ordinary plane of life, needs a stimulus to start it. Frederic Harrison used to write fifty letters before breakfast (I'd rather believe six impossible things, like Alice). Scott took an early morning ride, Samuel Butler "posted" his notebooks. Some habitual act chosen for the purpose is required to overcome inertia; even the businessman faced with the task of writing a report feels that he must elevate his heart with coffee. This explains the more destructive addictions, to drink or drugs, which artists and thinkers professionally and understandably fall into. The stimulant is indulged in not for pleasure, but for mental lubrication, to set the wheels going at a pace above normal, for the sake of a product also above normal.

This brings us to perhaps the least suspected fact of the intellectual life, certainly the least publicized. It is that thinking is inwardly a haphazard, fitful, incoherent activity. If you could

---

[4] The English historian E. A. Freeman used to work at a table of great length on which his notes and books lay open at the proper place. By moving around the table he could physically and mentally grasp masses of materials which otherwise might have been far harder to co-ordinate.

peer in and see thinking going on, it would not look like that trimmed and barbered result, A Thought. Thinking is messy, repetitious, silly, obtuse, subject to explosions that shatter the crucible and leave darkness behind. Then comes another flash, a new path is seen, trod, lost, broken off, and blazed anew. It leaves the thinker dizzy as well as doubtful: he does not know what he thinks until he has thought it, or better, until he has written and riddled it with a persistence akin to obsession.

Young scholars should believe all this if only in order to overcome their too frequent discouragement at the sight of their first thoughts or their first drafts. Too much has been talked about "cold reason" and "orderly processes of mind." The impression has got about that Euclid began with a fresh sheet of paper, wrote down "Proposition I," and pushed on through to the end of the book without an erasure. Even if his manuscript was neat, which I doubt, his previous fits and starts were doubtless many. The momentary glimpse that shows a relation, a truth, or a method of proof does not come at will. It is watched for like big game, and only when captured and tamed with others like it can it be shown off in orderly sequence. All this is unanalyzable interior work. Men of science who feel free to look into themselves and report what they see admit the same thing. "How did you get *that?*" I heard someone ask of a Nobel Prize winner. "I got it by intestinal fiat," was the reply. And another volunteered the fact that of several minute experimental determinations he always chose the one that "felt" most accurate, most happily executed, rather than trust to an average of the series.

In art, of course, we are familiar enough with the same elements of confusion and gradual ordering of the chaotic. Beethoven's notebooks are always cited as showing the patience that hammered out a lovely theme from a trivial beginning. But it was not patience so much as successive birth pangs, of which all trace remained inside the conceiving organ. De Maupassant first jotted down impossibly dull and trite ideas for stories which later bore the mark of his characteristic "originality." Coaxing the Muse, as I have said, is no metaphor, or rather it is no *fanciful* metaphor; it is an image of the mind delving into its own contents for the thread which, when spun out, will lead other minds straight to the end of their search, to the solution of their problem, or to the recognition of their own latent thoughts.

It may appear to some that in speaking of art and science to a young man who is going to be a teacher — perhaps a teacher in the elementary grades — I am flying over his head and mixing kinds. This is not so. Intelligence is a single power taking protean forms, hence its products are akin; there is only one kind of human thought, however different the substances it uses to make itself concrete. The teacher, the scientist, the musician, the scholar, the architect, are all thinkers, even though the one may be inarticulate in words, the other in figures, and the rest in sounds or in forms.

And conversely, all are or should be artists, meaning by this craftsmen in love with their work. Unless this is true, unless the teacher feels that besides breadwinning he has "his own work to do," he is cheating himself of freedom and joy, and reducing the worth of his toil as a teacher. For what he will infallibly convey to a class is his awareness of Quality or his blindness to it. Quality is what, apart from certain techniques, is common to art and to teaching; and it is indefinable. The Lord saw that his creation was good. Similarly the end of education is "knowing a good man when you see him." [5] The details vary with the occasion, but what is called in athletics Form, in literature Style, in social and animal life Breeding — that is Quality, and its presence fills a human need as great as that for food and drink. The word "art" used as praise refers to this same good, which is found or not found in even the trivial things of life — a gesture, a greeting, a

[5] The phrase is James's and he is careful to say that he chose it "after a certain amount of meditation" about the use of a college training. *Memories and Studies*, p. 309.

gadget. Compare the doggerel that recommends Burma Shave with the Alka-Seltzer ads. One has quality, the other not.

If instead of passing this kind of judgment, we are overawed by a sense of the conventionally great and small, we miss the point. In the intellectual life there is equality of function side by side with varying degrees of power. For the sake of the best in quality we must also have the humblest; which is not the same as the tawdry. There must be a regular gradation of the genuine inside the republic of letters as well as outside. I have said that all kinds of men make good teachers; I repeat it, and add that for slow boys you may need slow teachers, while a man who sees only a little ahead of another can — if he sees truly — perhaps teach him more than a seer who virtually inhabits another planet. More than any other, our country needs a *dissemination* of intelligence. As with our good doctors, who crowd the city blocks and leave the hinterland to ringworm and pellagra, so with our good brains: they must be distributed, both to serve the public and to create the fertilized soil in which the finest blooms can grow.

Serving the public is no vain phrase. It should even be: serving the republic. If teaching and learning have a practical goal and a patriotic function, it is this: to keep the men who run our national plant from being run by it — that is, to keep them men or, even better, to keep them artists. *Techne* is the Greek root for "art," but *technique* has degenerated into a synonym for thoughtless routine. Technique, technology, routine, does no harm when applied to inanimate matter; on the contrary, it saves time and work and makes possible mass production. The danger is in aping the machine with our brains, in thinking like an assembly line, fed from a storeroom of cheap interchangeable parts. Clearly we are all impressionable enough to become robots, so that industrial slavery is not only a fact of the body which we must prohibit, it is a state of mind which we must forestall. There is only one way, which is to pit intelligence against it, to make a dead set for qualitative work, to strengthen the Mark Twain and Whitman tradition against factuality, to make education the proudest feature in the American personality, instead of an alien minority trait. For the purpose, we must get into the habit of distinguishing citizens from mere inhabitants, true engineers from "mere" engineers, businessmen with ideas from the hardheaded impervious kind, and the college-*trained* person from the standardized alumnus.

This is a large order; we have a long way to go and time presses; economic and political sphinxes with sharpened claws demand answers that only this sort of intelligence, if spread wide throughout the land, can invent. American culture as a whole is being challenged and as a whole must respond. Fortunately, the quality of true culture is contagious precisely in proportion to its diffusion and its intensity. It grows as it goes, and the more it gets to be "in the air," the easier for teachers to galvanize others into educating themselves. No one can do it for another, just as no one can make a bad actor cry "Murder" with conviction — short of shooting him. How does education "take" and culture grow? When a man has been singled out by the Fates for education, what happens is that he first disgorges all the facts he has learned. He forgets on a really magnanimous scale. It is a spring cleaning in which he sorts out his true intellectual interests from the temporary or imitative. The true he pursues on a plan of his own, unacademic, no doubt, though not necessarily without order or system. Little by little, he takes aboard once more some of the cargo he jettisoned, but in new contexts and with a new command of his own ship. He rereads old books, thinks out again old principles. The work is slow and often unconscious, but it follows patterns laid down in previous instruction. This is proved by the importance that an educated man ordinarily ascribes to the chance remarks or helpful hints dropped by this or that teacher.[6]

[6] It is one of the pleasures of teaching to discover what trivial things, un-remembered by the speaker, will effect unpredictable "revolutions" in the

They stand for much more which lies below that surface. The whole reorganizing of a fine and well-stocked mind may seem a haphazard, uncertain process; but it has its logic; it is an instance of thinking in the widest meaning of the term; which means it is the working of a strong wish, early implanted — a passion — and out of it comes a characteristic work of art — a Person.

In spite of the silly phrase, "wishful thinking," all genuine thought starts in a wish, and the stronger the wish the farther goes the thought. You must wish for an answer if you tackle a problem, wish for a visible shape if you start drawing on a piece of paper, wish to prove or disprove a hypothesis if you set up an experiment. Even simple perception requires a will behind it and you will most likely fail to recognize your friend in a crowd unless you are looking for him — that is, wish to see him.

To become educated is above all things the result of wishful thinking; but the wish must be for the true state, not for its trappings. Wish is in fact too weak a word, so I have called it a passion. In *Candide*, Pococurante owns a veritable museum of art but he is not an educated being. He cares too little. If a passion is feeling and thought successfully fused, we can understand why relatively few people are passionate and fewer educated. The common meaning of "passion" is unqualified desire — usually love or anger — but these are notoriously inconstant and chaotic in their objects. Hence men seek firmer goods. Some rise to real passion in the pursuit of trade or power — the empire builder, the statesman, the Napoleon of finance, is a passionate man. Others, spurred by a dumb natural urge, become the artists, thinkers, and scientific discoverers of the world, whose self-denial

---

mind of a student. One recent instance comes to my mind, from the mouth of a particularly brilliant person, and hence doubly gratifying: "Do you know what changed my whole attitude to study?" "No." "Well, when I was a freshman, you assigned some readings in Samuel Butler, and when I came back to report, I began telling you what I had learned. But you broke in and said 'Yes, yes. What I want to know first is, Was it fun?'"

and toil, seemingly superhuman, are made almost easy by passion.

What is less frequently acknowledged is that on a lower degree of the same scale, every educated man shares their experience — the same toiling over oneself and over subject matter, the same sacrifice of usual pleasures, the same sense of never being satisfied, of never having done, in a span which dwindles as its purpose becomes clearer. Because of this common experience, it is the educated — and I do not mean the learned — who save novelty from neglect and propagate it, out of love and admiration and pride. Next come the teachers, more or less happily ordered souls, more or less passionate in their desire to emulate the quality of life which their work gives them glimpses of, but ready at any rate to interpret it to the young and thus insure its continuance.

III

To add to culture means simply more art, more science, more thought and knowledge finding a niche in the structure we have raised. Even if I had the space, I have not the power to say anything about the making of art or science. But in the department of scholarship which is one field of creation occupied mainly by the college teacher, I can offer some suggestions of possible use to the young scholar as well as to the ultimate consumer — the educated reader.

Time was when no one in an American university had any doubts about the uses of research. Everyone was as busy as a bee bringing back to the hive his load of distilled information. Learned societies and periodicals absorbed and distributed this mass to those hungry for it — fellow scholars in the four corners of the earth.

But for some time past, doubts have been expressed. "Knowledge for what?" asked Robert Lynd in a forthright series of published lectures. In one branch of the humanities, another scholar pointed out, production is four times as great as consumption.

He meant that the learned journals appearing quarterly had one whole year's material for publication in advance of the current date: scholars were writing four times as much as they could read. Mutterings have been heard, too, of the need for an Alexandrian burning of libraries. This is sardonic humor merely, but indicative of the fact that commentaries have swamped originals and that scholarship is now a task of slogging through a jungle of books. We have felled the Canadian forests for paper to print on, and we cannot see the truth for the woodpulp. As one man put it, evolution has endowed books with reproductive powers and we suffer from overpopulation. Count the books on a shelf, and pretty soon you discover that a new little one has appeared between two big ones, and bearing clear marks of its parentage. The academic way of putting it is that the newcomer is "carefully documented," though it hardly adds to our knowledge.

At the same time, the world wags on, still rather short of needful information, rather bloated with downright misinformation. Consider current discussions of Germany and Japan here and abroad. Regardless of their point of view, they nearly all betray a standard of knowledge at the bare subsistence level. They form only one instance, but it is sufficient to justify the demand, both lay and academic, for a newer conception of scholarship — a scholarship that would keep our civilization more nearly abreast of its own achievements and take a working part in shaping life through right opinion.[7]

The latest of these calls for a new start, Mr. Arnold Nash's *University in the Modern World*, says without mincing words

[7] The present split personality within the scholar is shown in the "double talk" at the head of an excellent anthology of classics in translation: there is a "Sober Preface for Professors" and a "Pleasant Preface for Students Only." The former apologizes: "The editors have no delusions about the originality of their work. We readily agree that it is a thing of paste and scissors, and we blush to think what some of our learned colleagues may say. . . ." But what are the students to think when they read this? And why are selection and translation not important scholarly acts?

that the Fascists and the Communists are ahead of us because they know what learning is for. Learning is to aid man in fulfilling his purpose upon earth, and for Mr. Nash only Christianity defines that purpose: Fascists and Communists have chosen the wrong ideal. He therefore bids us reorganize the life of mind around the dogmas of Christianity.

To a student of history this exhortation seems futile though not irrelevant. A ready-made ideal is always artificial, unlifelike, infertile. With it we can *make* nothing, for we know the traveled road. Militant Christianity was once a hope and a force which did inform learning and did create art and science; but its eternal truths are in those things and not in us. They can still arouse individual zeal and are so far fruitful, but cannot be reassumed en masse or reimposed from outside so as to unify our intellectual life.

The unity so much desired today will not come out of any one brain or any one book. It will be a collective result; others will see its clear outline; we shall not. Its coming will depend on the convergence of a million minds, provided these are now busy doing, instead of groaning for the completed edifice to which they themselves should bring some handiwork. The great architect is History, and contrary to childish desires History appoints no press agent to publicize its plans. There is no lack of unity in our intellectual life, but too many men lack faith in their own relation to it.

Even this is an overstatement. In the corner I dwell in, one can already see a community of mind concerning the duty of the man of knowledge and the role of scholarship. In its least aggressive form, it looks like nothing more than a desire to make scholarship readable. In reality this is a great step forward, particularly when it is taken by the young in opposition to their elders.[8] There is, besides, a desire to make scholarly work fit some

[8] Or to *some* of their elders, for the real leaders of the movement are the late James Harvey Robinson and Carl Becker.

conceived or conceivable need. This does not in the least mean that every piece of research must answer the problem behind today's headlines. Often, the conceiving of a new problem that no one else has seen is itself a great contribution. No one for example knew that there was such a thing as the American frontier until F. J. Turner and others created and criticized the concept. The *facts* were known, even to the Indians, but the meaning was the result of scholarly thought.

In short, constructive scholarship not only suggests ideas useful in our bedeviled condition, but tells us where it is that we live, whence we have come, and what we must now attend to. It is the nation or the world becoming aware of itself in an explicit form paralleling those of art and religion. For this reason, scholarship must be addressed to more than specialists: it must address itself to what I have called the head of the nation. If this broad definition should come to be adopted by the university scholar, our lives might in no distant time feel the effect. Not only would it strike a blow at the highbrow fact-for-fact's-sake tradition, but it would be a return to the greater tradition of the "classics" that we so profess to admire. For the classics have usually been books written by passionate men in answer to some felt need drawn from a given time and place. They are books for the most part addressed to other men and not to experts. They are books written in the idiom of the street rather than in the jargon of the schools. They contain "eternal truths" only because their authors saw into the present world with more than noting eyes: their authors were sublime journalists.

If enough modern scholars should take them as models, forgetting as beyond their control the difference between a comprehensive genius and a modest worker, the result might well supply the "synthesis" which our Jeremiahs seem to expect to find curled up in a formula. It is really too simple to talk as we do of a "crisis" which will be cured by a "synthesis." If the "crisis" is indeed a single ill, it is bound to be correctly diagnosed. If diagnosed, we are much more likely to find a remedy by work than by complaint. More likely still, there are many evils requiring as many correctives. These can only come from a variety of talents, whose works will then constitute *for other observers* a synthesis comparable to the medieval, the neoclassical, or the romanticist.

Meanwhile let us be clear about the role of the classics: they are worth studying as examples of *how* to think, not of *what* to think. We shall be acting most like Dante or Newton or Pascal if we think thoughts very different from theirs but having the same potency for our times that their thoughts had for their times. This does not exclude adoption and adaptation of former wisdom, it merely stresses the need for rethinking as against rehashing. The intellectual life justifies itself when, having embraced the common facts, it asks and answers the question, What does it all mean? There lies the true responsibility of the scholar — not to a ritual or a routine but to the reality of a subject. To find out whether a subject is real is to chart reality itself, as the mythical professor discovered after twenty years of work upon his "Essentials of Oblivion."

IV

All this implies new obligations and new freedoms. Let me suggest a few. We can begin by tossing off the burden of indoctrinating ourselves into a system. Salvation will not come to us by being docile little fellows. We must be master builders. If the dwelling proposed to us is already as perfect and broom-swept as a system must be, it cannot become our permanent intellectual abode. We can at best walk through it, or preserve the shell, as we do with our colonial farmhouses: the plumbing — and I mean to play on the word — must be new.

Again, we can throw off without a second thought the incubus of Europe's profundity. I do not mean Europe's thought, nor art, nor living genius; I mean the secondary-school patter that certain Europeans try to dazzle us with. The visiting or transplanted professors have flattered themselves too often and too long with their clichés about our mental incapacity and our lack of reverence for culture. We have, if anything, too much reverence for it — and for them. Certainly their effectiveness on the American campus — *exceptis excipiendis* — has been no recommendation of *their* powers. Egotistical, inobservant, cheaply superior, they have only demonstrated once again that it is easier to be wise at home than abroad, and I fully agree with the young American who in one of the pauses of a foreign lecturer's tirade on the worthlessness of the college that harbored him, said in a loud whisper, "If he knows as much as all that, why doesn't he step off that creaky board?"

True, the remark is justified only by the offense, but since offense does come — from arrogance, from pomposity, from imported hokum — it is good that America still has a strong vein of the Tom Sawyer spirit.[9] Used negatively it should rid us of bores and highbrows; used positively, it should help us recognize Quality in whatever guise it may be found. We defer too much to experts, we believe in the guarantee of a big name or a big place. With all our distrust of political and social titles, we are too much impressed by intellectual ones. Doubtless we mistrust our own judgment, as we saw deans and directors inclined to do, but that is mistrust in the wrong place. Every man should judge for himself what is offered to him as a man. If this could be achieved — the only true democracy of minds — we should not find the intellectual medium so sluggish, so resistant. Our first-rate thinkers would not so often lie neglected, or be falsely re-

[9] A typical instance of inexcusable behavior, whether judged for intelligence or for manners, is that of a man who was engaged to teach beginners the elements of architecture. He was warned that they were complete, utter beginners; yet in the Faculty dining room, after his first class, he indicted the whole of American education because these "wretched students could not even handle a T-square."

duced to one idea, or stand condemned wholesale for faults that merely screen their worth. The result would be greater pleasure, more gayety, and fewer formal dinners of the mind, in starched bosoms and fossil company. In a free state of culture, John Jay Chapman would not stay unread, though so readable; and T. W. Surette would not be an unknown name simply because he blazed a trail along which no honorary degrees hung.

Lastly, we should more readily make room for the young. That the youngest teachers are the best, I am certain; but young scholars are also to be preferred, other gifts being equal. They have the energy, the normal rebelliousness, the freedom from hindering habit, the zeal for establishing truth and their own name. Hear Sir William Osler, who besides being a revered physician was a student of the intellectual life: "As it can be maintained that all the great advances have come from men under forty, so the history of the world shows that a very large proportion of the evils may be traced to the sexagenarians. . . ." [10] He uttered this as he neared his sixtieth year and proved his good faith by proposing a "fixed period" for professional tenure of power.

This may come in time, but it is not administrative rules we need; only different expectations. Let the presumption be in favor of younger men. Let the judgment of scholarship shift to qualities of freshness, of insight, of substantial rather than accidental truth. In his excellent *Life of Jefferson*, Mr. Albert J. Nock makes the point by a simple comparison: "There are qualities that outweigh occasional and trivial inaccuracy, and Parton has them, while the other biographers of Mr. Jefferson, as far as I can see, have not. . . . A book should be judged on the scale of its major qualities. . . ."

This is of course the attitude of the true critic towards art, and the integrity of truth is not in the least impaired by it. The decisive question is, Does the truth lie in the details, as to which a

[10] *Aequanimitas*, p. 382.

man is fallible, or does it lie in the proportions, the form, the style, the quality beyond the mere mass? I have expressed the hope that the presence of musicians and plastic artists on many campuses will help familiarize scholars with this way of looking at raw materials. It would be a pity if, on the contrary, academic habits in a bad sense infected the artist. To forestall the evil and promote the good, I would urge the artists to become aggressive, to make converts. They will be the first to benefit, and we may then see that miracle hoped for but never realized, of the university sheltering living genius — not merely canonizing the dead, while its own peculiar gift to mankind, scholarship, acquired the virtue which alone can inspire to learning and to self-education. At that moment, provided science has succeeded in humanizing itself, we shall behold a true university, a mirror of the world, accessible to all true seekers; each institution a planet within the universe of mind, creating and shedding light upon a darker world which looks for it there, and would look for it elsewhere in vain.

Bibliographical Note

Parts of this book have appeared in the *Atlantic Monthly*, the *Magazine of Art*, the *Nation*, and the *Saturday Review of Literature*. For permission to reprint, I thank the editors of these periodicals. My thanks are also due to Henry Holt and Company and Longmans, Green for permission to reprint copyright material by William James.

The literature concerning education is immense and it would be futile to cite here a few dozen books as if they might furnish — unchecked — a broader base of knowledge for the reader to judge by. As for the nature and conditions of teaching, that is a subject which should be caught fresh, on the spot, and I cannot refer the curious to some of the best sources, because they are either unpublished or unwritten. Let the reader whose interest has been aroused visit a school, read its catalogue, and consort with men and women teachers.

But since I have made mention of some few books in my footnotes and chapter mottoes, I now formally suggest that they be read, and without listing them again, fill out a little more the two categories to which they belong — the category of "particularly good reading" and that of "easily overlooked." Heading the first are James's *Talks to Teachers* (1899) and A. J. Nock's *Theory of Education in the United States* (1932). Persons who do not live in Baltimore and have never read Ezekiel Cheever's columns in the *Sunday Sun* might enjoy looking up his *Fads and Fallacies in Present-Day Education* (1931). John Jay Chapman's books contain much wisdom on all aspects of the intellectual life, but the reader ought to begin with *Learning and Other Essays* (1910), following it up with Stephen Leacock's "Oxford as I See It" in *My Discovery of England* (1922) and John Erskine's "Moral Obligation to Be Intelligent" in the volume bearing that title. He may then conclude with the short book by Sherman Kent, *Writing History* (1941), which is much more than its title suggests: it is a brilliant definition and illustration of the new scholarship.

Not so much for reading as for consultation on special matters, I recommend *Redirecting Education*, edited by Tugwell and Keyserling (1935). In the second volume of that work are concise accounts of European and Canadian school systems — Robert Valeur and I contributing a description of the French *lycée*. Two other collections of essays worth looking into are J. Wells's *Oxford and Oxford Life* (1892) and *Five College Plans* (Harvard, Columbia, Chicago, Wabash, and Swarthmore) (1931). Cambridge, England, speaks on an important topic through the distinctive prose of the late Sir Arthur Quiller-Couch in his *Lecture on Lectures* (1928); the eminent Princeton chemist, Hugh S. Taylor, has a concise statement on "The Organization, Direction, and Support of Research in the Physical Sciences" in the American Philosophical Society Proceedings for January 1944; and a characteristic phase of American educational thought is recorded in Alexander Meiklejohn's *The Experimental College* (1932). As for statistics and other more intimate facts about teachers, Logan Wilson's sociological study, *The Academic Man* (1942), will repay attention.

Finally, I suggest the reading or rereading of a few well-known and well-neglected classics, such as Montaigne's essay on the instruction of children, in Donald Frame's modern translation (Classics Club Edition); the school portions of *Nicholas Nickleby* or *Dombey and Son;* Newman's several volumes on universities; and Rousseau's deceptively simple *Emile*, including the essay on "Travel."

DATE DUE

MY 19 '01			
GAYLORD			PRINTED IN U.S.A.